REASONING WITH RULES

Law and Philosophy Library

VOLUME 27

The titles published in this series are listed at the end of this volume.

JAAP C. HAGE
Department of Metajuridica,
University of Maastricht,
Maastricht, The Netherlands

REASONING WITH RULES

An Essay on Legal Reasoning and Its Underlying Logic

KLUWER ACADEMIC PUBLISHERS
DORDRECHT / BOSTON / LONDON

A C.I.P. Catalogue record for this book is available from the Library of Congress

ISBN 0-7923-4325-5

Published by Kluwer Academic Publishers,
P.O. Box 17, 3300 AA Dordrecht, The Netherlands.

Kluwer Academic Publishers incorporates
the publishing programmes of
D. Reidel, Martinus Nijhoff, Dr W. Junk and MTP Press.

Sold and distributed in the U.S.A. and Canada
by Kluwer Academic Publishers,
101 Philip Drive, Norwell, MA 02061, U.S.A.

In all other countries, sold and distributed
by Kluwer Academic Publishers Group,
P.O. Box 322, 3300 AH Dordrecht, The Netherlands.

Printed on acid-free paper

Printed in the Netherlands

To Loes and Suzanne

TABLE OF CONTENTS

PREFACE

This book deals with a number of issues which are connected to reasoning with rules, in particular legal rules. Its main line of argument runs that rules are constitutive, not descriptive, and that therefore reasoning with rules works fundamentally different than reasoning with statements (chapter I). It is proposed to replace the traditional deductive approach to reasoning with rules by a different framework based on adducing and weighing reasons. In this connection the book contains a chapter (II) on reasons and a chapter (III) on how legal reasoning can be analysed in terms of reasons, rather than in terms of deduction. Then follows a proposal for a logic based on the notion of a reason for or against a particular conclusion (chapter IV). Chapter V contains a number of examples that illustrate both the possibilities of the logic and how reasoning with legal rules can be analysed by means of the instruments provided by this logic. Chapter VI, finally, deals with some logico-philosophical issues in connection with rules. It contains also a comparison between the logic proposed in this book and some competitors.

As may be seen from this summary, the issues that are dealt with belong to different fields. The chapters I and III deal with topics that are familiar in the theory of Legal Justification. The topics of the chapters I, V, and VI also belong to the field of Logic and Law. The 'technical' chapters (IV and V) have subjects which are familiar in the field of Artificial Intelligence and Law. Issues in the chapters II and VI, finally, are relevant for the field of Philosophical Logic. It is not without dangers to write a text that deals with such different fields, and the author hopes that it does not contain too serious deficiencies in any one of these fields.

Readers with different backgrounds may be primarily interested in different parts of the text. Chapter I, which contains the introduction, is recommended to all readers. Chapter II is rather philosophical. It may be skipped by readers who are primarily interested in the logical and AI aspects of this work. This holds in particular for part B of chapter II. Legal theoreticians will primarily be interested in the analysis of legal reasoning as it is given in chapter III. This chapter does not contain a full-fledged theory of legal justification, but it sketches the consequences of the replacement of the deductive paradigm by a reason-based one. Chapter V is the technical counterpart of chapter III and can be read by workers in the field of AI and Law as an abstract study in legal knowledge representation. Those who are primarily interested in logical issues are referred to the chapters IV, which contains an exposition of Reason-Based Logic, and chapter VI which places this logic against the background of some problems that arise in connection with logics for rules. Readers should be warned, however, that the text was not written to be read partially. It may be difficult to understand some passages if previous parts were skipped.

The text contains a large number of cross-references which should make it easier for the reader's to keep track of the connections between the different parts of the argument.

The author encourages readers to comment on the text and make suggestions for improvement.

ACKNOWLEDGEMENTS

The research for this book was partly made possible through financial support by the Dutch Foundation for Knowledge Based Systems (SKBS).

The Law Faculty of the University of Limburg has provided me with the opportunity for working on this book by giving me leave from part of my educational duties during the period of writing.

I have profited from comments on earlier versions of the text by (in alphabetical order) Arno Lodder, Aleksander Peczenik, Henry Prakken, Giovanni Sartor, Bart Verheij, and Kees de Vey Mestdagh.

Most of the writing was done at home, and my wife Loes contributed there to a good working environment. During the last few years my daughter kept drawing my attention to the fact that there are more important things in life than writing a book.

I. INTRODUCTION

1. THE LEGAL SYLLOGISM

There will be few lawyers that seriously defend the thesis that legal decision making comes down to subsuming the facts of a case under a rule and deduce the legal consequences. However, it is sometimes argued that the justification phase of legal decision making can be *reconstructed* as a syllogism, with a rule as the major premise, and the facts of the case as the minor.[1] The complications of legal decision making are then part of establishing the precise content of the rule and the classification of the facts (cf. Aarnio 1987, p. 120). Given these decisions on the content of the rule and the classification of the facts, the legal consequences of the case follow 'logically'.

Although this view seems at first sight attractive, it has some important drawbacks. Suppose that John is a thief, but that he is also a minor. We must decide whether John ought to be punished. There is a statute to the effect that thieves ought to be punished, but there is also a statute saying that minors ought not to be punished. We face a dilemma, because it seems that the combination of the rules and the facts is inconsistent: it seems both derivable that John ought and ought not to be punished.

On the syllogistic model, this dilemma can be solved by a manoeuvre which we will encounter rather frequently, namely *adapting the premises*. If, for some reason, we decide that John ought not to be punished, we use the second regulation to deduce that John ought not to be punished, and add a condition to the first regulation to the effect that it does not apply to minors. As a consequence, the first regulation cannot be applied anymore, and the seeming inconsistency has disappeared. The complications of legal decision making were diverted to the interpretation of the first regulation. Given this interpretation, the solution of the case can be reconstructed as a simple syllogism on the basis of the second regulation.[2]

---

1 Cf. Alexy 1978, pp. 273f. and MacCormick 1978, pp. 19f. MacCormick does not speak of a syllogism, but of a deductive argument. For the purposes of the present investigation, this difference is immaterial.

2 Of course it is also possible to solve this conflict by means of a priority rule, such as Lex Specialis. Notice that this way to 'solve' the conflict is hard to reconcile with the deductive model of legal reasoning, because leaving a premise out of consideration does not fit well with deductive logic.

This book has two main aims:

- first I want to show that even in simple cases, the syllogistic model of rule application is not correct, and
- second I hope to provide an alternative for this syllogistic model.

At the end of the chapter, I will give an overview of this book. Before that, I want to give a first impression of my objections against the syllogistic model of rule application.

2. THE SEMANTIC NOTION OF LOGICAL VALIDITY

My main objection against modelling rule application as a syllogism is that the syllogism is a form of reasoning based on the semantic notion of logical validity, which is not suitable for rules.[3]

The most elementary form of the syllogism is an argument of the form Modus Ponens[4]:

If *A* then *B* [5]
A
----
therefore: *B*

If, for instance, we replace *A* by 'John is a thief' and *B* by 'John ought to be punished', we obtain:

If John is a thief, then John ought to be punished
John is a thief
----
therefore: John ought to be punished

Arguments of this form have the characteristic that if their premises are true, their conclusions must also be true. So, if it is the case that if John is a thief, then John ought to be punished, and if it is also the case that John is a thief, then it *must* be the case that John ought to be punished. This characteristic defines the *semantic notion of logical validity*. According to this notion, an

---

3 The semantic notion of validity and the related container metaphor of arguments are the main subject of part D of chapter VI.

4 A more complex form of the syllogism is:

All *A*'s are *B*'s
x is an *A*
----
therefore *x* is a *B*

5 In this work I use *italics* both for variables of the object language and for sentence-schema's of the metalanguage.

argument is logically valid if its conclusion must be true in case all its premises are true.

The semantic notion of logical validity derives much of its attractiveness from a particular way of looking at deductive arguments. We may call this way of looking the *container metaphor* of arguments. The central idea behind this metaphor is that every premise of an argument contributes a piece of information to a container. This information derives from the meaning of the premise. For example, the premise that John is a thief contributes the information that John is a thief. All the premises of an argument taken together provide us with a container full of information. If this information includes what is stated by the conclusion of the argument, the argument is valid; otherwise it is invalid.

The semantic notion of logical validity may be considered as a specification of the container metaphor. That the conclusion must be true if the premises are true is nothing else than a more precise formulation of the demand that the information contained in the conclusion was already present in the premises of the argument.

Since the syllogism as a valid argument form is based on the semantic notion of logical validity and since this notion is a specification of the container metaphor, the fate of the syllogism is connected to the adequacy of the container metaphor. An argument that can be seen as making the information of the premises explicit in the conclusion, can be cast in a deductive form, for instance that of the syllogism. However, if an argument cannot be seen in that way, it is questionable whether it can be modelled as a syllogism.

As I hope to convince my readers, rules are not statements or propositions, and they do not contain any information. Therefore, my argument will run, 1) the container metaphor does not suit reasoning with rules, 2) the semantic notion of logical validity is not the adequate notion of logical validity if rules are concerned, and 3) the syllogism is not the correct form of rule application.

In the following chapters I will sketch a picture of rules that gives support to the thesis that rules do not contain information. Running ahead of this more fundamental exposition, I discuss the defeasibility of reasoning with rules to illustrate why the semantic notion of logical validity is not suitable for reasoning with rules.

3. THE DEFEASIBILITY OF REASONING WITH RULES

Consider again the case of John who is a thief. We have a rule to the effect that thieves ought to be punished. Normally this means that we can conclude that John ought to be punished. Suppose, however, that we have the additional information that John's theft is prescribed. As a consequence, the rule that thieves ought to be punished cannot be applied to John's case, and we cannot conclude that John ought to be punished.

This phenomenon, that additional information can make a conclusion underivable which would be derivable in the absence of this information, is called the *defeasibility* of arguments.[6]

3.1 Defeasibility and Modus Ponens

Defeasibility of arguments can neither be reconciled with the container metaphor nor with the semantic notion of logical validity. In the container metaphor, every premise of an argument contributes the information contained in its meaning to the contents of the container. The amount of information in the container can only increase by the addition of more premises. As a consequence, it is not possible that information that was already available in the container disappears, if the information in the container only increases.

For the semantic notion of validity this means that if an argument is logically valid, it is not possible that all the premises of the argument are true, while the conclusion is false. If a new premise is added to the original set, the truth of the old ones does not change. Hence it is not possible that the conclusion of the argument becomes false. The addition of a new premise cannot change the truth of the conclusion. The semantic notion of logical validity leaves no room for defeasibility.

Arguments of the form Modus Ponens are valid according to the semantic notion. Such arguments cannot have true premises and a false conclusion. Moreover, such arguments are not defeasible. Still reasoning with rules is defeasible. Therefore, Modus Ponens, or the legal syllogism, is not the suitable logical model for reasoning with rules.

3.2 Reformulating the rule

There is an obvious objection to this argument, namely that the so-called defeasibility of reasoning with rules only shows that the rule was not formulated correctly. In our example the rule should not run that thieves ought to be punished, but rather that thieves ought to be punished unless the theft was prescribed. If we would use the correct rule formulation, additional informa-

---

[6] The term 'defeasible' appears to be introduced in legal theory in Hart 1949, where the term is applied to concepts. Cf. also Baker 1977 and Loui 1995. The applicability of certain concepts such as 'valid contract' is the conclusion of defeasible arguments, and this makes it tempting to ascribe defeasibility to the concepts instead of the arguments.

In the literature on nonmonotonic logics, one also finds the distinction between strict and defeasible rules. E.g. Geffner and Pearl 1992, where the distinction is made between sentences (L) and defaults (D) in the background theory (K). The notion of a defeasible rule suffers from the same drawback as that of a defeasible concept.

tion cannot invalidate the conclusion, reasoning with rules is not defeasible, and can therefore still be modelled as arguments of the form Modus Ponens. Thus runs the objection.

Although this objection is not very strong, it cannot be refuted completely, because it is always possible to argue that if the conclusion of a deductively valid argument is false, one of the premises must have been false. For example, since the conclusion of the present argument is false (it is not the case that John ought to be punished), one of the premises must have been false. It is true that John is a thief, so it is not the case that all thieves ought to be punished.

Therefore, the objection continues, the rule does not run that all thieves ought to be punished, but rather that thieves whose crime is not prescribed (or to whom no other exception applies) ought to be punished. If we choose the correct rule formulation, it becomes clear that the rule is not applicable to the case of John, and that we cannot conclude that John ought to be punished. In other words, if the conclusion of a rule-applying argument turns out to be false, this proves that we worked with an incorrect formulation of the rule (assuming that the facts were described correctly).

This approach can in two ways be put to practical use. If a rule seems applicable but its conclusion is nevertheless false, we can add one or more conditions to the rule that are not satisfied in the case at hand. Then it turns out that the rule was not applicable after all, and the falsity of the rule conclusion can be accounted for. If a rule seems not applicable, but its conclusion should nevertheless apply to the case at hand, it is possibly to drop one or more conditions of the rule, or replace them by different conditions, so that the conditions are satisfied by the case at hand. In general, it is possible to modify the rule conditions so that the rule conclusion can or cannot be derived, as circumstances require.

The flaw in this argument that the rule must be different from what it seemed at first sight, is that the argument *presupposes* that rule application has the form of Modus Ponens (or some other deductively valid form). Only on this presupposition does the falsity of the conclusion guarantee the falsity of at least one of the premises.

This presupposition is not necessary, however. Either we adopt Modus Ponens as the form of rule application, in which case we must be prepared to adapt the formulation of rules if there turn out to be exceptions. Or we stick to the formulations of rules as they seem to be at first sight, and give up Modus Ponens as the logical form of rule application. We might, for instance, adopt a way of reasoning with rules in which rules can be applied even though not all of their conditions are satisfied (analogical rule application), and in which they need not be applied even though all their conditions are satisfied (defeasibility). If we do this, as I propose to do in chapter III, it is not possible anymore to conclude that we have the wrong rule formulation if a rule conclusion turns out to be false although the rule conditions are satisfied.

We find that there are two options.

1. We can adopt Modus Ponens as the model of rule application. If we choose this option, we must sometimes adapt the rule formulation to make it account for the (non)drawing of some conclusions.
2. We can stick to the rule formulation as it appears at first sight. Then we must abandon Modus Ponens as the logical form of rule application and look for a different model that can account for, amongst others, the defeasibility of reasoning with rules.

3.3 Rules as means to draw conclusions

There is no one correct solution. Sticking to Modus Ponens keeps the logic relatively simple, at the cost of having to 'fiddle' with the premises of arguments to obtain the right outcomes. Such fiddling will for instance be the inclusion of additional conditions in the rule, to cope with exceptional circumstances.

Being orthodox with regard to the premises of arguments, and in particular with regard to the rule formulations, goes at the cost of complicating the logical form of rule application. In chapter IV, where I propose a logic to deal with rules, we will see how far these complications may go.

In this work, I will assume that rules usually are as they seem to be, that many exceptions must be handled by the logic rather than by the rule conditions, and that as a consequence the logical form of rule application is more complex than Modus Ponens.

There are two related reasons for this choice. The first one is that in my view a logic must not only provide us with means to evaluate an argument with hindsight, but also with guidelines about which conclusions we can correctly draw. Exceptions to rules cannot all be foreseen on beforehand. If these exceptions are to be built into the rule conditions, this means that we can never be sure about the rule conditions. It always remains possible that exceptions, or exception to exceptions .. etc. necessitate reformulation of the rule conditions.

This means that we never know how a rule runs at the moment at which we want to apply it. Only with hindsight, if we already know the conclusion of our argument, we can determine whether the rule conditions were correct. If we stick to Modus Ponens as the logical form of rule application, we can never use a rule to draw conclusions; we can only reconstruct the rule on the basis of the conclusion that we have drawn in some other way. As a consequence, we can never be sure which legal conclusions can be drawn given a particular case, because we do not know the precise contents of the relevant rule. All we can do is logically assess the validity of the conclusion given a hypothetical rule formulation. This is, in my view, a very serious objection, because we should be able to use legal rules to draw legal conclusions, instead of use independently drawn legal conclusions to reconstruct rules.

3.4 Similarity of structure

The second reason to abandon Modus Ponens is that in my opinion the logical structure of arguments as they are evaluated by logical means, should be as similar as possible to the natural language rendering of these arguments. Fiddling with the premises to obtain the wanted conclusion is in conflict with this demand.

Let me explain what I mean with similarity of logical structure. The following argument provides a traditional example that illustrates why propositional logic should be expanded to predicate logic (cf. Copi 1978, p. 340):

All humans are mortal
Socrates is human
----
therefore: Socrates is mortal

If this argument is represented in the language of propositional logic, we obtain:

P
Q
----
therefore: *R*

Arguments of this form are invalid in propositional logic. Still we judge the original argument to be valid. To account for this in logical terms, it is necessary to uncover the 'hidden' structure of the argument in the more powerful predicate logic:

All *A*'s are *B*'s
x is an *A*
----
therefore: *x* is a *B*

This is a valid argument form in predicate logic. The possibility to account for the validity of such arguments, which would count as invalid in propositional logic, is given as a reason to adopt predicate logic to deal with arguments of this kind.

Yet it would be possible to account for the validity of our example argument in propositional logic by adding a 'hidden' premise:

P
Q
if *P* and *Q*, then *R*
----
therefore: *R*

The problem with this approach is, however, that the 'hidden' premise does not seem to be part of the original argument. It is only added because it is needed to account for the validity of the argument.

Again we find ourselves facing two possibilities. We can stick to propositional logic and fiddle with the premises (in this case: add a 'hidden' premise) to obtain the result that we want, or we can change the logic (from propositional to predicate logic) and leave the premises as they are. Given that our example argument is often used as an illustration why we need predicate logic for this kind of arguments, we may conclude that the desire to keep the premises as they originally seemed to be is rather strong; strong enough to adapt the logic to make *it* account for the (in)validity of arguments in their original form.

The same kind of reasoning can be used to argue why we should abandon Modus Ponens as our preferred form of reasoning with rules, and look out for a more powerful logic that accounts for the defeasibility of reasoning with rules.

3.5 Adapting the premises

We have seen how it is possible to stick to a particular logic and account for seemingly unwanted conclusions by adapting the premises. We have also seen that this possibility illustrates a trade-off between the premises of arguments and the logics that are used to evaluate them. If a logic seems not to work, it can be made to work by adapting the premises to obtain the correct results.

We found two objections against adapting the premises. First it makes it impossible to use the premises for drawing conclusions, because the precise nature of the premises depends on the acceptability of the conclusions that follow from them. In the law this would imply that the contents of legal rules can only be reconstructed from the conclusions that follow from them. This is not acceptable as a general characterisation of reasoning with legal rules.

The second objection is that adapting the premises violates the demand that arguments as used in logical evaluation should have a similar structure as their natural language equivalents. If for arguments of a particular kind there is a *structural* discrepancy between their natural language renderings and their reconstructions for the purpose of logical evaluation, this goes to show that a wrong logic is used.

In my opinion, these two objections, taken together, are strong enough to refrain from adapting the premises as a means to account for the desired outcome of arguments. This does not mean that it is never allowed to have a look at the premises if an argument turns out to have a strange conclusion. A wrong conclusion *may* be a sign of wrong premises. If, however, there is a structural need to adapt the premises for arguments of a particular kind, this is in my opinion a sure sign that the wrong logic is employed. I think that the defeasibility of reasoning with rules is such a sure sign that Modus Ponens is the wrong logical model of rule application, and that we have good reasons to look for a different model.

In the remainder of this book, we will encounter several cases where it is necessary to fiddle with the premises of an argument, to show that a particular logic can 'deal with' this kind of argument. Where this is the case, I will keep my refutation short, and refer by means of the phrase 'adapting the premises' to this section to argue why the concerning logic is less suitable.

4. OVERVIEW OF THE BOOK

The defeasibility of rule applying arguments provides us with at least a good reason to search for new models of rule application. This search will take most of the present book, because it takes a detour to arrive at the desired model of rule application. I will argue that rules are best understood as derived from underlying principles and goals. This means that we must first develop a model of reasoning with principles and goals. This model can then be adapted to take rules into account.

Reasoning with principles and goals turns around reasons. I will argue that the application of a principle or goal generates a reason for the conclusion of that principle, respectively for an act that contributes to that goal. The other way round, principles and goals are best understood as the logical reconstruction of the phenomenon that facts of a particular type are reasons for facts of another type. Principles and goals are then to be understood in terms of reasons.

I will start my argument in chapter II by an extensive analysis of the notion of a reason, and the related notions of principles and goals. In chapter III I apply this account to legal reasoning, and there I will pay much attention to the distinction between principles and rules. In chapter IV I develop a logical theory that takes reasons for a conclusion as its starting point. This so-called Reason-Based Logic (RBL) has extensive facilities to deal with principles, rules and goals. These facilities are demonstrated in chapter V, that consists of a large numbers of applications of RBL. Because RBL can both be considered as a logic and as a way of modelling legal arguments, chapter V can also be read as a study in legal knowledge representation. In chapter VI, I will consider some modifications of RBL and compare RBL to other logics which can deal with defeasible reasoning. Moreover, I will offer a model-theoretic semantics for rules. And finally I will return to the container metaphor of reasoning and its related semantic notion of logical validity. There I will propose the pragmatic notion of validity as an alternative.

II. OF REASONS

This chapter lays the philosophical foundations for the theory about reasoning with (legal) rules and its logical elaboration which takes up the remainder of this book. In my opinion, the notion of a reason (rather than that of an argument) is the most fundamental one for a theory of reasoning.

The notion of a reason is closely connected with the notions of a principle and a goal. These connections are elaborately described in the second half of this chapter (part C). But first comes an account of the work of some philosophers that has inspired the present theory about reasons (part A), and an attempt to analyse the notion of a reason (part B). The chapter closes with an inventory of different kinds of reasons and the contexts in which they occur, and with an overview of the main conclusions of this chapter (part D).

A. PHILOSOPHICAL ROOTS

Reasons function in argumentation, when somebody tries to convince his audience by giving reasons to accept a particular conclusion. The work of Toulmin and Naess belongs to the rhetorical tradition and provides insight into the role of reasons in argumentation (Toulmin 1958 and Naess 1978). Moreover, reasons have their role in deciding how to act, that is, in the theory of practical reasoning. An important proponent of the so-called 'good reasons approach' in ethical theory and jurisprudence is Raz (1975, 1978a and b, and 1979). The role of reasons and the need to weigh them is also stressed in (Peczenik 1989). Finally, reasons play a role in certain ontological and epistemological theories in which it is argued that some facts depend for their existence on rules and on other facts. The phenomenon of the so-called 'institutional facts' plays an important role in this connection (cf. Anscombe 1958, Searle 1969 and 1995, and MacCormick and Weinberger 1986), but ontological/epistemological positions as the ones defended by Goodman (1978) and Putnam (1981) are relevant too.

In the following sections I will discuss the work of many of these authors with two purposes. First I want to acknowledge the sources that inspired much of the following, and second I will use my discussion of earlier theories as a stepping stone to introduce parts of my own views.

1. RAZ ON REASONS

In his book *Practical Reason and Norms*, Joseph Raz aims to give an analysis of norms by explaining their relation to reasons for action. In this connection he starts with a discussion of reasons.

1.1 Reasons are facts[1]

One of the first things Raz notices is that reasons are facts, rather than statements or beliefs. Facts are everything that can be *designated* by what follows after 'the fact that .....'. That reasons are not statements, or - for that matter - propositions, becomes clear from that you can act for a reason, but you cannot act for a sentence or a proposition. The fact that it is raining can be a reason to take your umbrella, but the sentence that it is raining cannot.

To this analysis of Raz's I would add that the category of facts that can be reasons should be taken broadly. The fact that this picture is beautiful is a reason to buy it, just as the fact that Mary ought not steal is a reason to prevent her from stealing. In short, reasons are not confined to brute, purely material facts.

I think that in general reasons are not beliefs, but some beliefs, or - better - facts of the type that somebody has a belief, can be reasons. They can be reasons in two senses of the word. One sense is reason as a *cause*. The reason why the stone fell to the ground is that I dropped it. If beliefs are reasons, this is most often in the sense of causes. The fact that I believed that it was raining is the reason why (the cause that) I wore my raincoat. That I believe that it is raining is, however, not a reason to wear my raincoat. It is not a reason *to act*, although it may be the reason, in the sense of cause, *why I acted*. This becomes clearer if we consider the case that I falsely believe that it is raining. My false belief is surely not a reason to act on, although it may be the reason why I acted. In the case of reasons that function as causes, Raz speaks of *explanatory reasons*.

In some exceptional cases, my belief may be a reason to act. Suppose I promise a friend to call him as soon as I believe that he was won the lottery. This promise makes the fact about my belief into a reason to call my friend. My belief has become a reason to act. Yet, situations like these are exceptional and do not warrant the general conclusion that reasons are beliefs. In the case of reasons to act, Raz speaks of *guiding reasons*, as opposed to explanatory reasons.

1.2 Complete reasons

In actual argumentation, a speaker will often confine himself to what is needed to convince his audience. Raz gives the following example:

---

1 Most of the following discussion of the work of Raz is based on Raz 1975, pp. 15-84.

When asked why he goes to the station, John may say that
a. James will be arriving there, or that
b. James will be pleased to be met at the station, or that
c. he would like to please James.

These three statements somehow belong together. They do not state independent reasons, as would the statements that John promised James to meet him at the station and that the station is a good meeting place. Reason-giving statements sometimes belong together and describe one reason, while at other times they describe several reasons. This phenomenon brings Raz to introduce the notion of a *complete reason*. Raz defines a complete reason as follows:

> The fact that p is a complete reason to ϕ for a person x if, and only if, ... necessarily, for any person y who understands both the statement that p and the statement that x ϕ's, if y believes that p he believes that there is a reason for x to ϕ, regardless of what other beliefs y has ....[2]

Two things about this definition are notable. First that there is a close connection between this definition of a complete reason and the semantic notion of logical validity. The definition of a complete reason boils down to that one should *necessarily* belief that x has a reason to ϕ if one believes that the complete reason is present. In other words, the relation between the statements that describe the facts that go into a complete reason and the statement that says that there is a reason should be one of logical entailment.

It seems that in defining a complete reason, Raz confuses part of a (complete) reason with the principle that underlies the reason. Suppose that the *facts* that are part of the complete reason are summarised in the statement that F. F would for instance be that John is a thief. To complement this into a complete reason in the sense of Raz, we must add that if F, there is a reason to ϕ. In the example this would for instance be that if John is a thief, this is a reason why we should arrest him.

In my opinion, this latter 'statement' is not part of the reason, but the principle that makes the fact F into a reason to ϕ. (Thieves ought to be arrested.) As Raz mentioned himself, rules[3] are not facts, and yet only facts are consid-

---

2 Actually the definition is more complex, but I have left the complications away because they only relate to technicalities and do not change the essence of the definition.

It should be noticed that Raz is only concerned with reasons for behaviour. He recognises that there are also other reasons, such as reasons to believe something, but he does not deal with them. This explains why Raz analyses the notion of a reason to ϕ, rather than the notion of a reason in general.

3 In *Practical Reasons and Norms*, Raz writes about rules where I would prefer to write about principles. In the discussion of the work of Raz, I will use the words 'rule' and 'principle' intermittently, without assigning much importance to their difference in meaning. The distinction between the two will become important in chapter III.

ered to be reasons. It may be that the combined mentioning of facts and the rule that makes them into a reason leads to more effective argumentation, but that does not prove that all the elements of effective argumentation are parts of a reason. Therefore I prefer to call only facts reasons, and to distinguish between on the one hand facts that are reasons, and on the other hand rules that make them into reasons.

Although I do not fully agree with Raz's analysis of a complete reason, I think that Raz is right where he notices that sometimes there goes more than one fact into a reason. Take for example the case of somebody who committed a tort that caused damages. A reason based on the rule that anybody who commits a tort by which damages are caused, must compensate for these damages, will contain two facts, namely the fact that a person committed a tort and that this tort caused damage. Neither one of these facts by itself is a reason to pay for the damages, but taken together they are a reason. Notice also that these facts together still do no entail the conclusion that the damages must be paid for. To achieve an entailment relation, the formulation of the rule must be added.[4]

The second thing to be noted about Raz's definition of a complete reason is that the presence of a complete reason cannot be defeated by additional beliefs. This again illustrates the close connection between complete reasons and deductively valid arguments. In a deductively valid argument, the truth of the premises guarantees the truth of the conclusion, no matter what the other facts are. Such arguments are not defeasible. Complete reasons are not defeasible either. There is a difference, however. In the case of deductively valid arguments, the truth of the premises guarantees the truth of the *conclusion*, while in the case of a complete reason the only thing that is guaranteed is the *presence of a reason*. This difference will return in section III.13, where different kinds of defeat are distinguished.

1.3 Potential reasons and actual reasons

The notion of a reason is ambiguous. If a fact A is a reason for some particular conclusion B, this may on the one hand mean that facts like A are reasons for conclusions like B. In this sense of the word 'reason', the fact that A is a reason for B does not say anything about whether this fact A actually obtains.

---

4 I do not think that the addition of the rule would really lead to entailment of the conclusion, because in my opinion the rule has no truth value and traditional logic cannot be applied to it. Moreover, as we have seen in chapter I, reasoning with rules is defeasible. This means that even the addition of the rule would not lead to an entailment relation between the reason and the rule on the one hand, and their conclusion on the other hand.

It only says that facts like A are reasons for facts like B. However, it may also mean that the fact A actually obtains, and provides a reason for B.

We can express this distinction by saying that the first situation deals with *potential reasons*, while the second situation deals with *actual reasons*. For instance, if it is somebody's birthday, this is in general a reason to congratulate him. So the state of affairs that it is John's birthday is a potential reason to congratulate John. This is in general true, even if today it is not John's birthday. If, however, today is John's birthday, this fact is an actual reason to congratulate John now.

In case of conflict, only the strength of the actual reasons is relevant. The fact that it is John's birthday is a reason to congratulate him, while the fact that his grandmother died is a reason not to congratulate (but rather to condole) him. Suppose, moreover, that the latter reason overrides the former one. If both reasons are actual, John should not be congratulated, but if it is John's birthday and his grandmother did not die, John should be congratulated. Potential reasons, reasons that do not actually occur, do not influence the relative weight of reasons, just as potentially winning the football pool does not make one rich.

Potential reasons are really no reasons at all. If, for instance, we say that being a thief is a reason for being punished, we do not say anything more than that we accept the principle that thieves ought to be punished.

1.4 The strength of reasons

According to Raz, reasons can conflict and such a conflict can be solved on the basis of their strength. Two reasons conflict if one is a reason to ϕ, and the other is a reason to not-ϕ. If a stronger reason conflicts with a weaker, the stronger reason overrides the weaker. If the reason to ϕ overrides the reason to not-ϕ, the result of the combined reasons is, according to Raz, a reason to ϕ.

On the basis of the notions of complete reasons and the strength of reasons, Raz defines some other notions:

- p is a *conclusive reason* for x to ϕ, if, and only if, p is a reason for x to ϕ (which has not been cancelled) and there is no q such that q overrides p;
- p is an *absolute reason* for x to ϕ, if, and only if, there cannot be a fact which would override it; that is to say, for all q, it is never the case that when q, q overrides p;
- a *prima facie reason* is a reason that is neither conclusive nor absolute.

1.5 Cancelling conditions and exclusionary reasons

If a reason is overridden, it should not be acted upon. This situation is to be distinguished from another one in which one should not act upon a reason, namely when there is a *cancelling condition*. Suppose that I promised to lend you a book, which is a reason to lend you the book. I need not act upon this reason if you told me later that you don't need the book anymore. Your telling me that is a cancelling condition, which takes away my reason to lend you the book.

Cancelling conditions need not be reasons for action themselves, but their effect is to take away the reason-giving force of the facts that would normally be reasons. Cancelling conditions have a temporal aspect; facts that were reasons until a certain point in time cease to be reasons because of a cancelling condition.[5]

Cancelling conditions are to be distinguished from *exclusionary reasons*, which may, according to Raz, be seen as a kind of second-order reasons. Second-order reasons are reasons to act for a reason or to refrain from acting for a reason. An exclusionary reason is in his view a reason to refrain from acting for a reason.

Raz gives three examples of exclusionary reasons. The first example is about Ann, who is offered an interesting investment, about which she is given only a few hours to decide. Since Ann is very tired and does not trust her judgement, she refuses the offer, even though on the balance of reasons she might have accepted it. According to Raz, Ann has an exclusionary reason not to act on the balance of reasons.

The second example concerns Jeremy, who is in the army. His commanding officer orders him to appropriate and use a van belonging to a certain tradesman. If the order is regarded as a normal reason, Jeremy should, on the balance of reasons, not take the van. But orders are orders and should be obeyed whether there are good reasons against what they command or not. In the view of Raz, Jeremy also has an exclusionary reason not to act on the balance of reasons.

The final example deals with the case of Colin, who promised his wife that in all decisions affecting the education of their son, he will only act for their son's interest. This promise is, according to Raz, a reason not to take his own interests (and the reasons based on them) into account while making decisions about his son's education.

The essential difference between an exclusionary reason and a cancelling condition is, in the view of Raz, that an exclusionary reason leaves the facts that are not acted on their status as reasons, while cancelling conditions take the reason-character of those facts away. Moreover, an exclusionary reason is often itself a reason for acting, while a cancelling condition is not. An exclu-

---

5 The existence of a reason is an institutional fact in the sense of MacCormick 1974. It is brought about by institutive facts, and terminated by cancelling conditions. Cf. section 4.3.

sionary reason is both a first-order reason to act, and a second-order reason not to act on other reasons.

Although the notion of an exclusionary reason is in my opinion very fruitful, I doubt whether Raz's analysis of exclusionary reasons is fully correct. Before stating where I have doubts, let me discuss the examples given by Raz, to illustrate how they can be interpreted differently.

REASONS FOR PERSONS VERSUS SOCIAL REASONS

In the case of Ann, it seems that the reasons pleading for and against the investment remain in force, independent of whether Ann considers them or not. That may lead to the impression that Ann did not act for the reasons which were still present. Moreover, since Ann had a reason for acting as she did, it seems that she had a reason not to act on other reasons.

It is true that there are reasons based on standards for investments that exist independent of Ann. Given these standards, which are accepted in the community in which Ann lives, there are reasons to make the investment, regardless whether Ann employs the standards or not. These reasons, based on socially accepted standards, may be called *social reasons*.

Yet, these social reasons are not reasons *for Ann* in her present situation. Given Ann's tiredness, she should not consider the facts about the investment as reasons at all. In other words, Ann's tiredness is a reason *for her* not to employ the normal standards for judging the investment. Moreover, if she does not employ these standards for judging the investment, the social reasons do not become *reasons for her*.

The situation is comparable to that of a person who considers to have a cup of coffee to overcome his sleepiness. For most people, there would be a reason to drink the coffee. However, *for this particular person*, the reason does not exist, because coffee makes him sleepy.

Facts that are in general reasons, or - in other words - that are social reasons, need not be reasons for every individual. Therefore, the social reasons for and against the investment do not have their reason-character for Ann, because of the exclusionary reason. If a fact is not a reason, this is something different than that there is a reason not to act on the reason. In the example about Ann, Raz seems to confuse the possibility that a social reason is not a reason for a particular person, with the presence of a reason not to act on another reason.

REASONS FROM A POINT OF VIEW

Reasons, and the principles on which they are based, often belong to *points of view*, and are relativised to them. Facts that are reasons from one point of view (e.g. the legal one), need not be reasons from another point of view (e.g. the aesthetic point of view). In deciding what one should do, one may take reasons from all points of view into consideration, but this does not mean that all reasons are reasons from every point of view.

For the case of Jeremy, who considers to appropriate the van, the distinction between different spheres of reasons is decisive. The balance of the military reasons is different than the balance of reasons from the point of view of the average citizen. In normal, non-military, circumstances, there may be overriding reasons not to take the van. However, these reasons loose their relevance in the context of military service, as soon as an order has been given. Outside the context of the army these reasons still exist, but in the context of the army they are not reasons. Their relevance as reasons is excluded by the order. As a consequence, the balance of reasons from the military point of view will be different. This does not mean that the order forms a reason not to act on the other reasons. The order prevents the other reasons from becoming reasons *from the military point of view*. Jeremy can still act on the balance of the available *military* reasons, but - because of the exclusionary reason - this set of reasons does not include reasons that would be there if there were no order. The example of Jeremy illustrates how exclusionary reasons can delimit points of view by preventing some facts from becoming reasons from a particular point of view.

REASONS AND CAUSES

Finally, consider the example of Colin. In deciding about his son's education, he will only take his son's interests into account. When Colin made this promise, he abolished a number of reason-creating facts as such. Facts that used to be reasons are not considered as reasons anymore. This does not mean that Colin might not be tempted to act on those 'reasons', or even be moved by them to act against his promise; it is only that he cannot adduce them as a justification for his decisions anymore.[6]

Compare this to the possibility to 'convince' a jury that a person committed a crime by pointing out that he is a Jew. This manoeuvre might be effective, but most juries would not dare to mention the fact that the suspect is a Jew as a reason for their decision. It is not a reason, although it may still be a cause. Again, it turns out that an exclusionary reason is not a reason against *acting* for some other reasons. An exclusionary reasons rather *prevents other facts from becoming reasons* (from a particular point of view) at all.

---

6 The possibility that somebody is tempted to act on 'reasons' which he does no acknowledge as reasons anymore is discussed in section 11.2.

Summarising we can say that exclusionary reasons are not reasons not to act on other reasons, but rather reasons why other facts do not become reasons. Exclusionary reasons differ from cancelling conditions in that the latter take away the reason-character from facts that have been reasons. If I make a promise to lend out a book, I have a reason to lend the book. This reason can disappear again when I am released from my promise. In the case of exclusionary reasons, the reasons do not even come into existence, so there is no need for making them disappear again.

There is still another objection against Raz's analysis of exclusionary reasons as reasons not to act on other reasons. If there can be reasons for not acting on other reasons, there will probably also be reasons to act on other reasons. It seems that this leads to an infinite regress: if one needs reasons to act on a reason for acting, these former reasons will also be reasons for acting, and will in their turn need other reasons why they should be acted upon. It seems more adequate to assume that a reason for acting (or for whatever else) does not need an additional reason to act upon this reason. There are no reasons to act for other reasons. Analogously, I think that there are not reasons not to act on other reasons either. Exclusionary reasons are not reasons not to act on other reasons, but reasons why other facts which would normally become reasons, do in a particular case not become reasons.

An exclusionary reason not only prevents others reasons from coming into existence; often an exclusionary reason is also itself a reason to act. In that case it excludes other facts as reasons for incompatible behaviour. For instance, Colin's promise to act in educational matters in his son's interest only, is both a reason to act in his son's interests and a reason not to consider other facts as reasons.

It depends on the scope of the exclusionary reason how many and which other reasons are excluded. It is certainly not always so that a reason to act which is also an exclusionary reason, excludes all reasons for incompatible behaviour. Such an exclusionary reason has still to be weighed against those conflicting reasons that are not excluded (Raz 1979).[7]

1.6 Exclusionary reasons and mandatory norms

Raz uses the notion of an exclusionary reason to analyse the phenomenon of mandatory norms, norms that prescribe behaviour. A typical example of such norms are rules of law that demand that one acts or refrains from acting in a particular way.

7 Cf. also the discussion of the relation between rules and principles in section III.9.

According to Raz, mandatory rules, or - better - the fact of their existence (Raz 1978b, note 11), are both reasons to act as the rules prescribe and exclusionary reasons that prevent other facts from becoming reasons to act differently. For instance, the norm that forbids religious processions on all weekdays except on Sundays is both a reason against having a procession on Wednesday and a reason why other factors such as the freedom of religion and the interests of the traffic do not count anymore. The exclusionary nature of mandatory rules explains why mostly it is not necessary to balance reasons if one can apply a mandatory rule. The potential reasons against which the norm would have to be weighed are excluded by the exclusionary nature of the mandatory norm.

I agree with Raz where he writes that mandatory rules have an exclusionary character, although I disagree with Raz's view of what the exclusionary character of reasons amounts to. We also disagree about what are precisely the reasons.

According to Raz, the existence of the rules is the reason to act conform the rules. I doubt this. Consider again the rule that if somebody commits a tort which causes damage, he must pay for the damages. The mere existence of this rule is not a reason why anybody should pay for damages.[8] The real reason is that one has committed a tort that has caused damage. These facts are a reason because of the rule, but neither the rule, nor the fact of its existence provide *by themselves* any reason. A rule does not lead to a reason, unless it is applied to a particular case and makes the facts of that case into a reason.

1.7 Some conclusions about Raz's analysis of reasons

The work of Raz provides us with valuable insights into the nature of reasons. First there is the insight that conclusions are drawn as a result of balancing reasons. Raz confines himself to reasons for acting, but the idea that the right action is the result of the interaction of all relevant reasons can easily be extrapolated to drawing any conclusion.

---

8 It might be objected that the existence of the rule is a reason why one should pay for the damages if one has committed a tort that caused these damages, and that therefore the existence of the rule is the reason. This objection misses the point. The existence, or - better - the validity, of the rule may be a potential 'reason' to behave according to this rule. (Although even then it would be better to say that the validity of the rule generates the potential reason to behave according to the rule.) This potential 'reason' does, however, not entail that one has an actual reason to pay for the damages in a concrete case. To obtain this latter conclusion, one needs to apply the rule, which in its turn makes the facts that one committed a tort that caused damages into an *actual* reason why one ought to pay for the damages. In other words, the potential 'reason' which is based directly on the rule does not entail the actual reason to fulfil the rule's conclusion in case the rule conditions are satisfied. Therefore, the mere existence of the rule is no reason to pay for damages.

It is important to see how fundamentally Raz's view differs from the traditional logical one. In that latter view, a conclusion follows if it can validly be derived from true premises. This means that one only needs to consider these premises and the form of the argument to determine which conclusion follows. All other information is irrelevant, because a sound argument guarantees the truth of the conclusion. Balancing reasons is quite a different matter, because the presence of a single reason does not say very much about the conclusion yet. Even the presence of a set of reasons does not determine the conclusion. Only if *all* relevant facts are taken into consideration, it is possible to determine which conclusion must be drawn. Adding new reasons may lead to different conclusions. In short, the idea of balancing reasons almost automatically leads to the defeasibility of arguments.[9]

A second important insight is that facts that are normally reasons, need not have that status under all circumstances. There can be exclusionary reasons that take their reason-character away. This means that it is also necessary to take all available information into account in determining which facts are reasons. Again we find a cause of the defeasibility of arguments. Facts which at first sight seem to be reasons that lead to a particular conclusion, may turn out not to be reasons at all, and the conclusion that is based on them may turn out not to be justified.

Finally, the idea that mandatory rules are (or - better - generate) exclusionary reasons explains why applicable legal rules seem to guarantee their conclusions. Because of the exclusionary nature of reasons based on a mandatory rule, these reasons will have no competition of conflicting reasons. As a consequence, they monopolise the case to which they refer. The exclusionary nature of the reasons generated by rules of law will be a main topic in my discussion of legal reasoning in chapter III, section 8.

Next to these valuable insights, Raz's theory has also some drawbacks. The analysis of exclusionary reasons as reasons not to act on the balance of reasons is not fully satisfactory. Moreover, Raz does not make a clear distinction between reasons and rules. He is sometimes inclined to consider (the existence of) rules as reasons, although he also explicitly states that all reasons are facts. The relation between rules and reasons is more clearly exposed in the Toulmin's analysis of arguments.

---

9 A similar insight can be found in Peczenik 1989, which stresses on the one hand the need to weigh reasons, and on the other hand the importance of transformation rules which are the basis for defeasible arguments ('jumps').

2. TOULMIN ON ARGUMENTATION

We have seen that Raz's account of the relation between reasons and rules is somewhat strange. On the one hand, rules would be part of complete reasons, next to the facts that are (in my view) the real reasons. On the other hand, mandatory norms - which are a kind of rules - or the fact that they exist, are said to be reasons too.

A more satisfactory account of the relation between reasons and the rules on which they are based, is given by Toulmin in his paper on the layout of arguments (Toulmin 1958, chapter 3). Toulmin does not write about reasons and rules, but rather about respectively data and warrants. In his paper, Toulmin presents the now well-known scheme of the elements of argumentation. Cf. figure 1.

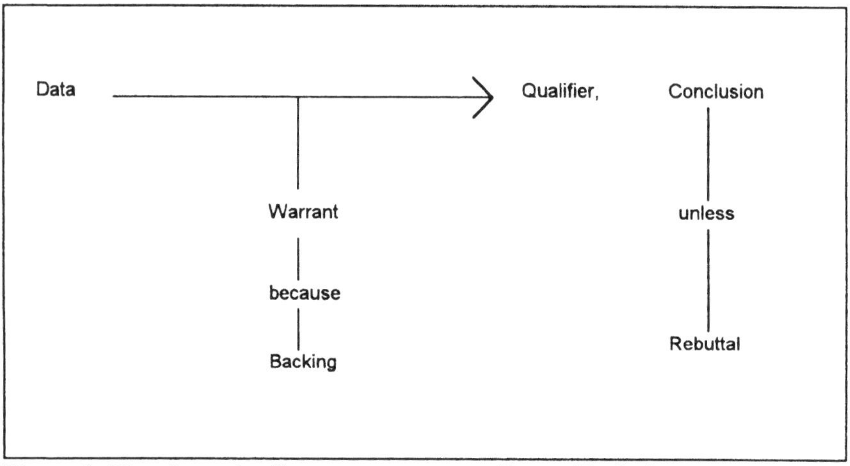

Figure 1: The elements of an argument according to Toulmin

A conclusion is argued by adducing data that plead for it. These data can be considered as the reason for accepting the conclusion. The connection between the data and the conclusion is created by something called a 'warrant'. One of the important points made by Toulmin is that the warrant is a kind of inference rule, and in particular *not* a statement of facts.

Toulmin discusses amongst others the example in which the fact that Petersen is a Swede is adduced to argue that Petersen is not a Roman Catholic. The connection between the fact that Petersen is a Swede and the conclusion that he is not a Roman Catholic is made by the warrant that a Swede can be taken to be almost certainly not a Roman Catholic. This warrant is explicitly distinguished from the more statement-like 'Scarcely any Swedes are Roman Catholic', and from the clearly factual statement 'The proportion of Roman Catholic Swedes is less than 2%'.

The fact described by this last sentence could very well function as the so-called *backing* for the warrant. A backing consists of facts that make a warrant acceptable. Warrants are not true or false, but rather they are accepted or not. Backings provide the facts that make a warrant acceptable. If we replace the word 'warrant' by the more common 'rule of inference', the facts mentioned in a backing could well be described as reasons to adopt a rule of inference, or as reasons why the rule of inference is justified.

Another important point made Toulmin is that the data need not guarantee the truth of the conclusion. This is expressed by allowing a qualifier and a rebuttal in the argument scheme. The *qualifier* can be added to the conclusion if the truth of the unqualified conclusion cannot be guaranteed. In the example of the Swede Petersen, the conclusion would more justifiably be that Petersen is *almost certainly* not a Roman Catholic. The phrase 'almost certainly' functions as the qualifier.

By mentioning a rebuttal, it is possible to specify a reservation in drawing the conclusion. The facts mentioned in the rebuttal would make the inference from the data to the conclusion unreliable. A good rebuttal in our example would be 'unless Petersen has Roman Catholic parents and was raised in Italy'. Notice that the rebuttal as described by Toulmin has much in common with an exclusionary reason as described by Raz. The fact that Petersen is a Swede can, in the terminology of Raz, be seen as a reason to assume that Petersen is not a Roman Catholic. The facts that both of his parents are Roman Catholic and that he was raised in Italy would then - again in the terminology of Raz - be an exclusionary reason not to act (in this case: not to conclude) on the reason that Petersen is a Swede.

The parallel between rebuttals and exclusionary reasons becomes even more clear if we replace Raz's analysis of exclusionary reasons by mine. In my opinion, the facts of the rebuttal withhold the data from becoming a reason at all. If we know that both Petersen's parents are Roman Catholic and that Petersen was raised in Italy, we are not anymore inclined to attach any value to the fact that Petersen has the Swedish nationality.

It is interesting to notice that if we change the rebuttal a little, to make it only contain the information that Petersen was raised in Italy, this fact now looks more like a conflicting reason than like an exclusionary reason. If we both know that Petersen has Roman Catholic parents and that he was raised in Italy, we are apt to assume that he was raised completely outside the Protestant sphere of Sweden, and that his Swedish nationality is hardly characteristic for Petersen anymore. As a consequence we are not inclined to draw any conclusions from this accidental characteristic.

If, however, we only have the information that he was raised in Italy, we can still imagine that both of Petersen's parents were Protestant, and that they might give him a Protestant education. On the other hand, the fact that he was raised in Italy makes it more plausible that he was raised Roman Catholic. Now we have conflicting reasons, which must be balanced to draw a conclusion. The layout of arguments as presented by Toulmin does not open the possibility to distinguish between these different reasons why the conclusion of the argument must be qualified.

3. NAESS ON BALANCING REASONS

In his teaching book 'En del elementaere logiske emner'[10], Naess explicitly discusses the balancing of reasons. He even develops a special notation to indicate the role of reasons in an argumentation-tree. The conclusion of an argument is for instance called 'F'. Reasons that plead directly for and against F are called P_1 ... P_n, respectively C_1 ... C_n. Each of these reasons can be considered as the conclusion of a sub-argument. Reasons that plead for, or against for instance P_2, are called P_1P_2 .... P_nP_2, respectively C_1P_2 .... C_nP_2. There can be reasons for and against reasons for and against .... etc.

If the coded reasons are represented in a tree-like structure, we obtain something like figure 2.[11]

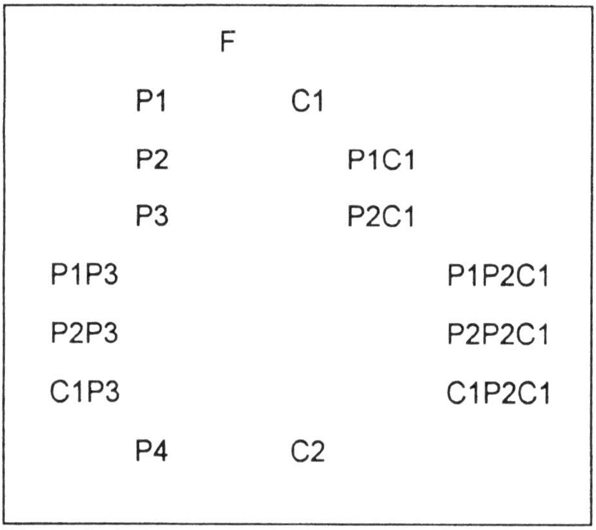

Figure 2: A pro et contra scheme according to Naess

---

[10] I have based my discussion on the Dutch translation of this book Naess 1978. Because of the different editions of the book that will be accessible to different readers, I have refrained from referring to page numbers.

[11] A related type of scheme is presented in Aarnio 1987, p. 117.

Schemes like these are called *pro et contra schemes*. The advantage of these schemes is that they clearly indicate how different reasons relate to each other. A disadvantage is that they cannot indicate the strength of reasons. Naess distinguished two elements that contribute to the strength of a reason. On the one hand there is the question to which extent the fact that forms the reason is itself defensible. On the other hand there is the question of the relevance of the reason. An ideal reason is a fact that is undoubtedly the case, and very relevant.[12]

To illustrate the strength of first order reasons (reasons that plead directly for or against the main conclusion), Naess proposes the use of *pro aut contra schemes*. In these schemes the tenability of reasons is indicated symbolically by the length of a vector, while their relevance is symbolised by the angle of the vector. Another important advantage of these schemes is that they correctly suggest that the outcome of argumentation is determined by the conflict of *sets of reasons*, rather than individual reasons. Cf. figure 3.

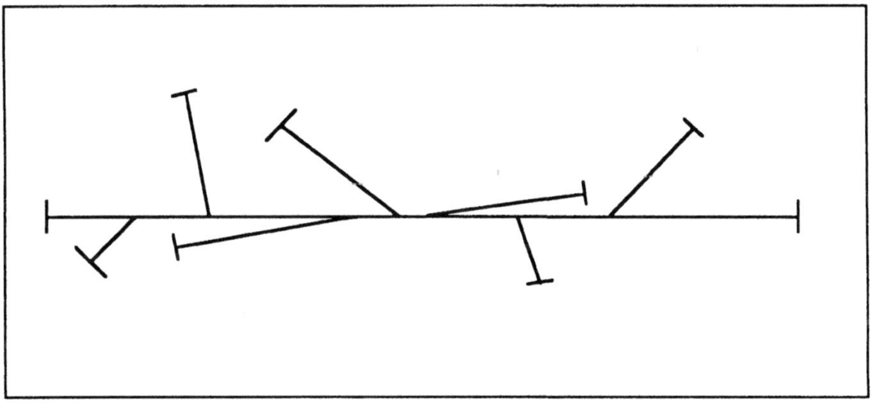

Figure 3: A pro aut contra scheme according to Naess

Although Naess recognises the importance of relevance, he does not indicate how relevancy can be used to determine which set of reasons wins.

4. INSTITUTIONAL FACTS

Toulmin and Naess consider reasons mainly from an argumentation-technical point of view. Yet, there is another important aspect of reasons that is often overlooked, and that is that reasons are *constitutive*. They make that the facts for which they are reasons, are the case. Such facts may be called *reason-based facts*. To facilitate the discussion, I will call the facts for or against

---

12 In section VI.5.2 I distinguish between the relevance and the probability of reasons, and the degree to which the facts which are the reasons obtain.

which reasons plead the *conclusions* of these reasons, even though there need not be an actual argument that has these facts as its conclusion.

For one particular kind of facts, it is now widely recognised that they are reason-based. These facts are the so-called institutional facts. I will start my account of the relationship between reasons and their conclusions by a discussion of institutional facts, mainly with the purpose of showing that there is no sharp boundary between institutional facts and other (reason-based) facts.

4.1 Anscombe on brute facts

The Scottish philosopher David Hume held that a sentence might be true for one of two reasons. Either it was true because it expressed a true relationship between ideas, or because the ideas expressed in it corresponded to the facts. Examples of the first form of truth are theorems of mathematics and (other) statements that are true by definition. Examples of the latter form would be provided by the statements that London is the capital of the United Kingdom and that my dog is named 'Sappho'.

In her paper *On Brute Facts* Anscombe remarks that this view leaves little room for the truth of statements like 'I owe the grocer one pound for the potatoes I bought from him'. For, on the one hand, it is not clear what matters of fact correspond to the expression 'owe', and, on the other hand, I do not owe the grocer a pound just because of some relation between ideas.

Anscombe grasps this dilemma by one of the horns by stating that there are facts that make these statements true, namely institutional facts. She does not use the expression *institutional facts* herself. Instead she writes that it is in the context of our institutions that the fact that I bought the potatoes from my grocer, makes true the statement that I owe him a pound.

The facts that underlie an institutional fact are called *brute* relative to it. If A describes an institutional fact, and the facts xyz are the brute facts underlying it, the following will according to Anscombe usually hold:

1. There is a range of facts xyz such that a set out of it must be true for A to hold. However, this range can only roughly be indicated, preferably by means of examples.
2. The truth of A presupposes the existence of an institution. A is *not* a description of the institution behind it.
3. If a set out of the range xyz holds, then *in normal circumstances* A holds. The statement that A, does not include that the circumstances were normal.[13]

---

[13] The italics replace quotation marks in the original. Notice the recognition of defeasibility in connection with institutional facts.

Applied to the example of the bought potatoes and the obligation that follows from it, these three characteristics come down to the following:

a. There is a range of facts such that some of these facts must obtain in order that I owe the grocer one pound for the potatoes I bought from him. This range of facts will cover the diverse circumstances that would amount to my buying potatoes. It is not possible to enumerate all the different ways in which I can buy potatoes from my grocer, although it is possible to provide a limited number of examples that covers most possibilities.
b. If I owe the grocer money for the potatoes I bought from him, this presupposes the institution of a sales contract. My obligation is not a description of this institution, although it exists thanks to it.
c. Not always when I do things that normally lead to an obligation based on a sales contract, I really incur such an obligation. For instance, if the contract I engaged in was the result of fraud, I would normally not have the obligation to pay. Yet, the statement that I owe the grocer one pound for the potatoes I bought from him does not *mean* that there was no fraud involved in the contract.

4.2 Searle on constitutive rules

In his paper *How to derive 'Ought' from 'Is'* and later, in his book *Speech Acts*, John Searle elaborated on the theory of Anscombe, most notably by introducing the notion of *constitutive rules*.[14] Searle opposes constitutive rules to regulative ones. The latter ones are said to regulate antecedently and independently existing forms of behaviour. Constitutive rules, on the contrary, not merely regulate, but *create* or define new forms of behaviour. The activities regulated by regulative rules exist independent of the rules; the activities constituted by constitutive rules are logically dependent on the latter rules.

Games are classical examples of behaviour made possible by rules. The rules of a game do not only prescribe how the game is to be played; they also constitute the game. Very gross violations of the rules of the game may even imply that one does not play the game anymore (e.g. soccer becomes an ordinary fight). Constitutive rules are not confined to games; they also underlie all kinds of speech acts, such as marrying, promising, issuing warnings, ordering, asking questions etc.

Facts based on constitutive rules are, in the view of Searle, institutional facts. Institutions are systems of constitutive rules; every institutional fact is based on a rule of the form 'X counts as Y in context C' . The presence of a

---

[14] Cf. Searle 1964 and 1969. The following discussion is based on Searle 1969. Recently, Searle has published an entire book about institutional facts: Searle 1995. A discussion of this book is outside the scope of this work.

particular context C is necessary to make the transition of the brute fact X to the institutional fact Y.

Searle uses the phenomenon of institutional facts to argue that one can derive 'ought' from 'is'. Such a derivation is, according to Searle, possible because institutional facts do not fit neatly in the classical empiricist picture of facts. This classical picture is essentially the Humean picture which was discarded by Anscombe. Institutional facts have something extra in comparison to the brute facts on which they are based. In the case of some institutions, such as promising or property, this extra involves an obligation. As a consequence it is, according to Searle, possible to derive conclusions about institutional facts from purely descriptive sentences, and to derive ought-statements from statements about institutional facts.

4.3 Law as institutional fact

In his paper *Law as Institutional Fact*, MacCormick finds that law exists on the level of institutional fact. But he directly reminds us that this finding is at once commonplace and confusing; the latter because no one quite knows what it means.

To clarify his position MacCormick distinguishes between, on the one hand, legal institutions in abstract, such as private property, crime, public officer etc., and, on the other hand, concrete instantiations of these institutions, such as this house being my property, Roger committing a crime, and Rosa being a public officer. The institutions in abstract might be called *institution types*, and then the concrete manifestations of the institutions are *tokens*. In this terminology, institutional facts are tokens of institution types. By this position, MacCormick distances himself from Searle's view that institutions are sets of constitutive rules.

Institutional facts exist according to MacCormick in time, but not in space. A contract or a corporation comes into existence and terminates again. Therefore there will be rules stating under what circumstances institutional facts come into being and terminate. MacCormick calls these rules *institutive rules* and *terminative rules*.

Institutive rules are closely connected with *legal powers*. Institutional facts often come into being as a consequence of an act-in-the-law. Such acts-in-the-law usually are some kind of illocutionary act, that is, an act with a conventional meaning. As Searle has pointed out, illocutionary acts must fulfil preparatory conditions, conditions which must be satisfied in order for the illocutionary act to succeed. In the law, a common preparatory condition for an act-in-the-law is that the actor has the necessary power.[15]

While an institutional fact is present, there are consequences attached to it. For example, the existence of a contract brings rights and obligations for the parties involved. The rules which attach legal consequences to the presence of institutional facts are called *consequential rules*.

Institutive rules and consequential rules combine in a standard way to create legal consequences. The former state under what circumstances an institutional legal fact obtains, and the latter indicate which consequences are to be attached to this existence. Since there is often more than one way to achieve certain institutional legal facts, and since the presence of such facts often has more than one (conditional) consequence, institutional facts can function as an intermediary between institutive facts and legal consequences. Cf. figure 4.

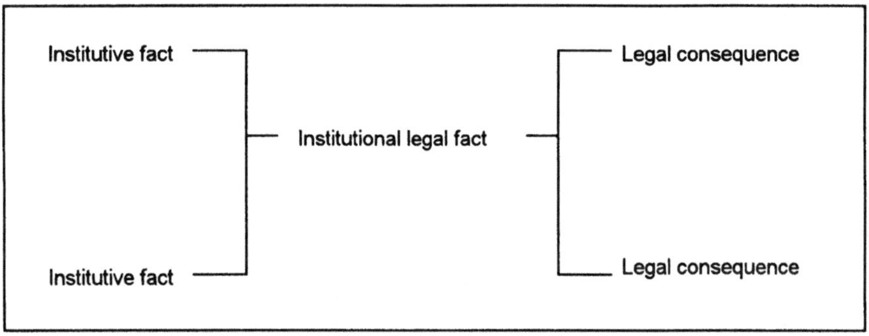

Figure 4: The relation between institutive and institutional facts, and their consequences according to MacCormick

Anscombe and Searle on the one hand, and MacCormick on the other hand differ as to the question whether institutional facts are institutional because they are instances of an institution (MacCormick), or because they are based on rules that belong to an institution. Which of them is right is not very important for our purposes. They all appear to agree that there are facts which depend on rules.

The facts called institutional by Searle and MacCormick are not only based on rules, but also on other facts. A promise is not only a promise because of the rule which defines what counts as a promise, but also because of the facts to which the rule is applied. It is, for instance, the fact that I told Jones that I would pay him a hundred dollars for his bicycle that is made into

15 An extensive analysis of acts-in-the-law in the light of speech act theory and an institutional theory of the law can be found in Ruiter 1993.

a reason for the existence of my promise to Jones to pay him a hundred dollars. Indeed, this very fact constitutes the promise.

The constituting facts are normally called the reasons why the constituted facts exist. These reasons often have little to do with social institutions. The reason why I should eat an ice-cream is that I would like to have one. The reason that I would like to have an ice-cream has nothing to do with social institutions. Clearly, there exist reason-based facts that have nothing to do with institutions. Therefore, I prefer to speak about 'reason-based facts', instead of 'institutional facts'. I will reserve the term 'institutional fact' for a special category of reason-based facts, namely those facts that are based on institutional rules (cf. section 15).

5. REASON-BASED FACTS

Building on the insights developed by Anscombe, Searle and MacCormick, reason-based facts appear to have the following characteristics:

1. Reason-based facts do not exist by themselves, but only thanks to the presence of other facts.[16] These other facts are the reasons for the existence of the reason-based facts. A reason-based fact is not identical to the reasons on which it is based.
2. The relation between a reason-based fact and the reasons on which it is based is one of the following two: Either the reason *amounts to* the reason-based fact, such as when a particular position on the chess board amounts to a player being check-mated. Or the reason (non-physically) *causes* the reason-based fact, such as when a promise causes the existence of an obligation.[17]
3. The presence of reason-based facts presupposes a background of rules[18] which make that particular facts count as reasons for the existence of the reason-based facts. The sentence that denotes the reason-based fact does not state that these rules exist, are valid, or something of the kind (Anscombe). The rules may define an institution (such as property; MacCormick), or belong to an institution (such as the law; Searle), but this need not be the case.
4. A reason-based fact normally obtains if the reasons for its existence obtain. There may, however, be exceptional circumstances which make that a reason-based fact does not obtain, although the normal conditions for its

---

16 In this connection, Hare speaks of the *supervenience* of some facts on other facts (1952, pp. 80f.).

17 Readers who object against a non-physical use of the notion of causation are free to substitute a neologism of their own choice.

18 The background can also exist of principles, goals, values, etc. Cf. section III.6.

existence obtain (e.g. contracts based on fraud). The sentence that expresses a reason-based fact does not state that such exceptional circumstances are absent, although its truth *presupposes* this absence (Anscombe).

Reason-based facts as described here are similar, but not identical to *humanly conditioned facts* as described by Weinberger (1986). Weinberger gives as examples of humanly conditioned facts such facts as the existence of the state, of religion, of social groups and institutions, knowledge, the facts of culture and the like. All of these facts have in common that they can only exist thanks to the presence of human culture. According to Weinberger, these facts cannot be appropriately characterised without recourse to practical (in the sense of action-related) concepts and practical sentences which enable us to express 'ought'-characteristics, value-characteristics and teleological relations.

These characteristics of humanly conditioned facts as described by Weinberger hold for very many reason-based facts. Still there are some reason-based facts, such as some modal ones, which are not typically 'practical'.[19] Think, for instance, of such facts as that it is *necessary* that 3 plus 5 equals 8, and the fact that *probably* the train will be late. Such facts are supervenient on other facts which are the reasons for them, such as respectively the facts that the axioms of arithmetic are true, and the fact that there is a railway strike. Therefore these are reason-based facts. Still they are not immediately related to practical concepts and/or sentences, and therefore they do not seem to be humanly conditioned facts in the sense of Weinberger. It seems that institutional facts as described by MacCormick, and humanly conditioned facts as described by Weinberger are subkinds of the more general kind of reason-based facts.

6. INTERNAL REALISM

The phenomenon of reason-based facts fits nicely with a theory about human knowledge, called *internal realism*, which was proposed by Putnam.[20] Internal realism is best opposed to another theory which Putnam dubbed *metaphysical realism*, and which assumes that 'the world consists of some fixed totality of mind-independent objects'. According to metaphysical realism, there is exactly one true and complete description of 'the way the world is'. Truth involves some sort of correspondence relation between words or thought-signs and external things and sets of things. Putnam speaks in con-

---

19 Cf. the introduction to part D of this chapter.

20 The theory of internal realism is most extensively exposed in Putnam 1981, pp. 49f. The following discussion is therefore based on that book.

nection with this view of the so-called 'God's Eye point of view of knowledge', because knowledge is considered as standing apart from the world that is known.

Putnam's alternative, internal realism, considers truth as a kind of idealised rational acceptability. There is no knowledge from outside the world that is known, no God's Eye point of view. Instead truth is 'a sort of ideal coherence of our beliefs with each other and with our experiences *as those experiences are themselves represented in our belief system*'. An important difference with metaphysical realism is that there is no privileged point of view. Knowledge, including the objects of knowledge, is always also influenced by the knowing subject, with the employed conceptual scheme in an important role.

This does not deny the existence of an independent reality; internal realism is still a variant of realism. What is denied is that objective, mind-independent knowledge of this reality is possible. The world as far as captured in a conceptual scheme, that is a world divided in objects that have characteristics and stand in relations to each other, is relativised to a conceptual scheme. An extreme consequence of this view is that conflicting *true* versions of the world are possible (Goodman 1978, pp. 1f.). Cf. figure 5.

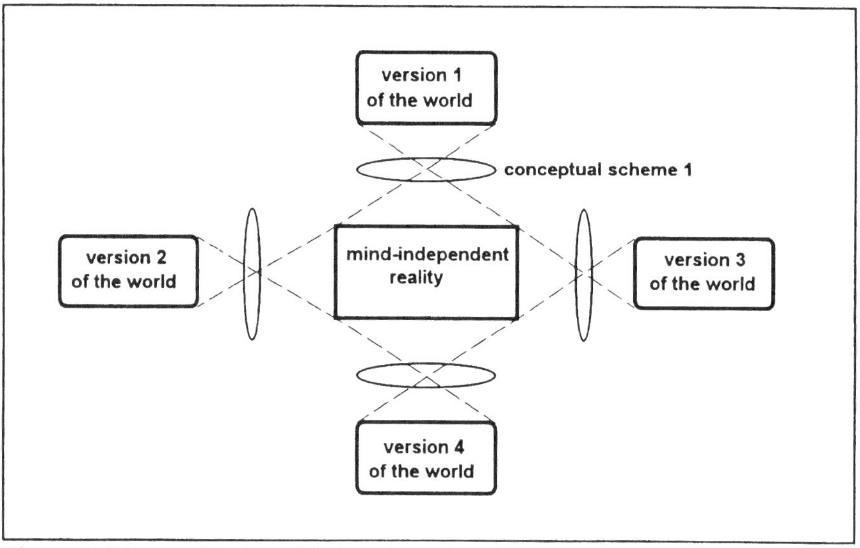

Figure 5: The world view of internal realism

Knowledge is human knowledge, and as a consequence influenced by the human cognitive apparatus. A notable characteristic of internal realism is that it reflects this insight back to the object of knowledge. On the one hand, *reality* is there independent of our knowledge of it. On the other hand, *the world* as we know it is not only determined by reality, but also by our cognitive instruments. This world, as opposed to the mind-independent reality, is mind-dependent.[21]

The consequences of the distinction between metaphysical realism and internal realism for a correspondence theory of truth would be the following. According to metaphysical realism, the truth of a theory is determined by whether the sentences of the theory describe the facts that obtain in a reality that is completely mind-independent. According to internal realism. however, the truth of a theory is determined by whether the sentences of the theory describe the facts that obtain in a world that is the result of the interaction of a mind-independent reality and the human cognitive apparatus. In other words, human knowledge is partly *made true* by means of the tools by which this knowledge is acquired. Therefore internal realism has a typical Kantian flavour.

If metaphysical realism were correct, the world would contain mind-independent objects and mind-independent facts. As a consequence, the relations between facts must be mind-independent. For instance metaphysical realism allows that one fact may be the cause of another fact. However, there would be no place in metaphysical realism for relations between facts which are based on the mind, such as reason-based facts.

Admittedly, reason-based facts need not be based on the individual mind of one person. Institutional facts such as the fact that I owe the grocer one pound illustrate how a social institution can underlie reason-based facts that do not depend on the mind of a single person. Still, social institutions are the results of human minds, and so are the facts based on them. Moreover, institutional facts are not the only reason-based facts. If the present temperature is a reason for me to eat an ice-cream, this reason is based on my own mind.

Internal realism, with its insistence of the role of the human mind in the creation of the world *as we know it*, leaves plenty of room for the existence of mind-dependent relations between facts. The relation between a reason and its conclusion is such a mind-dependent relation. Although somebody who holds that there are constitutive reasons needs not accept internal realism, internal realism provides a framework that has a place for the phenomenon of reason-based facts.

This framework is very liberal with regard to the number of fact types. Occam's razor may make sense when we are dealing with the 'objects' in a mind-independent reality (although I cannot imagine what these objects might be), but it certainly makes little sense if we allow reason-based facts. The human mind is able to construct as many facts as it wants on top of the 'brute' fact that two persons say 'yes' to each other. They may engage into a contract,

21 The present distinction between reality and the world is mine, not Putnam's.

play a word game, finish their education in the English language, or whatever meaning humans may assign to what actually happened. Even what 'actually' happened, two persons saying 'yes' to each other, is the result of conceptualisation that interprets certain physical events as the uttering of English words. And even the interpretation of what happened as physical events presumes some conceptualisation in which physics plays a role, in which events can occur, etc. In short, every attempt to do away with the conceptual framework on which a particular description of the world is based necessarily makes use of some (possibly the same) conceptual framework.

7. A FINAL REMARK ON CONSTITUTION

The lesson which we should learn from the theories about institutional facts and from internal realism is that many facts derive their existence from human classification. Often, this classification is based on reasons, and then the facts are dependent on the reasons that plead for or against their existence. These reasons constitute the facts that are based on them. A goal in soccer is constituted by the fact that the ball passed the goal line. A marriage is constituted by the fact that two persons say 'yes' to each other under the right circumstances. A book is constituted by pages that are bound together in the right fashion, ...etc.

Reasons themselves are the result of constitution too. A fact is made into a reason because it is considered in a particular light. This light may be provided by rules that belong to an institution, as is the case with many legal facts. It may also be more mundane, as when the fact that there are many dark clouds is seen as a reason why it will soon rain.

Constitution and the mechanisms that contribute to it will be central elements in the following part of this chapter.

B. A CAUSAL ACCOUNT OF REASONS

The notion of a reason plays a central role in this work. This notion is so elementary that it almost seems impossible to explain what a reason is without taking recourse to the notion of a reason itself. It might be possible to continue my analysis of reasoning with rules by taking the notion of a reason as a primitive term. Each time when a particular characteristic of reasons would be invoked, such as their universalisability and the need to weigh them, I might invoke our intuitive understanding that reasons have indeed the characteristic that is ascribed to them and continue as if this were evident.

Instead I have tried to 'reduce' reasons to a level that might seem more understandable, that is the level of causes and dispositions. It may seriously be questioned whether we understand the notions of a cause and a disposition better than we understand the notion of a reason, and therefore I do not think that the present analysis of reasons really explains what reasons are. Still, by indicating how reasons, causes and particular mental dispositions appear to be related to each other, I hope to shed at least some light on the nature of reasons.

Those who disagree with my analysis of reasons, or even find it incomprehensible, should know that the remainder of this work does not depend on the causal account of reasons as it is given here, that is in part B of the present chapter. They are invited to treat the notion of a reason as a primitive term in the way described above.

8. EXPLANATORY AND JUSTIFYING REASONS

We found that Raz distinguishes between what he called 'guiding reasons' and 'explanatory reasons'. Both types of reasons occur in connection with behaviour. Explanatory reasons for behaviour are reasons in the sense of causes. Knowing what are the explanatory reasons for a particular specimen of behaviour is knowing what moved somebody to behave in that particular way. For example, if Julia thought that it was raining, this was the reason why she took her umbrella. Because explanatory reasons are actually causes, there cannot only be explanatory reasons for behaviour, but also for all other caused events. For instance, the (explanatory) reason why this stone falls, is that I dropped it.

Guiding reasons are not causes of actions, but they are reasons why one *should* perform a particular action, or why one *should* refrain from it. For instance, the fact that it is raining is a reason why one should take ones umbrella. Guiding reasons specifically deal with behaviour. There cannot be a guiding reason why the stone falls.

Not all reasons which are not causes are reasons to act or to refrain from acting.[22] In other words, not all reasons which are not explanatory reasons are guiding reasons. There are also reasons why something falls under a particular category (vehicle, tort), there are reasons to (dis)believe something, and there are reasons why something is (im)possible. All of these reasons can be used to justify judgements. For instance, the facts that this object has wheels and is propelled by an engine justify our classification of it as a vehicle. The facts that John had a motive, and no alibi (weakly) justify our belief that he is a thief. And the fact that the velocity of light is finite justifies our judgement that we cannot (that it is impossible for us to) see images of the present. Be-

---

22 But cf. section 17.3 where all kinds of reasons are, *amongst others*, treated as reasons for some kind of mental behaviour.

cause of these justifying uses, I propose to call reasons which can be used to justify judgements *justifying reasons*.

Explanatory reasons do not justify the facts that they explain. My mistaken belief that Geraldine is a murderer explains why I turned her in to the police, but this belief does not justify my behaviour. My belief would not even justify my behaviour if the belief were correct, because it is not my *belief* that Geraldine is a murderer that would justify my turning her in, but rather the *fact* that she is a murderer.

There is a fundamental difference between explanatory reasons and justifying reasons. This difference is one of the many manifestations of the distinction between *is* and *ought*. Explanatory reasons deal with causal connections between types of facts: which fact explains which other fact?[23] Justifying reasons, on the contrary, deal with normative connections: Which facts justify our judgements regarding other facts?

While factual relations between facts are often assumed to be sufficient clear[24], normative connections seem to ask for additional explanation. In this chapter I will try to analyse the notion of a justifying reason in terms of causes of mental behaviour, and therefore also in terms of explanatory reasons. This analysis will not be reductionist in the sense that it argues that justifying reasons are 'actually nothing else but causes of mental behaviour'. Still, by giving the analysis I try to make it more easy to understand what I mean by the notion of a reason.

My account of reasons in causal terms is indirectly also an analysis of the 'ought' in terms of the 'is'. Later on I will argue that an action ought to be performed if the reasons that plead for it outweigh the reasons that plead against it. If these reasons can themselves be analysed in terms of facts, this means that the ought is, in some sense, analysed in terms of facts. I will return to this aspect of my analysis in section 18.7, and implicitly - in the completely different setting of model-theoretic semantics for a system of logic - in section VI.14.

---

23 I assume that even teleological explanations are (indirectly) causal explanations. For instance, my buying an ice-cream is explained teleologically by my wanting to eat an ice-cream, and causally by my psychological state of wanting to have an ice-cream. These two explanations coincide in my view. This does not mean that there are not other kinds of explanations, also called teleological, which cannot so easily be 'reduced' to causal explanations. Cf. Hull 1974, pp. 115f. These explanations have little to do with the explanatory reasons with which I am concerned here, however.

24 However, I often wonder why causal connections are often deemed to be more understandable than normative connections. In fact, in my opinion both are (the result of) significance relations imposed by the human mind on the world as structured by that mind, and as such equally easy or difficult to understand. Cf. also the introduction to part B of this chapter.

The present causal account of reasons mainly consists of the discussion of one extended example about a reason to believe. Moreover, the concerned reason is a reason for one particular person. Clearly there are other kinds of reasons than only reasons to believe, and most often when we speak of reasons we do not intend reasons for one particular person, but rather reasons that are recognised by most persons, or which even belong to some institutionalised system such as the law. My present account (in part B of this chapter) has therefore a very limited scope. For the purpose of exposition, this is only the more convenient, but it also means that the account must be adapted to deal with other kinds of reasons. This adaptation is a subject of part C of this chapter.

9. GLORIA'S CAR

Suppose that I have a neighbour called Gloria. She has a red sportscar that she uses on weekdays to go to her job. On Sundays, Gloria and her sportscar stay with Gloria's friend in another town. If Gloria is at home, she parks her car before her apartment.

Knowing this, I have developed a simple strategy to determine whether Gloria is at home or not. I just look whether I see her sportscar before her apartment. If it is there, Gloria is probably at home; if it is not, Gloria is almost certainly away. Of course my knowledge will never be quite certain, because the car may be serviced in a garage while Gloria is at home, or Gloria may be making one of her exceptional walks in the park. Still, looking for her car provides me with a fairly reliable clue as to whether Gloria is at home.

One way to describe this situation is to say that if Gloria's car is before her apartment, this is a *reason for me to assume* that Gloria is at home. Why would this be a true description of the situation?

If we believe that there is a reason to believe something, this increases the chance that we believe it. In our example this means that if I believe that Gloria's car is before her apartment, the chance that I also believe that Gloria is at home is bigger than if I did not have this first belief. Moreover, this increased probability should be *caused* by my belief; it does not suffice that there is only a positive correlation between my believing that Gloria's car is before her apartment and my believing that she is at home.

Notice that it is not the reason to believe itself that increases the probability of my believing; it is the belief that this reason is present. The mere fact that Gloria's car is before her apartment does not increase the probability of my believing that Gloria is at home. Only if I *believe* that her car is there, my other beliefs will be influenced.

Not every increase in probability of my believing that Gloria is at home suffices for the presence of a reason to believe. The increase should be so big that normally I should believe that Gloria is at home when I believe that her car is before her apartment, *unless I know of facts* that break the connection between my two believes. Belief in a reason to believe should normally cause the belief for which it is a reason: I should normally believe that Gloria is at home if her car is before her apartment.

My belief in the existence of a reason will often be caused by the reason itself. For example, my belief that Gloria's car is before her apartment is caused by the presence of the car: I see it standing there. This belief in turn causes my belief that Gloria is at home. The relation between the reason and the belief based on this reason normally contains two causal steps, one from the reason to my belief in the reason, and one from the belief in the reason to my believing the conclusion of the reason. Cf. figure 6.

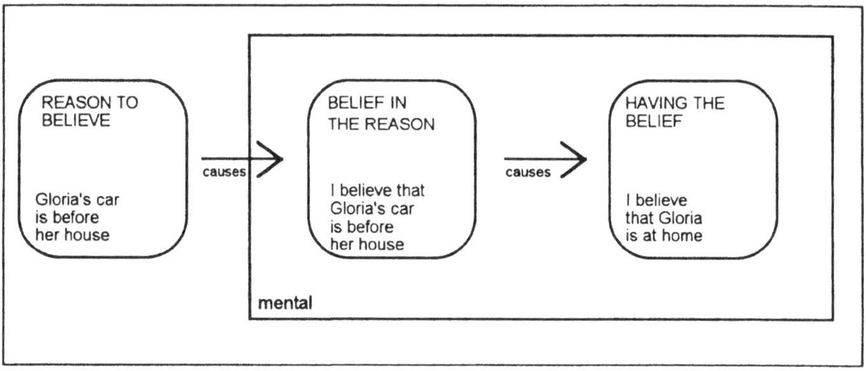

Figure 6: The causal relation between a reason to believe and the belief based on that reason

Only the second of these steps is relevant for the definition of a reason to believe. It does not matter how the belief in the reason has come into existence. What matters is the causal connection between the belief in the reason and the belief in the conclusion of the reason. If a suitable causal relation between these two beliefs exists, the *content* of the first belief is the reason that has the second belief as its conclusion. So the *fact* that Gloria's car is before her house is a reason to believe that Gloria is at home, if there is a suitable causal connection between my *belief* that Gloria is at home and my belief that Gloria is at home.

10. INTERRUPTIONS OF THE CONNECTION

Clearly not every fact that causes a belief is a reason for that belief, nor does every reason to believe cause the belief for which it is a reason. The relation between a reason to believe and the belief for which it is a reason is in a complex way dispositional.

10.1 Kinds of interruption

First, the existence of a reason to believe will often not lead to belief in its existence. For instance, the presence of Gloria's car before her house will often go unnoticed. If this belief in the presence of the reason is absent, it cannot lead to the belief for which the reason pleads. This disconnection is not important for our present purposes, however.

Second, even if somebody believes in a reason to believe, there are several possible causes that interrupt the chain between the former and the latter belief. The belief in the reason is a mental state that is realised by a configuration of the brain, and the same counts for the belief in the conclusion of the reason (if it exists). If the latter belief is caused by the former belief, the connection between these two beliefs is realised by means of brain processes. If something is a reason to believe, the configuration of the brain will be such that belief in the reason most often leads to belief in the conclusion of the reason. The dispositional connection between the two brain states is itself realised by a brain state.

It is, however, not necessary that these connections between belief-realising brain states are always the same. There will probably be many configurations of the brain that embody belief in the reason, and also many configurations that embody belief in the conclusion. As a consequence, there will also be many different brain processes that lead from the one functional state (belief in the reason) to the other one (belief of the conclusion), and there will be many factors, in the form of brain states, that can disturb these processes.

Moreover, disturbances in the process that lead from one brain state to another need not be conscious. One need not realise it, if belief in a reason does not lead to the belief of the reason's conclusion. For instance, if I know that Gloria's car is before her apartment, but nevertheless do not believe that Gloria is at home, I may not even be aware that something exceptional happened. If I do not think about it at all, it just happens that I believe the one thing but not the other thing, without realising the (dis)connection between the two. As soon as I come to think of it, however, I may realise that the combination of my beliefs is irrational. Cf. figure 7.

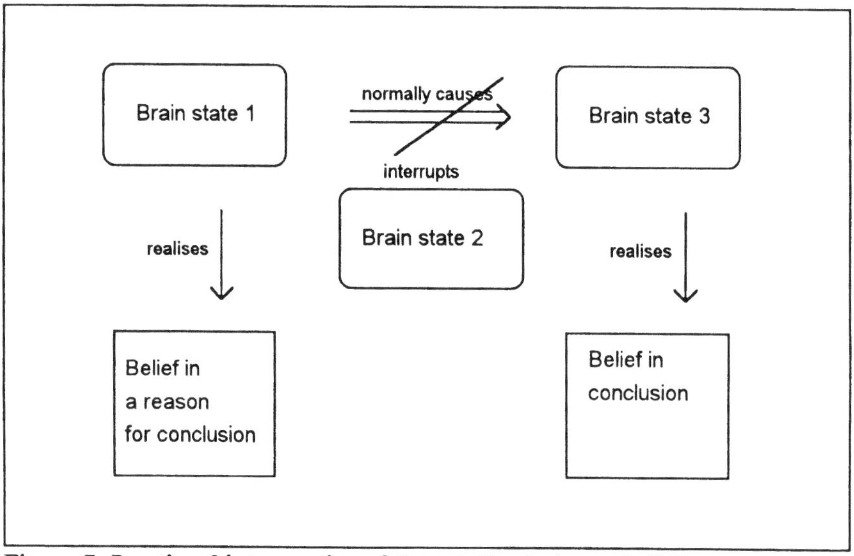

Figure 7: Irrational interruption of the relation between beliefs

Often, the factors that interrupt the causal chain between the belief in a reason and the belief in its conclusion can be made conscious, or - better - the knowledge or beliefs that were realised by these states can be made conscious.[25] For instance, I know that Gloria's car is before her apartment, but I do not believe that Gloria is at home. When asked why I do not believe that, I may recollect that I saw Gloria leave home in her jogging suit, probably on her way to the park. The brain state that embodies this memory interrupted the causal chain between my knowledge about the car and my belief that Gloria is at home. This interruption may have led to a conscious mental argument, but it may also have passed unconsciously. In the latter case, it is the question why I do not believe that Gloria is at home, that makes me remember that I saw Gloria leaving home, and that suggests that this knowledge withheld me from believing that Gloria is at home.

If a situation like this occurs, and if we approve of the interruption by facts like the ones that caused the interruption, we call such facts exclusionary reasons. Cf. figure 8

[25] The brain state that interrupts a connection cannot be made conscious *as such*. No brain state can be made conscious as such, but a brain state will sometimes realise beliefs, which can be brought to the level of consciousness.

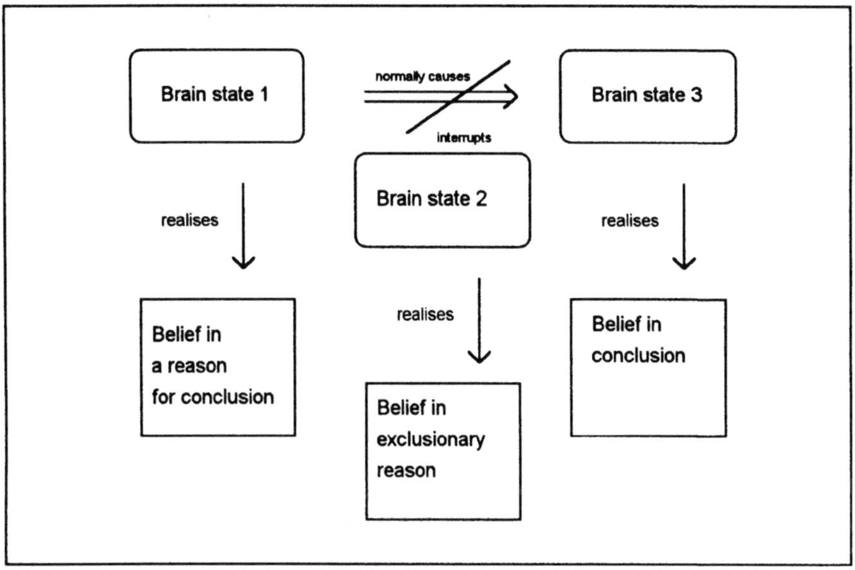

Figure 8: Interruption of relation between beliefs, by belief in an exclusionary reason

Another case in which the disturbing factor can be made conscious is when I do not only have a reason to believe something, but also a reason not to believe. Suppose that I know that Gloria always goes out shopping on Saturday mornings. Normally she takes her car for that purpose, but on rare occasions she takes the bus to the city centre. If I see Gloria's car before her apartment on a Saturday morning, this is a reason to believe that she is at home. The fact that it is Saturday morning, however, is a reason to assume that she has gone to the city centre. The conflicting evidence makes me suspend my opinion about Gloria's being at home or not. Cf. figure 9.

This last case differs from the former one, because my knowledge that Gloria's car is before her apartment still contributes to my believing that Gloria is at home. The contribution is not sufficient anymore to bring about the belief, but it is still there. If I saw Gloria go to the park, however, I know that the usual connection between the presence of the car and the presence of Gloria does not hold. My knowledge that the car is there does not even influence my belief anymore. In the one case, there is a conflict of reasons, while in the other case, there is no reason at all.

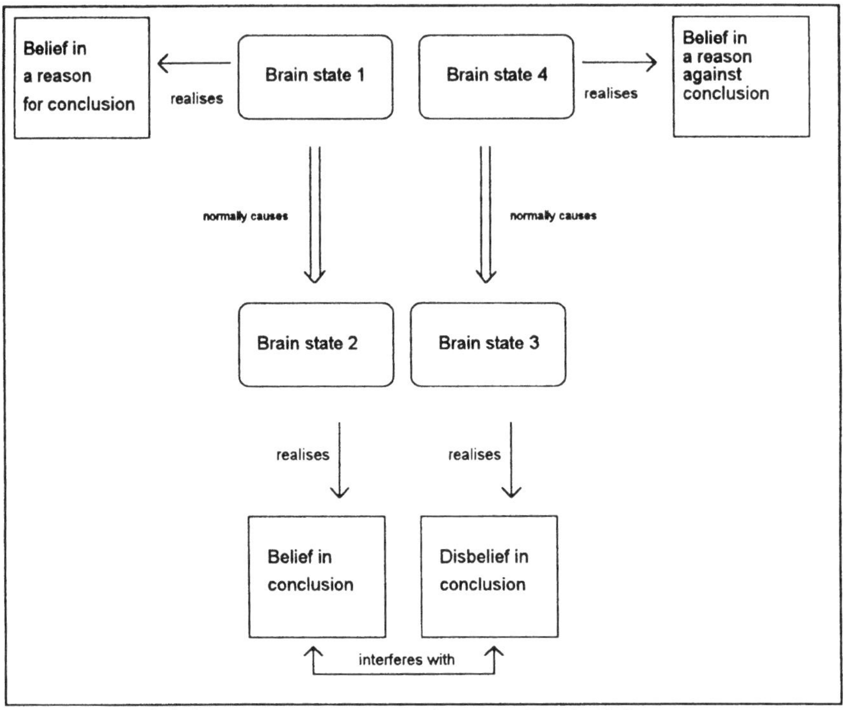

Figure 9: Beliefs in reasons for and against another belief

10.2 Consequences of the interruption

If, in a particular case, the causal connection between the belief in the presence of a reason and the belief in the conclusion of this reason is interrupted, this does not necessarily mean that the reason is not a reason anymore in general or even this particular case. To make this clear, we must fall back on the distinction between justifying reasons and explanatory reasons. If the causal chain between the two beliefs is interrupted, the second belief does not occur, or - if it occurs - it is not caused by the first belief. This means that the first belief is not the reason, *in the sense of explanatory reason*, why the second belief is held.

It does, however, not mean that the contents of the first belief are not a reason, *in the sense of justifying reason*, to hold the second belief. The relation between a reason to believe and the belief for which it is a reason depends on the existence of a *dispositional connection* between types of beliefs, and not on the existence of a causal chain between two beliefs in one particular case. If the dispositional connection still holds, facts of the one type are still potential reasons to believe in facts of the other type.

11. ADDITIONAL DEMANDS ON REASONS

Suppose that Gloria moved in with her friend, and that she has sold both her apartment and her car to Mrs. Hynde. I know that Gloria has moved, and have even made acquaintance with the new owner of the apartment. Still I have grown so accustomed to making inferences as to Gloria's presence on the basis of the presence of the red sportscar, that every time I see the car before my neighbour's apartment, I still think that Gloria is at home, that is, next door. The causal connection between my belief that the car is before my neighbour's apartment and the belief that Gloria is at home has remained, although the fact that the car is before the apartment is not a reason anymore to believe that Gloria is there.

Clearly the single presence of a dispositional connection between the two mental states is not sufficient for the existence of a reason to believe. The mere fact that belief in the presence of the red sportscar is causally connected to my belief that Gloria is next door, does not make the fact that the car is there into a reason for my believing that Gloria is next door. Two additional conditions must be fulfilled. First I must normally be able to make the connection between my two mental states (that realise the two beliefs) conscious, and second, I should approve of this connection.

11.1 Consciousness

If I do not know that I believe that Gloria is at home *because* I believe that her car is before her apartment, the fact that the red sportscar is before my neighbour's apartment is not a reason to believe that Gloria is at home. Consider, for example, the case in which I am hypnotised and have been told that if the bell rings, my dog has been hit by a car. If the bell rings and this leads me to believe that my dog has been hit by a car, while I cannot point out the correct (explanatory) reason for my belief, the fact that the bell rings cannot be considered as a justifying reason to believe that my dog was hit.

This is the case even though my hearing the bell ring is an explanatory reason for my belief. This is still true if there exists some objective connection between the ringing of the bell and my dog's being hit, as long as I am not aware of this connection, or if I am not moved by my awareness of the connection. Such a connection might make the ringing of the bell an intersubjective (social) reason to believe, but a connection that *I* do not know of, or by which I am not influenced, does not make the ringing of the bell into a reason *for me* (cf. the discussion of Ann's case in section 1.5).

Although it is necessary that the causal connection between belief states can be made conscious, it is not necessary that the connection has always a counterpart in consciousness. For instance, it is not necessary that each time that I believe that Gloria is at home because I see her car before her apartment, I realise that this belief is caused by my awareness of the car. It is necessary, however, that normally, if I am asked why I believe that Gloria is at home, I am able to explain this belief by my belief that her car is before her apartment. This is what I meant by writing that I should *know* about (rather than be aware of) the connection between my belief in the reason, and my belief in the conclusion of this reason.

11.2 Unwanted associations

Even if I am aware of the causal relation between my mental states, this does not suffice for there being a justifying reason. The example of Gloria's moving elsewhere illustrates the case in which I am aware of a causal relation between two belief states, but also know that this relation is there wrongly. In such a case, my knowledge that the car is before my neighbour's apartment explains why I believe that Gloria is next door, but the fact that the car is there is not a reason for me to believe that Gloria is next door. Only if I approve of the connection between the causing belief and the caused belief, the contents of the first belief can be said to be a reason for having the second belief.

In this connection it is still possible to distinguish between general approval of the connection between two beliefs, and approval of this connection in a particular case. It is possible to approve generally of the connection between believing that Gloria's car is before her apartment and believing that Gloria is at home, while disapproving the connection between my present belief that the car is there, and my present belief that Gloria is at home. General approval is necessary for the acceptance of a general rule of inference that connects the two beliefs. Concrete approval is necessary to make sure that I do not believe that there is an exclusionary reason that blocks the application of the inference rule in this particular case.

Notice that approval of a causal connection does not mean that one needs to have reasons for accepting the connection. If the presence of such reasons were necessary, this would lead to an infinite regress, where reasons can only be explained in terms of other reasons. Mere approval, or maybe even the absence of disapproval, suffices to make the presence of a conscious connection between belief states into a reason-giving connection.

Notice also that the necessity of approval (or of the absence of disapproval) does not mean that the causal connection between my belief states is there because of the approval, or that I decided to have that causal connection. It is very well possible that I got somehow accustomed to believing that Gloria is at home, when I see her red sportscar before her apartment. At some point in time I become aware of this connection, and I approve of it. This is sufficient to make the presence of the car into a reason to believe that Gloria is at home.

The element of self-reflection involved in the approval of the causal connection between mental states is very important for the existence of reasons. It precisely marks the difference between reasons and mere causes.[26] It would be wrong to assume a chasm between the physical on the one hand, and the mental and the rational on the other hand, but there is clearly a difference between what is purely physical and a-rational, and what is mental and (ir)rational. The 'bridge' between these two ways of considering the human brain/mind may lie in self-referential phenomena such as the approval of causal connections in ones own mind, that marks the difference between 'mere' causes and reasons.

12. SOME CHARACTERISTICS OF REASONS

By means of the example about Gloria and her car I have tried to illustrate the following characteristics of reasons:

- Reasons are facts that derive their status of reasons from a mental disposition that a belief in the reason causes a belief in the conclusion of the reason. This means that reasons are on the one hand facts, and therefore part of the world, and on the other hand mind-dependent.
- The causal connection in the mind that forms the basis for the existence of reasons is dispositional. The belief in the presence of a reason need not always cause a belief in the conclusion of this reason.
- If a dispositional connection between beliefs is to give rise to reasons, this connection must both be known and it must be approved of.
- If the causal connection between the belief in a reason and the belief in the conclusion of this reason is incidentally interrupted, there are three possibilities:
    1. the interruption is the consequence of belief in the presence of an exclusionary reason,
    2. the interruption is the consequence of the belief in the presence of a reason against the conclusion,
    3. the interruption is a case of irrationality.

Remember that the account of reasons given in this part of the chapter only refers to reasons to believe that count for a particular person. In the following part I will extend this account of personal reasons to believe into a general account of reasons and of principles.

---

[26] In this connection it is interesting to notice that Hofstadter proposes the hypothesis that high level mental phenomena involve self-reference. Cf. Hofstadter 1980, p. 709.

C. REASONS AND PRINCIPLES

There is a close connection between reasons, rules, principles and goals. In the following chapter, I will distinguish between rules on the one hand and principles and goals on the other hand. Until then, I will write about rules and principles as if there were no difference between them, and I will use the terms 'rule' and 'principle' interchangeable.

Very coarsely formulated, the connection between reasons and rules is that if somebody recognises facts of type A as reasons for facts of type B, he uses the rule 'If A then B'. For instance, if I consider the fact that Gloria's car is before her apartment as a reason to assume that Gloria is at home, I may be said to use the rule that if Gloria's car is before her apartment, Gloria is at home. Such a rule might be called a 'rule of inference'.

In the case of personal reasons it is not very natural to speak of corresponding rules or principles. It might be defended that I follow a rule of inference if I conclude that Gloria is at home because I see her car before her apartment, but this use of the expression 'rule of inference' is somewhat strained. The same would count for the expression of 'principle of inference'. However, in the case of social and institutional reasons, the connection between reasons on the one hand and rules, principles and goals on the other hand, is more natural. Therefore I will write about social and institutional reasons and rules, and to stress the continuity between personal reasons and social and institutional reasons, I will also write about personal principles.

In this part of the chapter, I will elaborate the account of personal reasons to make it cover social and institutional reasons too. Moreover, the connection between social and institutional reasons and between social and institutional principles and rules will also be analysed.

13. PERSONAL REASONS AND PERSONAL PRINCIPLES

13.1 Personal reasons

The causal account of when somebody has a reason to believe something, as it was developed in part B, comes down to the following:

The fact that F is a reason for a person P to believe that C, if and only if

1. normally if P believes that F, this causes him to believe that C;
2. normally if P believes that C as a consequence of his believing that F, P knows about this connection; and
3. P approves of his believing that C as a consequence of his believing that F.

It is important to notice that this circumscription only deals with facts that are reasons to *believe*. There are also reasons for e.g. classification and action, which will be discussed in part D of this chapter.

Notice also that the definition only concerns facts that are reasons for a specific person. Let us call such facts, that have the meaning of a reason for specific persons, *reasons for a person*, or *personal reasons*. In the sections 14 and 15 I will deal with reasons that are not confined to a single person. Reasons for a person will, however, form the basis for the description of these other categories of reasons.

13.2 Personal principles

The first element of the definition of F as a personal reason for P to believe that C is that *normally* if P believes that F, this causes him to believe also that C. The word 'normally' is important for two reasons. First, it indicates that the relation between a reason and its conclusion does not hold in every single instance. Here we find the basis for the defeasibility of reasoning with principles and rules.

Second, it indicates that the relation between a reason and its conclusion is not confined to this particular reason and its conclusion, but exists between the type of fact exemplified by the reason, and the type of fact exemplified by the conclusion. In the example about Gloria, around which the previous part was centred, every fact of the type 'Gloria's sportscar being before her house' is a reason for a fact of the type 'believing that Gloria is at home'. A particular fact cannot be a reason for some other fact or for a belief, unless facts of the former type are reasons for facts or beliefs of the latter type.

In ethical theory, Hare has described this phenomenon as *universalisability* (1963, chapter 2). If we know that a particular fact is a reason for something else, this can be universalised to the principle that all facts of this type are reasons for similar conclusions. The result of universalisation in the example of Gloria would be the principle that if Gloria's red sportscar is before her house, (I may assume that) Gloria is at home.

Clearly principles like this one have no universal validity. It is connected with reasons that only count for me, with personal reasons. In line with the term 'personal reasons', I propose to call principles of this kind, *personal principles*. As I already indicated in the introduction of this part of the chapter, the use of the term 'principle' for personal principles is somewhat strained. It is the analogy with social rules and principles that makes me nevertheless adopt this terminology.

It is not easy to give a definition of a personal principle in se. Therefore I prefer to give a contextual definition of personal principles in the form of a definition of the employment of a personal principle by some person:

A person P employs a personal principle 'If R_1, R_2, ... R_n, then C', if and only if
1. the facts r_1, r_2, ... r_n are a personal reason for P to assume that c, where
2. r_1, r_2, ... r_n are instantiations of respectively R_1, R_2, ... R_n, and where
3. c is the corresponding instantiation of C.

Suppose that Peter employs the personal principle that if somebody has no job, and still owns a fancy apartment, this person is a crook. Then, if Geraldine owns a fancy apartment, although she is jobless, these facts are a reason for Peter to consider Geraldine a crook.

13.3 Personal reasons and their consequences

Considering facts as personal reasons and employing a personal principle are two sides of one medal. The reason-terminology places emphasis on the individual cases in which facts are reasons for other facts, while the principle-terminology emphasises the universal nature of the dispositional connection between a reason and its conclusion. It is particularly important to notice that personal principles exist through being used. They cannot be the result of legislation or social convention. A personal principle is nothing else than the expression of a dispositional connection between mental states that exists in the mind of a particular person.

Whether a fact is a reason for somebody depends on the dispositional characteristics of the concerned person. If belief in the presence of some fact(s) normally generates belief in the presence of another fact, the former fact(s) are said to be reasons to believe the latter facts The presence of this disposition is expressed by saying that this person employs a personal principle to the effect that if the former facts are present, one may believe that the latter facts are present too.

This does not guarantee, however, that in a concrete case this person will believe the latter facts on the basis of the former. Only if the disposition is realised, and the person is at least motivated to believe, the principle is said to be applied, and the one belief occurs as a consequence of the other belief.[27] So we have a difference between employing a personal principle on the one hand, and applying it on the other hand. Employing the principle, that is having the suitable mental disposition, normally makes certain facts into justifying reasons to believe other facts. Application of the principle comes down to

---

[27] It need not be the case that the other belief actually occurs. It suffices for the application of the principle and the corresponding generation of a reason, that the person is motivated to have the second belief. Normally this motivation leads to the belief, but it is possible that there is also a reason to disbelieve which outweighs the reason to believe. In that case the application of the principle and the generation of the reason do not lead to the corresponding belief. Cf. the discussion of this case in section 10.1.

the realisation of this disposition in a particular case: the belief in the one fact causes (motivation for) the belief in the other fact. It is this application that makes the former belief into the explanatory reason of the latter belief.[28]

Exclusionary reasons are reasons not to apply a principle or rule. The presence of an exclusionary reason against the application of a principle prevents this principle from generating a reason. The *mere presence* of an exclusionary reason against the application of a principle prevents this principle from generating a *justifying* reason. So the fact that Gloria went to the park is an exclusionary reason that prevents the principle that if Gloria's car is before her house, Gloria is at home, from generating a reason. If Gloria is to the park, the fact that her car is before her house is not a reason anymore to believe that Gloria is at home.

Belief in the presence of an exclusionary reason will normally prevent the principle from being applied as a mental event, and from generating an *explanatory* reason. So if I believe that Gloria is to the park, this will normally prevent me from considering the presence of her car as a reason to believe that Gloria is at home. However, it may be the case that the dispositional connection between my belief in an exclusionary reason and the non-application of the rule of inference is not realised. In that case, I should not apply the rule of inference, and I do not have a reason to believe, but nevertheless, I do apply it, and the belief in the reason causes the belief in the conclusion. So it may be the case that I believc that Gloria is in the park, but that this belief does not prevent me from letting my awareness of Gloria's car cause my belief in Gloria's being at home. In that case, (my awareness of) the presence of the car is the cause of, but not a (justifying) reason for my belief that Gloria is at home.

14. SOCIAL REASONS AND SOCIAL RULES

If I am considered an irrational person, this does often not mean that I have no reasons for my behaviour or my beliefs, but rather that I have the wrong reasons. For instance, if I consider the facts that a woman has a wrinkled face and a crooked back as reasons to believe that she is a witch, I am irrational, because I consider the wrong facts as reasons. My reasons for believing that she is a witch are said to be not really reasons, or to be no good reasons. Still,

---

28 It is somewhat strange to speak of the application of a personal principle, since the use of a personal principle is a mental disposition which works 'automatically'. The existence of social and institutional rules is not purely a matter of individual mental dispositions, however, and in those cases it makes sense to speak of their being applied. It is again conformity of terminology that makes me write about application in the case of personal principles too.

for me they are good reasons. What does it mean that facts that are good reasons for me, are in some sense not good reasons?

The answer is that we must distinguish between personal reasons, and what might be called *social reasons*. 'Social reason' is a term of art; I will use it for facts that are considered as reasons by most members of a social group. Social reasons are reasons based on *social rules*.

If the wind suddenly becomes stronger, and the sky is quickly darkening with clouds, this is for most Dutch people a reason to believe that it will soon rain. These facts are *for a typical Dutchman* a reason to believe that it will rain. In other words, they are a personal reason, but not only for one person, but for most persons that partake in the group.

Moreover, most group members not only consider the increasing wind and the darkening sky as personal reasons to believe that it will rain, but also as reasons why others should believe that it will rain. Social reasons are perhaps the most important category of reasons in daily life. Humans that live together must harmonise their behaviour, and this brings the demand with it that behaviour is predictable. The best basis for harmonisation of behaviour is if people consider the same things as reasons for behaviour or for belief, that is, if they use the same rules. That is why members of a group not only often consider the same facts as reasons, but also exercise some social pressure for conformity. This pressure for conformity can take many different forms, from avoidance and ridiculing to punishment and banishment from the group. It is this pressure that distinguishes social rules and reasons from mere personal principles and personal reasons that count for many group members.[29]

14.1 Definitions

This leads to the following definition of social reasons to believe:

A fact F is a social reason in a group G to believe that C, if and only if:

1. for most members of G, F is a personal reason to believe that C;
2. most members of G approve of it if other members of G base their belief of C on the evidence provided by F, and disapprove of it if this does not happen.

Analogous to the relation between personal reasons and personal principles, we can define the relation between social reasons and social rules to believe:

[29] Clearly this account of social rules is inspired by Hart's account of social rules. Cf. Hart 1961, pp. 50f.

In a group G a social rule 'If R_1, R_2, ... R_n, then (it may be held that) C' is valid, if and only if

1. the facts r_1, r_2, ... r_n are a personal reason for most members of G to assume that c, where
2. r_1, r_2, ... r_n are instantiations of respectively R_1, R_2, ... R_n, and c is the corresponding instantiation of C; and
3. most members of G approve of it if other members of G base their belief of c on the evidence provided by r_1, r_2, ... r_n, and disapprove of it if this does not happen.

14.2 Social rules and points of view

Many social rules do not exist independently, but exist together and belong to a particular point of view.[30] Clear examples are moral rules or principles and the rules of etiquette, which belong to the moral point of view, respectively the point of view of etiquette. Legal rules and principles belong to the legal point of view.

There are social rules that do not belong to a point of view, such as for instance the rule about the prediction of rain that I mentioned just ago. Many rules of evidence will be social rules that do not belong to a particular point of view. Rules of games that have never been established officially still belong to a point of view, however, namely the point of view defined by the game in question. There are also in-between cases. For instance, the methodological rules that define scientific method might be said to belong to the scientific point of view, but they may also be subsumed under the larger category of rules of evidence that do not belong to a point of view.

Points of view are important, because reasons that belong to a point of view have often no force outside that point of view. The rules of a game may provide us with reasons to behave in a particular way, for instance not to touch the ball with our hands. These reasons have no force at all outside the context of the game, although there may be independent reasons to play the game and, consequently, to stick by the rules. Moreover, reasons from a particular point of view often exclude other facts as reasons *as far as this point*

---

30 Following Taylor 1961, I distinguish a point of view from a set of rules which define the point of view. For instance, both in the Netherlands and in China it is possible to evaluate behaviour from the legal point of view. Nevertheless, different rule sets will be involved in the evaluation. This is in agreement with the circumscription of a point of view given in Raz 1993, as 'any such perspective which we can assume and reason from, or turn away from and shun'.

of view is concerned. Reasons from the point of view of etiquette may be set aside completely while playing a competitive game.[31]

14.3 The relation between personal principles and social rules

There is no opposition between personal reasons and social reasons. In fact, most personal reasons will also be social reasons. If I consider the presence of thunderclouds as a forebode of rain, that is, as a personal reason to believe that it will rain, this does not exclude that the same holds for other persons, and that everybody thinks that thunderclouds are also a reason for others to believe that it will rain. In other words, there is a social rule to the effect that thunderclouds predict rain, and my adoption of this social rule is realised in my employment of the personal rule that thunderclouds predict rain. Many personal principles are but personal instances of social rules, while the existence of social rules to a large extent depends on the employment of the corresponding personal principles.

Still there is an important difference between personal principles and social rules in that the employment of personal principles is closely tied to the mind of individual persons. This closer connection manifests itself for instance in the smaller likelihood of irrational behaviour with respect to personal principles in comparison to social rules.

In connection with personal reasons I have already discussed the example of the irrational belief. If, after Gloria's moving in with her friend, I still believe that Gloria is next door when I see the red sportscar that used to belong to her, this is irrational, because I know that Gloria has sold the car and does not live next door anymore. The fact that the car is before the door is therefore not a justifying reason. Although I am still disposed to associate the presence of Gloria with that of the car, I do not employ a personal rule to that purpose anymore.

Situations like these are, however, exceptional. It will not often happen that we systematically disapprove of our own mental associations, because the very fact of this disapproval will usually influence our association patterns, so that the discrepancy will disappear. Our mind has mechanisms that preserve consistency. These mechanisms are certainly not perfect, but nevertheless they produce by and large harmony between what we tend to believe and what we think is rational to believe. As a consequence, believes that tend to induce other believes are usually also considered to be relevant, that is, to reflect personal reasons.

---

[31] Cf. also the example discussed in section 1.5 about Jeremy who had to obey an order in the army.

In the case of social reasons, discrepancies between our associations and the demands of (social) rationality will occur more often. The reason for this is that now the standards by means of which we evaluate infering behaviour are group standards. Group standards cannot make use of the mental mechanism to maintain consistency. A person can easily base beliefs on other beliefs and continue to do this for quite a long time, although this connection between these beliefs may be in disagreement with social standards.

The example of my believing in witches is a case in point. I might consider certain facts as reasons why a particular woman is a witch. That means that I might not only base my belief that somebody is a witch on the facts that her face is wrinkled and that she has a crooked back, but also that I might be aware of this connection, and approve of it. It might even be the case that I think that others should also consider these facts as reasons for assuming that somebody is a witch. Still, these facts are no good social reasons, because most group members do not approve of my basing the conclusion that the woman is a witch on my beliefs that her face is wrinkled and that she is hunch-backed.

14.4 The independence of social rules and reasons

In the case of social rules, we often do not speak of a rule that is being employed, but rather about a rule that is accepted or even valid. This difference already suggests the independence of social rules of their being employed by each and every member of the group. The existence of a personal rule is completely dependent on the mental dispositions of one particular person. The existence of social rules and reasons, on the contrary, is tied to groups. Not all members of a group need to recognise a social reason as a reason for themselves.

As a consequence social rules and reasons seem to exist more or less independently; a particular individual needs not recognise social reasons and still they are social reasons. Maybe this relative independence of social reasons of individual acceptance, and their dependence on rules that are also relatively independent of individual acceptance, give social reasons a semblance of objectivity. In this sense they represent a force that, from the perspective of a group member, is coming from the outside.

The relative independence of social rules and reasons of the mental behaviour of individual group members makes that social rules have some kind of ontological priority with regard to social reasons. The employment of a personal principle is nothing else than the reflection of certain facts being regarded as reasons for particular conclusions. One might say that the reasons were there first, and that the principle is nothing else than shorthand for the reason-giving relationship that exists between kinds of facts.

In the case of social rules, the situation is the other way round. Social reasons often take their character as reasons from social rules that existed independently; independently that is, from the perspective of the individual. These social rules are transmitted as such among the group members, and the reason-character of some facts is justified by invoking the rule. For these social reasons counts that they are reasons because of the application of the social rule that underlies them.

14.5 Exclusionary reasons, conflicting reasons, and social rules

The presence of exclusionary reasons prevents accepted social rules from generating reasons. In this connection, only *social* exclusionary reasons have this effect. Suppose, for instance, that I walk along a canal and in it I see a little child that obviously cannot swim, almost drowning. Then I have a social (moral) reason to jump into the canal to save the child. Maybe I do not like to get wet, and if I am a-social this may be a sufficient reason *for me* to block the application of the principle that tells me to jump and save the child. In that case, there is no reason *for me* to save the child. However, this reason to block the application of the rule is not socially recognised. Therefore, the application of the social rule is not blocked, and there still is a social reason why I should jump and save the child.

The determination of what is rational to believe is in the case of social rules and reasons also the result of weighing all the relevant *social* reasons. It will not do to balance a personal reason against believing and a social reason for believing. The outcome will be irrational from the social point of view. Suppose that in a particular group three black crows signify danger. Personally, however, I also believe that the absence of clouds means that there will be no danger. This opinion is not shared by the other members of my group, who think that my belief in the predictive value of clouds is superstitious. If I weigh the presence of the black crows against the absence of clouds, and postpone judgement, I will be considered irrational, because the group members only see a sign of approaching danger.

15. INSTITUTIONAL REASONS

Institutional reasons are even more independent of the mental dispositions of individual persons than social reasons. Institutional reasons are based on rules that are defined by and for a particular social institution. The most prominent of these institutions is the law. The legislator makes statutes and creates in that way rules of law. These rules define which facts count as legal reasons.

Suppose that the Dutch legislator makes a statute that prohibits smoking in public offices. As a consequence the Dutch law contains a rule that says that it is forbidden to smoke in public offices. Given this rule, the fact that some act would be smoking in a public office is a legal reason not to perform this act. Or, to take an example about making inferences: if there exists a legal rule to the effect that a deed is sufficient proof for the existence of a contract, then the fact that there is a deed stating that two parties engaged into a particular contract is a reason to assume that this particular contract exists.

15.1 Institutional facts and institutional rules

Let us call the rules that were made in the context of and in accordance with the criteria of a particular institution, *institutional rules*. A typical example of institutional rules are legal rules that were made by legislation. These rules are made as legal rules, that is, in the context of the institution of the law, and moreover, they are made in accordance with the rules (criteria) laid down by the law (the institution) for making rules of law.

The fact that John, who is a public servant, ought not to smoke in his office, is based on the institutional rule that it is forbidden to smoke in public offices. This fact, which is based on an institutional rule, may be called an *institutional fact*. This terminology differs from that of MacCormick, who only recognises instantiations of (legal) institutions as institutional facts (cf. section 4.3).

Institutional facts are reason-based facts, where the reasons are based on institutional rules. A special case of an institutional fact is the fact that a particular rule is valid because it is made in accordance with the rules of the institution. These latter rules (of recognition) are usually institutional rules themselves, and therefore the validity of institutional rules is often a matter of institutional fact.

15.2 Validity and effectiveness of institutional rules

Characteristically, in the case of institutional rules, it is possible to distinguish between a rule's validity and the rule's effectiveness. Whether a rule is valid, whether it is part of the institution[32], depends on whether it is made according to the correct procedure and was not abolished. It does generally not depend

[32] In my opinion, the notion of validity as used in connection with institutional rules, has nothing to do with 'binding force' or something of the kind. Almost on the contrary, I would say. Binding force is more typically connected with personal principles, because personal reasons for behaviour by definition tend to generate the correct motivations. Institutional rules, which generate institutional reasons (for behaviour) provide the least guarantee (in comparison to personal and social rules) that the obligations which stem from them are *experienced* as binding.

on its being effective in the sense of being followed (cf. Kelsen 1945, pp. 29f.; Hart 1961, p. 100).

Of course, the existence of an institutional rule depends on the existence of a social institution. If the rules that are institutionally valid are *on a large scale* not recognised by the persons for which they are meant, the existence of the institution itself has become dubious. There should at least be a common acceptance between the members of a group of the rules deriving from an institution. This demand has been formulated in legal theory by Kelsen (1945, p. 42) as the demand that the *legal system as a whole* should be effective. Hart (1961, pp. 97f.) formulates a comparable demand, namely that there should be a *social rule*, the Ultimate Rule of Recognition, among the participants in the legal system, which is used to identify rules of law.

In general, it may be said that the existence of social institutions depends on the existence of social rules that define these institutions. Even institutions that are created on the basis of institutional rules depend in the last instance on social rules, because there cannot be an infinite regress of institutions. Therefore we may say that the existence of institutional rules ultimately depends on the existence of social rules, which in their turn depend on the employment of personal principles.

Legal rules made by means of legislation are paradigmatic cases of institutional rules. The rules of soccer, of chess, and of hockey, are also institutional rules. There are organisations that have the power to modify the rules of these games.

Institutional reasons fully depend on institutional rules; their existence is independent of the mental dispositions of individual persons. Even if the existence of a deed would not make most persons believe that there is a contract, still this existence is a legal reason to believe in the existence of a contract. The consequences of an institutional rule obtain, whether the rule actually lives in people's minds or not. Only if the universal disuse of a rule leads to the removal of the rule from the institution - and whether this is the case depends on the institution - the rule does not generate reasons anymore.

15.3 Institutional rules and points of view

Institutional rules belong by definition to a particular *point of view*. If a rule of soccer prescribes that only the keeper is allowed to play the ball by means of his hands, this prohibition (for the other players) is only a prohibition from the point of view of soccer. In hockey, other players than the keeper are (subject to certain conditions) also allowed to play the ball with the hand. Legally there is normally no problem with touching a ball by the hand.

Institutions define points of view and the rules belonging to institutions constitute reason-based facts from that particular point of view. The power to make rules or to engage into contracts is a *legal* power. Statutory definitions make that some classifications are *legally* applicable, while the legal applicability of a concept may deviate from its 'normal' use. It is, for instance, imaginable that something which under common parlance would not be considered as a vehicle, legally counts as a vehicle.

Although all institutional rules belong to a point of view, the opposite need not be the case. A clear counter-example is the moral point of view, which does not contain institutional rules at all. But even sets of rules that belong to the legal point of view will often contain rules which are not institutional. Customary rules of law, for instance, are not institutional rules. There is no legislator for customary law, and still the rules of customary law are part of the law. This goes to show that an institutionalised social system need not only contain institutional rules; it can also have social rules as its constituents.

15.4 The objectivity of institutional reasons

The most fundamental difference between personal principles and institutional rules concerns their mode of existence. Social institutions have means to make, change, and abolish institutional rules. Rules made according to the procedures pointed out by the institution are valid, independent of their effectiveness amongst those who partake in the institution. Moreover, the power of institutional rules to generate reasons is similar to that of social rules: Only reasons not to apply an institutional rule which are recognised as such by the point of view defined by the institution can prevent an applicable institutional rule from generating an institutional reason.[33]

As a consequence, the existence of institutional reasons is to a large extent independent of the (mental) behaviour of the individuals that partake in the social institution, let alone those who do not even partake in the institution. Institutional reasons are so 'objective' that they almost seem to be mind-independent. Only if we go back to the social rules that define the institution, we can find the mind-dependent reasons on which even institutional reasons in the end rely.

---

33 There is a subtlety involved here in the case of points of view, such as the law, that contain social rules next to institutional rules. It is possible that a social rule that is part of the law (a legal principle) excludes the application of an institutional legal rule. In other words, it is sometimes possible (at least in the Netherlands) to review a legal rule against a legal principle. This is an exception to the principle that exclusionary reasons are always of the same type (personal, social, or institutional) as the rule the application of which they exclude.

15.5 The internal and the external perspective on rules

The distinction between personal principles on the one hand, and social and institutional rules on the other hand, is related to the distinction, popularised by Hart, between the internal and the (moderately) external point of view (Hart 1961, pp. 86-88). Somebody takes the internal point of view towards a rule, if he considers the facts corresponding to the rule conditions as a reason for the presence of (for behaving according to) the rule conclusion.

For example, the fact that somebody is a thief is considered as a reason for punishing this person. Somebody who takes an extreme external point of view does not 'see' anymore than regularities in behaviour. For instance, he sees that thieves are usually punished. From a moderately external point of view, the observer sees that the members of a group consider being a thief as a reason for punishing; the observer himself remains uncommitted regarding the issue whether being a thief is a reason for being punished.

The internal point of view as described by Hart can, in my opinion, more or less be identified with considering facts as personal reasons. If I take the internal point of view to the rule that thieves ought to be punished, I consider the fact that somebody is a thief as a reason *for me* to punish this person (or having him punished).[34]

The moderately external point of view is the point of view of someone who recognises the existence of a social or an institutional rule, without using this as a personal rule. For instance, I recognise that if somebody is a thief, this is legally a reason to punish him. Personally, however, I object against punishment in general, and against punishing thieves in particular.

16. PRINCIPLES AND REASONS

In the previous sections we have seen that there is a general relationship between reasons on the one hand, and principles and rules on the other hand. Principles make facts into reasons for their conclusions. This relation can be depicted as in the Toulmin-like figure 10. In section 22 I will extend this figure by incorporating the relation between a constitutive reason and the reason-based fact that is generated by it.

---

[34] If something is a personal reason for acting, this means that this reason probably motivates the person for whom the reason exists. It may, however, be the case that the concerning person is not the appropriate person to perform the action for which the reason exists. (This person is not the addressee of the norm.) In that case, the concerning person should not be motivated to perform the action himself, although he will tend to approve of the concerning action if performed by the appropriate person.

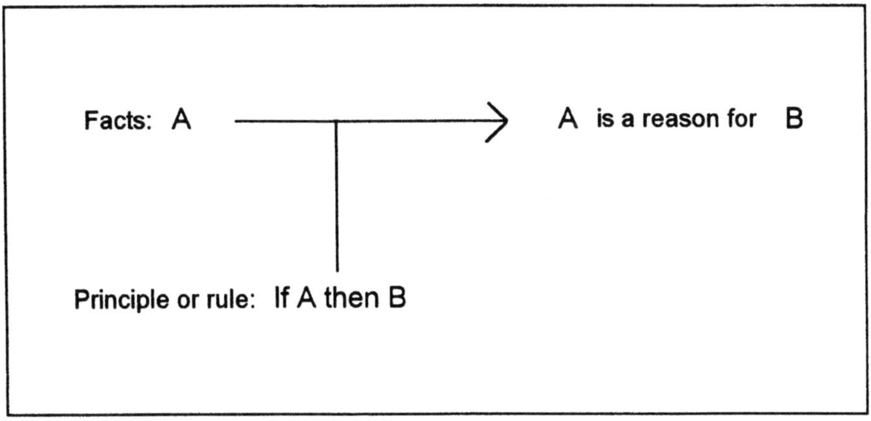

Figure 10: The transformation of facts into reasons

In the sequence personal principles, social rules, and institutional rules, we find an increasing 'objectivity' as far as the presence of reasons is concerned. This increase in objectivity is paralleled by a switch in the relation between reasons on the one hand, and principles and rules on the other hand.

Personal principles are little else than the result of universalising personal reasons; they have little or no independent existence. Social rules, on the contrary, are normally prior to social reasons. Social reasons are there because a social rule is applicable to a particular situation, and not the other way round. Still, the presence of social rules is still dependent on reason-recognising behaviour of the members of a social group. This dependency has in the case of institutional rules almost completely disappeared. Institutional rules exist, are valid, if they are made according to the relevant procedures defined by the institution. If facts satisfy the conditions of these rules, they will normally be institutional reasons, independent of whether these reasons have effects on the (mental) behaviour of people. Institutional reasons are as 'objective' as personal reasons are 'subjective'. Nevertheless, the mechanisms of exclusionary reasons and of conflicting reasons that are relevant in the field of personal reasons maintain their logical functions in the fields of social and institutional reasons.

D. KINDS OF REASONS

With some modifications, the account of reasons and the rules connected to them as it was given in the previous part of this chapter not only applies to reasons to believe, but also to other kinds of reasons. Running ahead of a more extensive discussion, I want to distinguish two main kinds of reasons, namely epistemic and constitutive reasons.[35] *Epistemic reasons* are reasons for believing in facts that obtain independent of the reasons that plead for or against believing them. *Constitutive reasons*, on the contrary, influence the very existence of their conclusions. In the discussion of reason-based facts (section 4) we have already encountered the phenomenon of constitutive reasons.

Constitutive reasons can be subdivided into two subcategories, namely classificatory reasons and modal reasons. Classificatory reasons are reasons why something belongs to a particular class, or falls under a category. The modal reasons can finally be subdivided into anankastic, deontic, and (again) epistemic reasons. Anankastic reasons are reasons why something is (im)possible or necessary.[36] Deontic reasons are reasons why something is permitted, obliged, a duty, or should or ought (not) to be done, or to be the case. Epistemic reasons are not only reasons why something may be assumed, but also reasons why some things are certain, or probable. Cf. figure 11.

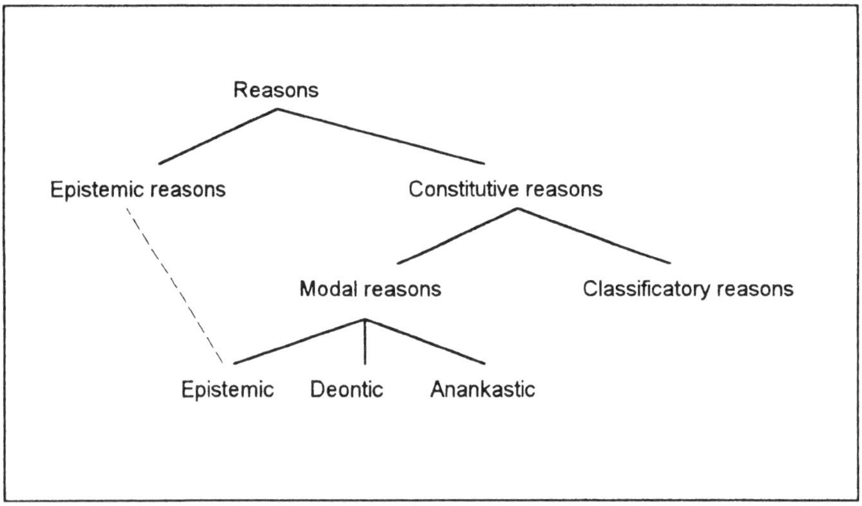

Figure 11: Kinds of reasons

The conclusions of modal reasons will be called 'modal facts', or 'modalities'. Following analyses of White (1975), I distinguish three main categories of modalities, anankastic, deontic and epistemic, that correspond to the three mentioned kinds of modal reasons.

---

[35] This distinction cuts across the distinction between causal and justifying reasons. Cf. section 8. I return to this distinction in the sections VI.6 and 7.

[36] The use of the term 'anankastic' follows a suggestion of Von Wright 1963, p. 10.

The distinction between kinds of reasons and their conclusions is in particular important because I want to argue that seemingly different phenomena such as classifications and deontic judgements are based on the same underlying mechanism and that, as a consequence, one and the same logic can be used to deal with these seemingly heterogeneous phenomena.

I will in turn discuss classificatory, deontic, anankastic and epistemic reasons, and in each case I will pay some attention to phenomena that are closely related to the concerning kind of reasons and rules. This chapter is closed with short discussions of the relations between reasons and the points of view to which they sometimes belong.

17. CLASSIFICATORY REASONS AND RULES

Classificatory reasons are reasons why a concept is applicable to a particular situation. Legal definitions and all other stipulative definitions provide a basis for classificatory reasons: The fact that John took Mary's purse is the reason why John is a thief; that this paper contains uncle Henry's declaration of what he wants to happen with his estate after his death, is the reason why it is his last will.

17.1 Classificatory rules

Not all classificatory reasons need to be based on explicit definitions. For instance, the facts that this piece of wood has a top and four legs are together a reason why it is a table. Or the fact that soldier X ran away as soon as the enemy appeared is the reason why he is a coward. (Or why he is prudent, depending on the classificatory standards used.) The criteria for being a table, a coward or for being prudent have never been stated (authoritatively) by means of an explicit definition. Instead they rest on social rules (conventions) that are accepted within a certain community involved in the practice of classifying pieces of furniture and evaluating behaviour in terms of (amongst others) cowardice and prudence.

For a while the theory has been popular that rules of language specify for each term a number of conditions that are individually necessary and together necessary for the term to apply. These conditions together were assumed to form the term's intension or connotation (cf. Carnap 1956, pp. 18f. and Copi 1978, pp. 142f.). Semantically ambiguous terms would have more than one intension, while synonyms would share an intension. On this theory, which is sometimes called the 'classical theory', classificatory rules specify the intensions of terms. Stipulative definitions are good examples of such rules. For instance: A thief is somebody who takes away a good that belongs to somebody else, with the intention to appropriate this good illegally.

It has turned out that the classical theory does not work satisfactorily for all cases, and consequently it has lost popularity to the prototype theory. The prototype theory holds that there are prototypical instances of a concept or category, and other instances that still belong to the category, but are less characteristic for the category than the prototypical cases (cf. Rosch 1978, Smith 1989 and 1990, and Lakoff 1987a and 1987b). Philosophical precursors of prototype theory are Wittgenstein's theory of family resemblances and Putnam's theory of stereotypes (Wittgenstein 1953, 67, and Putnam 1975, pp. 247f.).

On the prototype theory, classificatory rules would specify the characteristics of a prototypical instance of a category and the extent in which a concrete specimen may deviate from the prototype to remain a member of the category.[37] For instance, a classificatory rule may specify a prototypical table as a flat rectangular top of approximately 0.3 square metres, supported by four legs under the corners of the table. Deviations from this prototype may concern each of these characteristics in varying degrees, but not all of them at once and to a large extent.

If a particular piece of furniture has characteristics that make it sufficiently similar to the prototypical table, these characteristics are the reason why this piece of furniture is a table. It is then possible to construct a rule that says that pieces of furniture with these characteristics are tables. Such a rule would count as a classificatory rule.

On the prototype theory, classificatory rules must be reconstructed from reasons. It is not possible to determine prior to actual classifications all possible sets of facts which make a piece of furniture into a table. Yet, as soon as a classification has taken place, there will be a reason for it, and this reason also counts in other, similar situations. This makes it acceptable to speak of classificatory rules, although these rules cannot be formulated a priori.[38]

17.2 Classification and evaluation

The example of the fleeing soldier shows that there can also be classificatory reasons for applying evaluative terms. There is a difference between the reason why something is, for example, a last will and the reason why somebody is a coward, but this difference is not one between classificatory reasons and

---

[37] It is not impossible that a category has more than one prototype. I will leave this complication out of consideration here.

[38] It seems to me that classificatory rules only apply to non-prototypical instances of a category, and that the reasons why something belongs to a category refer to the characteristics of prototypical instances, or are based on relations between categories. A typical apple, for instance, is an apple just because this kind of thing is an apple (no particular reason at all). That the apple is also a fruit is because apples are fruits (a classificatory rule).

another kind of reasons. Classificatory reasons are always reasons for or against the applicability of a concept in a particular situation. If the classification serves some particular purpose, such as for instance evaluation, classificatory reasons are also reasons for something different, such as praise, admiration, or criticism. For instance, the fact that the soldier ran away as the enemy appeared is both a reason why he is a coward and a reason why he is to be blamed. However, the primary function of classificatory reasons is that they contribute to, or detract from the applicability of a concept. Classification covers both sides of the fact/value dichotomy.[39]

17.3 The two levels of constitutive reasons

Classificatory reasons function on two levels. On one level, the fact that soldier X ran away is the reason why he *is* a coward. The relation between the reason and its conclusion is depicted in the world; it is a relation between facts. This level may be called the *ontological level*, and the reason that functions on it is a constitutive reason.

The other level concerns human classification. The fact that soldier X ran away is the reason why *we should classify him* as a coward. In this view the reason is a reason for some form of mental behaviour, for making a particular classification. This second level may therefore be called the *behavioural level*, and the reason that functions on it is a deontic reason. Cf. figure 12.

That soldier X ran away as soon as the enemy appeared	is a constitutive reason why	Soldier X is a coward	The level of ontological relations in the world
That soldier X ran away as soon as the enemy appeared	is a deontic reason to consider	him as a coward	The level of mental behaviour

Figure 12: The ontological and the behavioural level of constitutive reasons

39 In fact, the phenomenon that both purely factual and value judgements are based on the same kind of reasons places the whole fact/value dichotomy in a dubious light. Cf. Hage 1986 and 1987.

The distinction between the ontological and the behavioural level occurs with all kinds of reasons. It should be noted that the two levels of consideration do not refer to different things. The reasons why something falls under a concept and why we should apply that particular concept, are identical. The two levels of consideration are just two ways of looking at the same phenomenon. This is, of course, in full agreement with the position of internal realism that the world and knowledge of the world cannot be completely separated (cf. section 6).

We will encounter the connection between the ontological and the behavioural level more often in this work and therefore section III.15 contains an additional discussion of this phenomenon under the heading of *deontic collapse*.

17.4 The three functions of classificatory reasons

The two levels on which classificatory reasons can be considered also indicate two of the three functions of classificatory reasons. First they are reasons why some facts (or things) belong to a particular category, and second they are reasons to classify these facts or things as belonging to this category.

Classificatory reasons can finally also give rise to inferences. From the fact that John took Mary's purse, we may infer that John is a thief. On the one hand, the fact that John took Mary's purse is a reason why John may be classified as a thief (why he is a thief). On the other hand, we can use this same fact to make inferences about John's status as a thief. The inferential function of classificatory reasons is parasitic on the classificatory function. Only because a fact is a reason to classify in a particular way, it is also a reason to assume that this particular classification is applicable. The fact that is inferred does in this case not exist independent of the fact from which it was inferred, as it would be in the case of proper epistemic reasons.

I will illustrate the three functions of classificatory reasons by means of a table:

1.	The fact that soldier X ran away as soon as the enemy appeared	is a reason why he *is*	a coward.
2.	The fact that soldier X ran away as soon as the enemy appeared	is a reason to *consider*	him as a coward.
3.	The fact that soldier X ran away as soon as the enemy appeared	is a reason to *assume*	that he is a coward.

The first two rows of this table represent respectively the ontological and the behavioural level on which classificatory reasons can be considered. The third row represents the parasitic inferential function of classificatory reasons.

18. DEONTIC REASONS, NORMS AND GOALS

Deontic reasons are reasons for the existence of duties and obligations, prohibitions, etc. For example, the fact that taking Mary's purse would be theft is the reason why John is legally prohibited to take the purse. The fact that Eric promised to visit Derek is the reason why Eric has a duty to visit Derek. These examples illustrate the ontological way of looking at deontic reasons: the reason is a reason why a particular deontic situation *exists*.

18.1 Deontic facts as a species of reason-based facts

The conclusions of deontic reasons are *facts*. It may seem strange that it is considered to be a fact if George ought to pay Geraldine a certain amount of money, because this duty seems to have no basis in material facts. Still we do not hesitate to speak about the fact that George ought to pay Geraldine an amount of money, and of, for instance, the consequences which this fact has for George's behaviour.

Moreover, the fact has a material basis in the ground for George's duty. Maybe he has made a promise or something like that. The existence of the duty is a reason-based fact, which is itself immaterial, but which has a material basis in the reasons that constituted it. If we are prepared to accept the existence of reason-based facts in general, there is no additional difficulty in accepting the presence of duties, permissions, etc. as facts. I propose to call this kind of fact *deontic facts.*[40]

18.2 Some terminological issues

In natural language, there are many different words to express deontic facts. Next to the traditional words such as 'ought', 'forbidden', 'duty', 'permitted' etc., there are terms like 'should', 'must', and 'may' which, at least in some of their uses, also express deontic modalities.

There are subtle differences between the deontic states expressed by the different deontic words. Often these differences are connected to the point of view to which the deontic modalities belong. Moral obligations are perfectly well expressed by the words 'ought' and 'duty', while these same words would often be too strong if the reasons are only based on my personal preferences. It is, for instance, somewhat odd to say that I ought to eat an ice cream, because I would like to have one. But it seems right to say that you *should* eat an ice cream if you like to (but cf. also section 18.6). In many legal cases, the

---

[40] Von Wright 1963, p. 106 uses the term 'normative statement' for what seems to me the same thing. Alchourrón and Bulygin 1981 write about normative propositions in distinction to norms.

word 'obligated' seems in place, such as when one is obligated to repay the loaned money.[41]

In the remainder of this work, I will not pay much attention to the different shades of the deontic modalities.

18.3 Norms as opposed to deontic facts

Deontic rules, or *norms*, are rules (or principles) with deontic facts as their conclusions. They indicate under which circumstances something is prohibited, permitted, or obligated, or when somebody has a duty. Notice that I use the expression 'norm' for a kind of rule. It is not uncustomary, especially among deontic logicians, to use the expression 'norm' for everything that contains a deontic component. In particular, what I would call deontic facts, such as the fact that John ought not take Mary's car, would also be called a norm.[42]

My choice for this terminology stems from the fact that I see the distinctions rule / fact, and non-deontic[43] / deontic as orthogonal, and do not wish to have another label than 'deontic' for the combination of deontic facts and deontic rules. Cf. the following table:

	fact	**rule**
deontic	deontic facts John ought not take Mary's car	deontic rules, or norms One ought not take another person's property
non-deontic **e.g. classificatory**	non-deontic facts John is a thief	non-deontic (e.g. classificatory) rules Who takes another person's property is a thief

---

41 Extensive analyses of the different deontic notions and their interrelations can be found in White 1984.

42 Cf. for instance the implicit adoption of the term 'norm' for both normative rules and normative propositions in the introduction of Hilpinen 1971. The use of one term for both deontic facts and deontic rules will often reflect an unwillingness to distinguish for logical purposes between statements and rules.

An elaborate discussion of the terminology concerning norms is given in Von Wright 1963.

43 I prefer not to use the word 'alethic' as the opposite of 'deontic', because *alethic* means 'concerning truth or falsehood', and because sentences that describe modal facts are also true or false. The distinction alethic/deontic rests precisely on the confusion between the distinctions rule/fact and deontic/non-deontic that I try to avoid here.

18.4 Goals and norms

In the deontic field, where reasons for behaviour are involved, not only rules, but also goals can underlie reasons. If, for instance, somebody wants to become a professional soccer-player, this goal makes for him the fact that smoking stands in the way of his professional ambitions, into a reason not to smoke. Similarly, the goal not to have lung cancer would make the fact that smoking increases the chance of having lung cancer into a reason against smoking. Cf. figure 13.

Having (pursuing) a goal functions in a similar way as having a norm (but cf. section III.6.4). In fact, goals can easily be 'translated' into corresponding norms. If somebody has the goal G, this can be translated into his using the norm that if some action contributes to G, this action should be performed.[44] In this connection, the notion of a goal should be taken in a broad sense. Goals include desires, needs, policies, values, interests, and - in some sense of the word - rights.

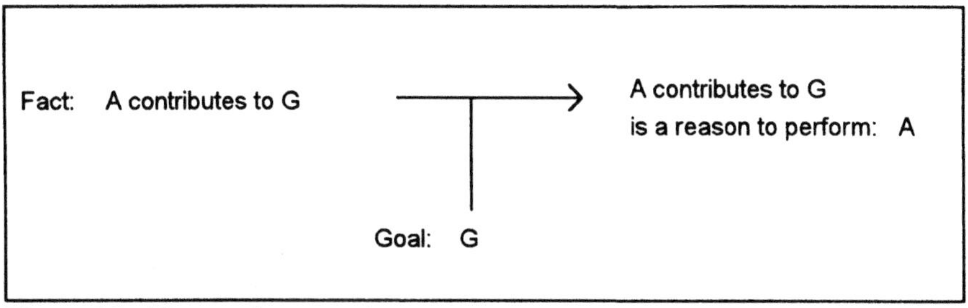

Figure 13: How goals generate reasons

The parallel functions of norms and goals reflect respectively the two classical types of deontic reasoning: deontological and teleological (cf. Summers 1978 and MacCormick 1993). In a deontological approach, duties or obligations are said to arise from a rule that tells what ought to be done. In a teleological approach, duties and obligations are attributed to the effects that pertain to (not) performing the concerned behaviour. In practical (deontic) reasoning, both types of arguments occur.

Because all (constitutive) reasons can be interpreted as reasons for mental behaviour (cf. section 17.3) reasoning with goals is potentially relevant on any occasion where reasons are involved. I will return to this in the discussion of deontic collapse in section III.15.

---

44 Cf. the identification by Dworkin 1978, p 22/3 of principles and policies, which works in a similar fashion. Cf. also the sections IV.6 and 7, where goals are translated into corresponding principles to simplify Reason-Based Logic.

18.5 Weak and strong permissions

In my opinion, permission with regard to some action or state of affairs is the 'normal' situation, where an ought of a prohibition are abnormal situations which require special reasons. Facts that involve an ought or a prohibition are reason-based, permissions are not. Clearly, permissions as described here are weak permissions in the sense that they are merely the absence of a prohibition (cf. Soeteman 1989, p. 97).

Strong permissions, in the sense that something is explicitly allowed, are in my opinion never deontic facts, but rather norms or goals. For instance, the right of freedom of speech underlies reasons why actions that fall under this freedom are permitted. The effect of this right is not only that it provides reasons why some actions are not prohibited, but also (and maybe even primarily) that it underlies reasons why the application of rules that prohibit these actions is excluded (cf. Dworkin 1978, pp. 186 f.).

18.6 The four functions of deontic reasons

The very facts that are reasons for the existence of deontic facts are also reasons for the corresponding kinds of mental behaviour. For instance, the fact that the owner of the garden forbade Geraldine to walk in the garden is a reason to consider her as being prohibited to walk through the garden. This is the behavioural level that corresponds with the ontological level as discussed in section 17.3. There is also the parasitic inferential use of deontic reasons. From the fact that taking Mary's purse would be theft, it may be *inferred* that it is prohibited that John takes Mary's purse.

Next to these functions of deontic reasons, that parallel the corresponding functions of classificatory reasons, there is an aspect of deontic reasons that remained unmentioned. *Deontic reasons are reasons for acting.* I have already said that deontic reasons are reasons for a form of mental behaviour, that is for recognising or accepting the presence of deontic states. But deontic reasons can also be reasons for other, non-mental behaviour, such as driving on the right side of the road, refraining from murder, paying ones debts, etc. So the reason why I ought to pay my taxes is ipso facto a reason to pay my taxes, and the reason why Geoffrey should not partake in the strike is a reason for Geoffrey not to partake in the strike.[45]

If a deontic reason is a reason for acting, is a deontic fact then also a reason for acting? For instance, suppose that the fact that some child threatens to drown is both a reason why I ought to rescue the child and ipso facto also a

[45] In this connection, the phrase 'for Geoffrey' means that Geoffrey is the addressee of the reason, and not that the reason is a personal reason, although it might be one.

reason for me to rescue the child. Can we then also say that the fact that I ought to rescue the child is a reason for me to rescue the child?

In my opinion not, for that would mean that if some child threatens to drown, I have two reasons to rescue it. The first reason is that the child is drowning, and the second reason is that I ought to rescue it. In my opinion the first reason is the only one, and the second 'reason' is only a repetition of the first one. Of course, if I ought to do something, this means that I have a reason to do what I ought to do. But this reason is not the fact that I ought to do it, but rather the reason why I ought to do it. An ought-judgement presupposes the presence of a reason for acting, but does not express it.

Although every deontic reason is a reason for acting, I doubt whether every reason for acting is also a deontic reason. For instance, if I would like to have an ice-cream, this is a reason for me to buy one. Is it then also a reason why I ought to, or should buy an ice-cream? I would think that it is certainly not a reason why I ought to buy an ice-cream, and maybe not even a reason why I should buy an ice-cream (cf. section 18.2). The ought-terminology seems inappropriate in the case of merely personal deontic reasons, as opposed to social and institutional deontic reasons.

The four ways in which deontic reasons can function are represented in the following table:

1.	The fact that taking Mary's purse would be theft	*makes it the case* that	John ought not to take the purse.
2.	The fact that taking Mary's purse would be theft	is a reason *to accept* that	John ought not to take the purse.
3.	The fact that taking Mary's purse would be theft	is a reason	for John *not to* take the purse.
4.	The fact that taking Mary's purse would be theft	is a reason *to assume* that	John ought not to take the purse.

Row one illustrates the constitutive function of deontic reasons, ontologically considered. Row two presents the mental behaviour way of looking at the same phenomenon. Row three is characteristic for deontic reasons: they are also reasons for behaviour. Row four, finally, illustrates the parasitic inferential function of deontic reasons.

18.7 Digression: the truth conditions of deontic sentences

There is a close correspondence between the behaviour for which deontic reasons plead, and the deontic facts that are constituted by these reasons. For instance, if the fact that I promised it, is a reason to pay you thousand dollars, this same fact is a reason why I ought to pay you thousand dollars.

That a reason for the existence of a deontic state is often also a reason for acting (depending on the kind of deontic state), explains the phenomenon pointed out by Raz that the sentences 'x ought to φ' and 'There is a reason for x to φ' are (approximately) equivalent (cf. Raz 1975, pp. 28f.). The truth conditions of the first sentence are more or less given by the second sentence.

There is, however, a small but important discrepancy, because the reason to φ can be outweighed by other reasons. If one knows that this is the case, one cannot any longer say that one ought to φ, even though the reason to φ still exists. Clearly we have hit here on the classical distinction between the prima facie ought, and the ought all things considered (cf. Ross 1930, p. 28; Hintikka 1971, pp. 91f.; Searle 1978; Alchourrón 1993, pp. 65f.; Morreau 1994).

A deontic sentence (not a norm) expresses, if it is true, a deontic fact. Such a fact is reason-based; it obtains because of the presence of other facts which are the reasons for its existence. This means that the truth conditions of a deontic sentence are given by the reasons why the deontic state of affairs[46] that is expressed by the sentence, obtains. For example, the reason why the sentence that John ought to be punished is true, is that John is a thief.

In general, a deontic sentence is true if the state of affairs that is expressed by it, obtains. This state of affairs obtains if (and only if) the reasons that plead for it outweigh the reasons that plead against it. So a deontic sentence is true if and only if the reasons that plead for the state of affairs expressed by that sentence outweigh the reasons against this state of affairs. Which facts count as such reasons depends on the principles, rules and goals that are adopted (valid).

Actually, this general description of the truth conditions of deontic sentences holds for the truth conditions of all sentences that express reason-based facts.

19. ANANKASTIC REASONS

Originally the concepts of necessity and possibility were just called modal ones. However, the notion of modality has broadened and now includes also

---

46 The notion of a state of affairs is a technical one. This notion and its relations to those of a sentence and of a fact will be discussed in section IV.1.

deontic and epistemic modalities. As a consequence we need a more specific concept to denote necessity and possibility and I follow a proposal of Von Wright by calling them *anankastic facts.*[47] As a further consequence of this convention, reasons why something is necessary or possible are called *anankastic reasons.*[48]

19.1 The three functions of anankastic reasons

Anankastic reasons are facts that make other facts necessary or (im)possible. For instance, the fact that I drop this stone is the anankastic reason why the stone *must* fall, and the fact that the speed of light (in vacuum) is 300,000 kilometres per second makes it *impossible* to travel faster than 300,000 kilometres per second.

Anankastic reasons also include reasons why something *can* happen, or why somebody has a particular *capability* or *power.*[49] Think for instance of the reason why Parliament has the legal power to make legislation (the power was attributed by the constitution), or the reason why James cannot validly engage into a contract (he is a minor).

It goes almost without saying that anankastic reasons are also reasons to *consider* things as necessary, possible, etc., and that they are parasitic reasons to infer that things are necessary, etc. I will give the usual table:

1.	The attribution of legislative power by the central government	*makes* it	*possible* that the municipal council makes by-laws.
2.	The attribution of legislative power by the central government	is a reason to *consider*	the municipal council *capable* to make by-laws.
3.	The attribution of legislative power by the central government	is a reason to *assume* that	the municipal council *can* make by-laws.

---

[47] Cf. Von Wright 1963, p. 10. The alternative, alethic modalities, has the disadvantage of suggesting that the other modalities, the deontic and the epistemic ones, would not be alethic. Cf. also note 43.

[48] Since anankastic reasons are used in making explanations, the category of anankastic reasons coincides with the category of explanatory reasons. Cf. the sections 1.1 and 8 of this chapter. Justifying reasons are either deontic, epistemic, or classificatory.

[49] Having a power comes, at least in one sense of the word, down to being capable of doing what one has the power to do. Cf. Hohfeld 1913.

19.2 Anankastic rules and laws of nature

Anankastic reasons go together with anankastic rules, but what are these rules supposed to be? If I drop a stone, the reason why the stone (necessarily) falls is that I drop it. Universalisation leads to the rule of experience that a stone falls if it is dropped. Of course there is physical law that underlies the falling of the dropped stone, but this law is not concerned with stones in particular. The laws of gravity deals with all bodies that have gravitational mass, and stones just happen to belong to this latter category. Yet, the reason that the stone falls is that it (the stone) was dropped, rather than that the stone has gravitational mass (and that it was not supported anymore, and etc.....).

Our feeling that a dropped stone *must* fall is based on a rule of experience, rather than on the relevant physical law. It is these kinds of rules of experience that determine our everyday experiences of necessity and possibility, and that underlie a large number of anankastic facts. They form a large proportion of what I propose to call *anankastic rules*.

Not all anankastic rules belong to the sphere of physics. A political anankastic rule would be that one *cannot* win elections after introducing impopular enactments without a convincing explanation. A psychological rule would be that one *needs* some self-confidence to be happy. In the field of mathematics it is a rule that the diagonals of a diamond *must* intersect orthogonally. And a legal example of an anankastic rule is that a government agency *can* only make valid regulations if the *power* to do so was attributed to it.

If we do not confine the notion of causality to physical causality[50], we can characterise many anankastic rules by saying that their conditions are causes of their conclusions. The fact that I dropped the stone is the cause why the stone fell. The facts that the government enacted impopular regulations just before the elections without providing a convincing explanation caused the electoral defeat of the government party. And the fact that the municipal council was not attributed the power to raise taxes is the cause that its tax measures are invalid. Only in the mathematical case it is a little strange to speak of causes. Can we say that the fact that this figure is a diamond causes its diagonals to intersect orthogonally?

---

[50] Kelsen 1960, p. 83 explicitly discusses the phenomenon of legal causality, although Kelsen prefers to speak about a normative rather than a causal connection between the conditions and the conclusion of a rule of law. Cf. also Kelsen 1945, p. 46.

Kelsen analyses a rule as ' If A, then *it ought to be* that B'. This means that the normative element is part of the copula. I prefer another analysis, where the normative element is part of the conclusion: 'If A, then B ought to be'. In this analysis, the parallel between laws of nature and legal rules becomes much stronger.

20. EPISTEMIC REASONS AND RULES OF INFERENCE

20.1 The four functions of epistemic reasons

Epistemic reasons are first and foremost reasons to make inferences, or for holding beliefs. If some masked person comes running out of a bank building, brandishing a gun, while the alarm system of the bank is working, this is a reason (possibly even more than one) to *assume* that he is a bank robber. Of course these facts do not make him into a robber; they are only clues that allow the conclusion that he (tried to) rob the bank.

Epistemic reasons in the first instance do not deal with the world itself, but with our knowledge of the world. They are reasons why our knowledge should include this, but not include that. Viewed in this way, epistemic reasons are closely related to rules of inference, that allow us to make certain inferences.

This inferential function of epistemic reasons is *not* parasitic on some other, constitutive function. The mentioned reason to assume that somebody is a bank robber is not a reason why this person is a bank robber. In this sense, the inferential function of epistemic reasons differs from the inferential function of constitutive reasons, which is parasitic.

Epistemic reasons deal not only with our knowledge of the world; they are also reasons why some facts *are* probable, certain, or possible. For example, the fact that Gloria's car is before her apartment makes it improbable that she is to her work. Viewed in this way, epistemic reasons are also a kind of constitutive reasons, that is, reasons that constitute epistemic modalities. The categories of the probable, the certain, and - in one sense of the word - the possible[51] are epistemic ones.

Here we encounter an interesting parallel with deontic reasons. A deontic reason is on the one hand a reason for the existence of a deontic modality, and it is on the other hand a reason for behaviour. Similarly, an epistemic reason is on the one hand a reason for the existence of an epistemic modality, and on the other hand a reason to make an inference. Where a reason why a particular form of behaviour is obligatory is also a reason to perform this behaviour, a reason why a fact is certain, is also a reason to believe this fact. This parallel can even be strengthened if we consider rules of inference as deontic rules that *permit* us to make particular inferences. In that case, the epistemic reasons would be a subset of the more comprehensive category of deontic reasons. The same counts for the mental behaviour functions of both anankastic and classificatory rules. I will not pursue this line of investigation here, however. To some extent the issue returns in the discussion of deontic collapse in section III.15.

---

[51] Cf. White 1975, pp. 5f. for an account of the two different senses of 'possible'.

The constitutive function of epistemic reasons can be considered both on the ontological and on the behavioural level. On the one hand, the fact that Gloria's car is before her apartment makes it improbable that she is to her work. On the other hand, this same fact is a reason to *consider* it improbable that Gloria is to her work. Moreover, there is also an inferential function of epistemic reasons that is parasitic on the constitutive function: The fact that Gloria's car is before her apartment is a reason to assume that it is improbable that Gloria is to her work.

The parasitic inferential function of epistemic reasons does not coincide with their primary inferential function. Suppose that the train's being late makes it probable that Mary will not be home in time for dinner. According to the primary inferential function of epistemic reasons, we may assume that Mary will not be home in time for dinner if we know that the train is late. According to the parasitic inferential function, we may assume that Mary will *probably* not be home in time for dinner. In the parasitic inferential function, the modal qualifier 'probably' is part of what we may infer, while this qualifier is absent from what we may infer primarily. That is because the train's being late does not constitute Mary's not being home in time, but it does constitute Mary's *probably* not being home in time.

It may be useful to give an overview in a table of the several functions of epistemic reasons, and the levels on which they can be considered.

1.	The fact that Gloria's car is before her apartment	is a reason *to assume* that	Gloria is not to her work.
2.	The fact that Gloria's car is before her apartment	is a reason that *makes it probable* that	Gloria is not to her work.
3.	The fact that Gloria's car is before her apartment	is a reason *to consider it as probable* that	Gloria is not to her work.
4.	The fact that Gloria's car is before her apartment	is a reason *to assume* that	it is *probable* that Gloria is not to her work.

The first row in this table illustrates the primary inferential use of epistemic reasons. The fourth row also illustrates an inferential use, but this is the parasitic use which reflects the constitutive function of epistemic reasons that is illustrated in row two on the ontological level. Row three, finally, illustrates the behavioural level of epistemic reasons.

20.2 Rules of inference

Anankastic rules, especially the physical ones, are often based on experience, and they make it possible to draw conclusions. Yet, they are not proper rules of inference, because their inferential role is parasitic on their constitutive role. Proper *rules of inference* are normally based on experience too, but their conditions and conclusions need not be causally related. Examples of such rules are 'On holidays, the number of traffic casualties is approximately 20 percent higher than normal' and 'Italians may be assumed to be Roman Catholic'. Sometimes rules of inference are based on legislation, as for instance legal rules of evidence ('A deed counts as decisive evidence of the facts described in it'), and the rules of logical languages such as predicate logic. Finally, some rules of inference have a statistical basis, such as the rules that specify what may be derived (with what probability) from the results of samples (cf. also section VI.6). It is these proper rules of inference that give rise to epistemic reasons.

21. KINDS OF RULES AND POINTS OF VIEW

Some rules, and in particular norms, belong to a *point of view*. There are legal and moral norms, but also norms of etiquette. Anankastic rules are also divided over several points of view. Something may be logically necessary (that A implies A), mathematically necessary (3 plus 4 equals 7), physically necessary (this stone is subjected to gravitational forces), or medically necessary (if the illness is to be cured you *must* take this medicine).

The distinction between classificatory, deontic, anankastic and epistemic rules is orthogonal to the distinction between points of view. This means that within one point of view, there can be rules that belong to different kinds. The following table illustrates this for the legal and the moral point of view.

	the legal point of view	**the moral point of view**
classificatory rules	definition of e.g. vehicle	criteria for being a coward
deontic rules	prohibitive rules	moral requirements
epistemic rules	rules of evidence	-
anankastic rules	power conferring rules	prerequisites of promises

22. SUMMARY

In this chapter I have given an overview of different kinds of reasons and their relation to rules, goals and principles. The main issues can be summarised as follows.

There is a fundamental distinction between facts on the one hand, and rules, goals and principles on the other hand. The latter do not give information about the world, but rather structure it by creating connections between kinds of facts.

These connections are based on reasons, where some facts are reasons for other facts. There are two main kinds of reasons, namely constitutive reasons and epistemic reasons. The former are reasons why their conclusions are the case (obtain), while the latter are reasons why their conclusions should be accepted (held true, believed). It should be noted, however, that constitutive reasons can be used for making inferences, while epistemic reasons constitute epistemic modalities.

Actually two kinds of constitution are involved. First facts are made into reasons by the application of a rule, goal or principle. And second these reasons constitute their conclusions. Cf. figure 14.

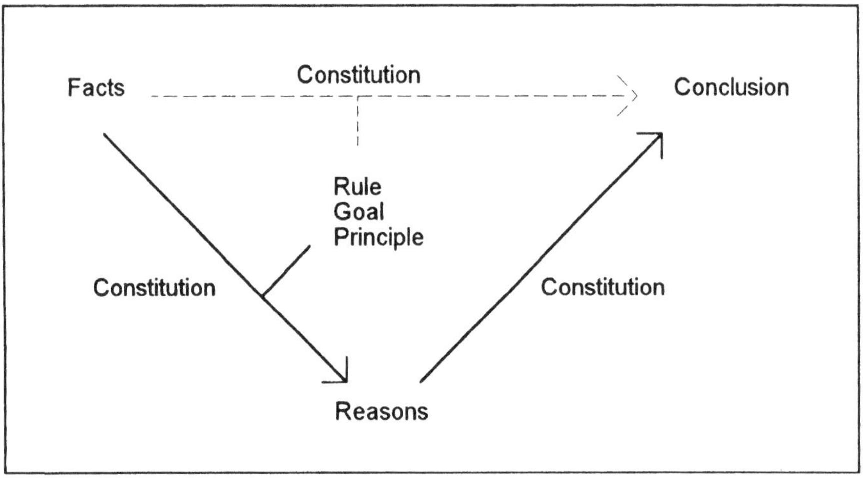

Figure 14: Two kinds of constitution

Constitutive reasons can always be considered on two levels. On the one hand there is the ontological level, where they make it the case that their conclusions obtain. On the other hand there is the mental behaviour level, where they are reasons to assume that the facts that they constitute obtain. Both levels are two sides of one medal.

Rules, principles, goals and the reasons that are based on them can be subdivided into three categories, that is institutional, social and personal ones. This order of categories is one in which the kinds of rules, etc. decrease in objectivity, and increase in motivating force. For instance, an institutional rule exists independent of whether it is accepted by a particular individual. The reasons based on it need, as a consequence, have little meaning for such an individual. A personal principle, on the contrary, depends for its existence completely on being used by the person for whom this principle exists. The reasons based on it will, consequently, normally motivate this person.

Social and institutional rules can, respectively will, belong to a particular point of view, and the reasons based on them will belong to the same point of view as the rule on which they are based. Legal rules, for instance, give only rise to reasons from the legal point of view, while methodological rules only give rise to reasons from the scientific point of view.

A rule or principle needs not always to be applied if its conditions are satisfied. Exclusionary reasons block the application of a rule or principle, and prevent it from generating a reason. The application of rules and principles that belong to a particular kind (personal, social, institutional) or to a particular point of view can only be excluded by exclusionary reasons that belong to the same kind, respectively point of view. This has the consequence that the exceptions to rules and principles are just as objective (subjective) as the rules to which they make an exception.

Cancelling conditions must be distinguished from exclusionary reasons. Reason-based facts can obtain because of the occurrence of their constitutive reasons. For instance, a contract comes into existence, because two parties gave their consent. If the consent was not freely given, this is an exclusionary reason that prevents the contract from coming into existence (at least from being a full-fledged contract). A cancelling condition, on the contrary, does not prevent the contract from coming into existence. It only ends the contract as soon as the cancelling condition obtains. Cancellation of the contract would be such a cancelling condition.

A general characteristic of reasons is that they do not guarantee their conclusions, but only contribute to them. This means that if there are reasons for incompatible conclusions, these must be 'weighed' to determine which conclusion obtains.

III. REASONING WITH RULES

According to the semantic notion of logical validity, an argument is valid if the truth of its premises guarantees the truth of its conclusion. In chapter I, I tried to make it plausible that this semantic notion of validity is not very suitable if we are dealing with rules. The elaborate discussion in chapter II of reasons and their relation to principles, goals and rules, should have substantiated this claim.

In this chapter I propose a different view on the role of principles in arguments. Principles are no longer premises which together with factual premises guarantee the truth of their conclusions. Instead they are generators of reasons which plead either for or against a conclusion, and which need to be weighed to determine which conclusion follows. This view is elaborated in the second part of this chapter.

In the previous chapters I did not make the distinction between rules and principles, because this distinction does not play an important role outside the law. However, as soon as we direct our attention to legal reasoning, as will be done in the present chapter, the distinction between legal rules on the one hand, and legal principles and goals on the other hand, becomes important. Ronald Dworkin, for instance, has argued that rules of law obey a different logic than legal principles. Where principles only generate reasons for their conclusions and must consequently still be weighed, rules would apply in an all-or-nothing fashion. If the conditions of a valid legal rule are satisfied, the consequence of the rule must follow, thus Dworkin (1978, pp. 22f.).

Although I do not think that Dworkin's views are fully correct, these views have drawn the attention the distinction between two kinds of entities in a legal system, rules and principles, one more forcing than the other. In the sections 1 and 2 of this chapter, I try to elucidate the difference between legal rules on the one hand, and legal principles and goals on the other hand, by positioning rules in between principles and statements. In that way, I make a beginning with the explanation of the logical differences between these two categories.

The elaboration of the logical difference between principles and statements leads to an abstract model of reasoning with rules, goals and principles, which contains the outline of a general theory of legal reasoning (section 4). In this theory, the central place of the syllogism (or - more general - the deductive argument) has been abandoned at the favour of reasons that plead for or against a conclusion. This model also forms the basis for the theory of Reason-Based Logic, that will be elaborated in the chapters IV - VI. The development of this abstract model of legal reasoning takes the sections 5 and following.

Before concluding with a list of recommendations for a logic for rules, I make a few remarks on the causes of defeasibility, on the phenomena of deontic collapse and deontic inflation, and on the shifting bounds of rationality.

1. THE STONE ON THE HILL

There is a clear difference between the principle that murderers may be punished and the statement that all murderers may be punished. The latter can only be true if literally *all* murderers may be punished, whatever the reason why they may be punished. The former, being a principle, cannot even be true, because principles have no truth value. The principle may be accepted, although its acceptance does not necessitate us to think that all murderers may be punished. Principles are best considered as a kind of instruments that we can use or not, and which only generate reasons if they are used.

Despite this clear difference, there is a connection between the acceptance of the principle, and the truth of the statement. If in fact all murderers may be punished, this is most probably because of the acceptance of the principle (or even the rule) that murderers may be punished. To illustrate on the one hand the difference between principles and statements, and on the other hand their interconnection, I will discuss an example from physics.

1.1 Description of the example

This example deals with a stone that lies on a steep slope. The stone is pulled down by gravitational forces. The movement downward is hindered by both frictional resistance and by a person who tries to pull the stone upward by means of a rope and a pulley block. Cf. figure 1.

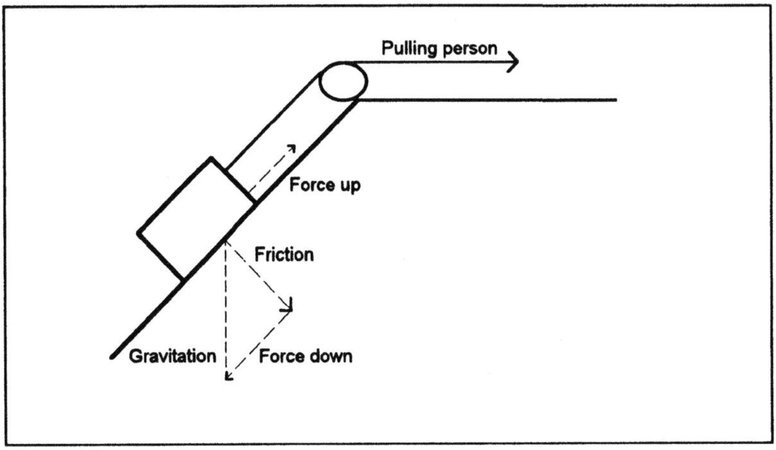

Figure 1: Colliding forces

The point of this example is that the forces that act upon the stone can be compared to reasons that are generated by principles. In this situation, there are four forces involved.[1] First there is the force upward (Fu), exercised by the pulling person. Let us assume that this force is constant. Second there is the gravitational force (Fg) exercised on the stone. This force can safely be assumed to be constant too. The gravitational force does not work in the direction of the slope and must therefore be dissolved into two forces, one of which downward in the direction of the slope (Fd), and the other one perpendicular to this direction. This latter force will give rise to frictional resistance (Ff). The force downward will be constant too, but the frictional resistance varies within certain confines.

Friction only exists if there is a tendency to movement. If the forces up and down are in equilibrium, the frictional force will be zero. If the equilibrium is disturbed, for instance because the force down is bigger than the force up, the friction comes in to prevent the stone from moving. In fact, as long as the difference between the force down and the force up is not too big, the friction will be just as big as the difference between the forces up and down, causing the stone to be in rest. Only if the difference between the forces up and down exceeds the maximum resistance (Ff_{max}), the stronger force will cause the stone to move. In fact, the resistance will increase from 0 to Ff_{max} as the difference between the forces up and down increases. Moreover, the direction of the resistance will always be equal to that of the lesser of these two other forces, causing the total amount of forces to be in equilibrium.

1.2 Two ways to characterise the situation

The effects of two of the relevant forces can be expressed by hypothetical if .. then-sentences:

- If there is a force upwards, the stone will move up.
- If there is a force downwards, the stone will move down.

Neither one of these two sentences is a true statement, but both express a factor that is relevant in determining the movements of the stone. Moreover, each of them, if it is the only relevant one, can be used in arguments *as if* it were a true hypothetical statement. Only, reasoning with them is defeasible. For instance, if there is a force upwards we can provisionally conclude that the stone will move up. This conclusion may have to be withdrawn on the basis of the additional information that there is also a force downwards.

To obtain an indefeasible outcome, all forces must be combined. Whether the stone will move (better: accelerate) and in which direction, can be com-

---

[1] The example does not aim at full physical correctness.

puted by adding three forces (Fu, Fd, and Ff). If the sum is not equal to zero, the stone will move in the direction of the biggest (combination of) force(s).

Until now, the example has completely been described in terms of colliding forces. It was indicated which forces are present, how their sizes are determined, and how the movement of the stone can be determined on the basis of these data. Neither one of the forces on its own determines the movement of the stone; only in their combination lies the determinant of the stone's behaviour. Still it is possible to describe that behaviour in three conditional statements, each of which is true, and which together exhaust the space of possibilities. These statements are:

- If $Fu > Fd + Ff_{max}$, the stone moves upwards.
- If $Fd > Fu + Ff_{max}$, the stone moves downwards.
- If neither $Fu > Fd + Ff_{max}$, nor $Fd > Fu + Ff_{max}$, the stone does not move.

Neither one of these three statements describes a force and its effects. Each of them describes a hypothetical situation in which the forces combine in a particular way. Given the nature of the relevant forces, and the fact that there are only three relevant outcomes, it is possible to describe the complete situation by means of these three hypothetical statements.

Because the last three sentences are statements, reasoning with them is not defeasible. If these sentences are true, and if the facts that correspond to the antecedents of one of these sentences obtain, we can with hundred percent certainty conclude that the consequent of the concerning sentence is true. If, however, a Modus Ponens argument in which one of these sentences is used, turns out to have a false conclusion, we can fairly assume that one of the premises must have been false.

We encountered two ways to characterise the situation of the stone on the hill. The first way uses the forces that act upon the stone and asks for a combination of these forces to compute for each particular case whether the stone would move, and if so, in which direction. The second way makes use of a description of the three possible ways in which the forces on the stone can interact, and gives for each of these situations the result of the interacting forces. The first characterisation refers to the effective causes that govern the events in the case. The second characterisation as it were describes the situation with hindsight. Knowing the result of the interaction of the three forces, it connects the relevant different starting positions with their actual outcomes. That is why the latter approach makes use of sentences that are true or false (were the different outcomes assigned correctly to the several starting positions?), while the first approach does not describe the events at all, but only indicates which factors are relevant in determining them.

1.3 Physical principles and legal principles

Reasoning with legal principles is similar to reasoning with forces. In fact, the forces are the result of the application of law-like entities to concrete fact situations in a way that is very similar to the application of legal principles to cases.[2] Where a physical principle leads to forces, a legal principle leads to reasons. The parallel even goes further: there may be reasons not to apply a physical principle, in particular if a fact situation is outside the scope of the principle. For instance, the principle that heavy objects fall if dropped should not be applied in a space shuttle. This is similar to the non-application of the principle that murderers may be punished to prescribed cases of murder.

In fact, legal principles and physical principles are not only comparable; they are legal and physical instances of the same phenomenon, namely the phenomenon of the principle. The examples I gave were cases of a deontic principle that belongs to the legal point of view, and an anankastic principle that belongs to the physical point of view. The parallels in reasoning between legal and physical principles reflect the same underlying mechanisms that apply both in the legal and in the physical field.

That is why my physical example can both be used to illustrate the relation between physical principles and statements that become true as a consequence of the application of these principles, and the relation between legal principles and statements. Just as it is possible to distinguish different situations depending on the different ways in which the physical forces interact, and to describe these situations by means of statements that are true or false, it is also possible to distinguish different legal situations, depending on how legal reasons interact. These situations and their legal consequences can be described in statements that are either true or false.

2. LEGAL RULES AND DESCRIPTIONS OF THE LAW

The Dutch law has the principle that nobody can transfer rights that he has not got himself. This is the so-called *Nemo plus*-principle, after the Latin *Nemo plus iuris transferre potest quam ipse habet*. If this principle is applied to the case that Joyce transfers the ownership of a book which she does not own to Casey, the legal consequence would be that Casey does not become the owner of the book.

The Dutch law also has a recognised goal to protect parties in good faith. In connection with the acquisition of property, this goal would promote that if a party in good faith through an act-in-the-law seeks to obtain the ownership

---

[2] In Toulmin 1953, pp. 23f. law-like entities like the ones under consideration are called principles. The difference between principles and laws is discussed on the pages 77f. of that work.

of some good, this party should become the owner. If this goal is applied in the case of Joyce and Casey, Casey should become the owner of the book.

Both the principle and the goal generate a reason in this particular case, and these reasons plead in different directions. The nemo plus-principle generates a reason why Casey should not become the owner, while the goal to protect parties in good faith generates a reason why Casey should become the owner. How is this conflict to be solved? According to the Dutch law it depends on whether Casey had to pay for the book. If she got the book for free, she should not be benefited at the cost of the original owner. If, on the contrary, she paid a reasonable price for the book, her interests are protected, and she becomes the new owner.

Here we have a nice parallel with the case of the stone on the hill. There are two colliding 'forces', that is the reasons based on the principle and on the goal. Moreover, there is a third factor that determines the outcome of the conflict. In the end, the outcome of the case depends on three factors, namely whether Joyce owned the book (corresponding on the Nemo plus-principle), whether Casey was in good faith (corresponding to the goal to protect parties in good faith), and whether Casey paid a reasonable price for the book. If Joyce owned the book, Casey becomes the new owner. Otherwise, Casey only becomes the new owner if she both acted in good faith and paid a reasonable price for the book.

These last two sentences (attempt to) describe the possible situations and their legal outcomes according to the Dutch law. Reasoning with these sentences is not defeasible, and can be handled by arguments of the form Modus Ponens. Notice that these sentences are not the original legal principle and the goal that determined the outcome of the case. They are only a summary of the possible situations and their outcomes which had to be established in some other way, namely by reasoning defeasibly on the basis of the principle and the goal. The principle and the goal are not true or false; they are *valid* or *accepted* as parts of the Dutch civil law. The sentences which aim to describe the outcome of the conflict of the principle and the goal for various situations, are true or false, depending on whether they succeed in correctly describing the outcome of the interacting relevant factors. Therefore, these sentences can be used to reason in an indefeasible way about who is the (new) owner of the book.

However, the conclusion that these sentences describe the different possible situations and their outcomes is itself defeasible. Its truth depends on the assumption that the principle and the goal that were involved in establishing the possible situations and their outcomes, were the only relevant ones. If other factors are also relevant, the description based on the outcome of the interaction of only two factors (the principle and the goal) will probably be false. So the sentences that describe the outcome of this interaction can only be conditionally true, with the condition being that the two factors that were taken into account are the only relevant ones. A similar assumption was made in the physical example, where it was tacitly assumed that there was, for instance, no other gravitational force that pulled the stone straight up in the air.

Such assumptions may turn out to be false, and in the legal example the assumption is false. The Dutch law also has the principle that the interests of somebody who did his best to protect them, deserve more legal protection than the interests of somebody who does not protect them very well. In the case of transfer of property by a non-owner, this principle means that somebody who lend out a book deserves less protection if it is sold by the borrower, than if the book was stolen and sold (by the thief or his legal successor) to a third party in good faith. More concrete it means that if the book was stolen, the original owner retains his ownership for at least three years. Only after these three years, a third party in good faith may become the new owner.[3]

A good description of the Dutch law must take this additional principle into account and would consequently be somewhat more complex than the description offered above. Notice, however, that such a new description would still only be true on the assumption that all the relevant factors have been taken into account. The introduction of additional complicating goals or principles would make the new description false. In fact, any description of the outcome of the interaction of legal principles and goals for the different possible situations would be fallible for this reason. There is no finite amount of information about the legal system that guarantees the truth of hypothetical descriptions of situations and their legal consequences. It always remains possible, at least in theory, that additional information about new principles or goals would change the situation. Only trivial descriptions, that would for instance have the condition that the factors mentioned are the only relevant ones, can be unconditional.

Of course, this fundamental fallibility need not stop lawyers from trying to give exhaustive descriptions of the legal system through identification of possible cases and their legal consequences. Only such descriptions will always be provisional under the assumption that all relevant goals and principles have been taken into account.

Legal *rules* may at first sight be interpreted as descriptions of the outcome of the interacting factors which are relevant in the type of case with which the rule deals. A legal rule can be seen as the formulation of the legal consequences that attach to a particular kind of case, with the pretension that it is

---

[3] In fact, the regulation is still more detailed, but the remainder of these details will be left out of consideration. Cf. the sections 3:86f. of the Dutch Civil Code.

exceptionless, unless the exception is mentioned explicitly. The Dutch statutory rules concerning the transfer of property by a non-owner, for instance, are the result of combining all goals and principles that are relevant for cases of transfer of property by a non-owner. As a consequence, their legal consequences cannot be refuted by factors that are relevant on the basis of these goals and principles, and therefore their application seems to proceed in an all-or-nothing fashion.

Appearances are deceptive, however, because even rules are only based on a finite amount of information concerning the legal system, and although there will not be frequent exceptions, reasoning with rules is still defeasible.[4] That is one reason why legal rules cannot be identified with descriptions of the outcome of interacting principles and goals for all the different relevant types of cases. Such descriptions would either be true or false. If they are false, they cannot be used in any deductive argument at all to derive conclusions. If they are true, reasoning with them is not defeasible. Reasoning with rules is neither reasoning with false premises, nor reasoning indefeasibly with true premises. Therefore, rules are not summary descriptions of the outcome of interacting reasons.[5]

3. THE ROLE OF EPISTEMIC AND CONSTITUTIVE REASONS IN ARGUMENTS

Because rules and principles differ from statements in a way that necessitates a different way of reasoning, we are left with the task to determine a model for reasoning with principles and rules. Before we can start to develop our model of reasoning with reasons, however, we must deal with a seeming problem. Any such model has to face the complication that constitutive reasons do not have their primary function in arguments, but in the constitution of the world. The rule that defines theft is meant to identify certain events as cases of theft. Its role lies primarily in the cognitive apparatus of humans, and in the conceptual schemes that give the world its structure. How can such rules and the reasons based on them play roles in arguments?

The answer is easy to give in the case of epistemic rules, or rules of inference. As their name indicates, their role is to indicate which inferences are

---

[4] It is, of course, possible to legislate on the subject, and determine by that means which factors count as relevant. The rule that results from such legislation seems to settle the matter definitively, because the legislator has the power to determine, rather than to describe, what is relevant and what not. However, see section 8 on the notion of a replacing reason and its significance for the relation between legal rules on the one hand and legal principles and goals on the other hand.

[5] Another reason why rules are not statements is that rules have a different direction of fit. Cf. section VI.8.

possible, or allowed. Epistemic rules can both be formal, such as the rule that allows arguments of the form Modus Ponens, and material, such as the rule that allows us to conclude that somebody is probably not Roman Catholic if both of her parents are Swedish. In both cases, inferences in accordance with valid inference rules and the reasons based on them, are ipso facto valid ones, although not necessarily in the sense that the truth of the premises guarantees the truth of the conclusion.

In the case of constitutive rules, we must relate to their parasitic function as rules of inference (cf. sections II.17.4, 18.6 and 19.1). If an event has the characteristics that make it into a case of theft, these same characteristics will also be a reason to *believe* that this event is a case of theft. Similarly, if the fact that John is a murderer is a reason why he may be punished, this same fact is also a reason to believe that John may be punished. And, finally, the facts that make that some agency has legislative powers are also a reason to believe that this agency has legislative powers.

In short, all kinds of rules can be used to make inferences. Rules of inference, because it is their primary function; constitutive rules, because they have a parasitic function to support inferences. So the problem that seemed to arise from the constitutive nature of many reasons can be circumvented by appealing to the parasitic inferential function of constitutive reasons. This does not mean, however, that the distinction between rules of inference and constitutive rules is unimportant where the validity of inferences is concerned. In section VI.7 we will see how the distinction has implications for arguments about the validity of rules.

4. THE TWO STEP-MODELS OF REASONING WITH PRINCIPLES AND RULES

Reasons have to be weighed in order to determine which conclusion follows. Principles contribute to the conclusions of arguments in that they generate reasons for their conclusions. An adequate model of reasoning with principles should therefore contain a step that deals with the interaction of the reasons generated by the principles.

As a consequence the model of reasoning with principles that is presented here contains two steps. The first step consists of the application of all relevant valid principles, in order to gather all reasons which plead for or against a conclusion. The second step consists of a 'weighing' process, that establishes which conclusion follows from the collected reasons.

The first step can be subdivided in three steps. For each possible principle which deals with the conclusion of the argument it must first be established whether it is valid. Second, it must be decided whether the conditions of the principle are satisfied by the case to which the principle is to be applied. And third, it is to be determined whether the principle, assuming the satisfaction of its conditions, is not excluded in the case at hand. Only non-excluded principles generate reasons for their conclusions.

The reasons which were found by applying principles are divided in a set of reasons which plead for, and a set of reasons which plead against the conclusion. The weighing of reasons can be dealt with in a rational manner if one of these sets can be argued to outweigh the other set. If this is not possible, there is no rational solution to the weighing problem.

The main elements of the two step-model are depicted in figure 2. This figure essentially holds for reasoning with goals too.

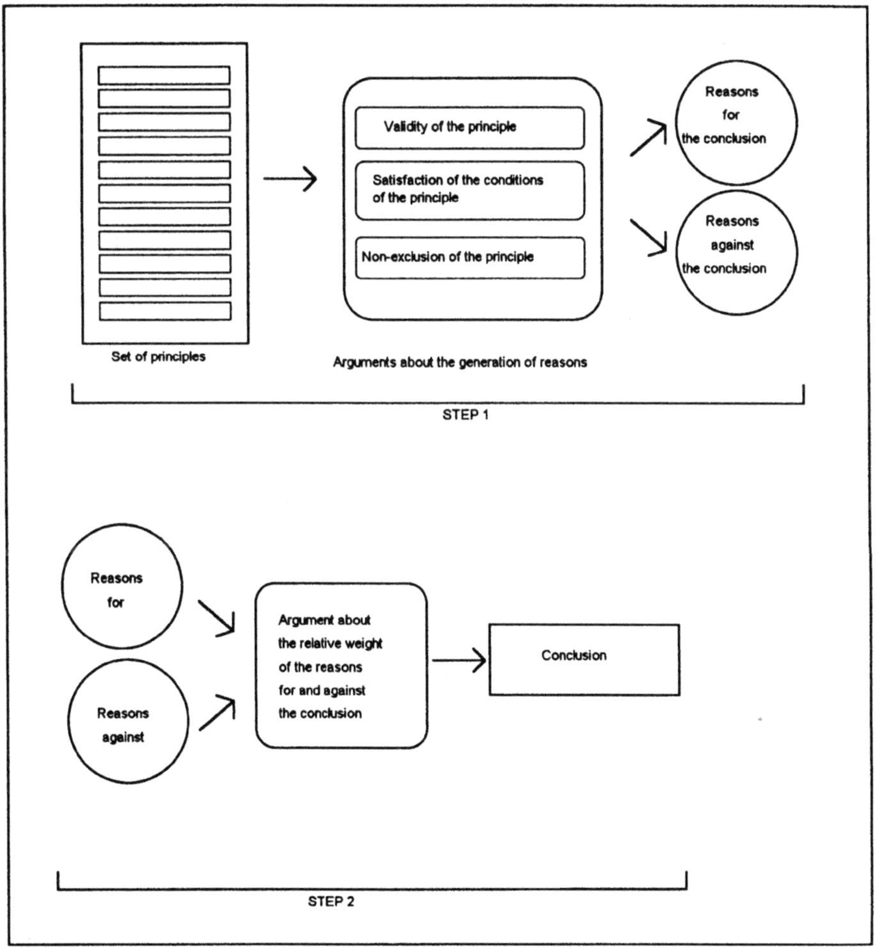

Figure 2: The two step-model of principle application

In the case of rules, the model is slightly different, because - as I will argue in section 10 - a rule that is applied to a case guarantees the truth of its conclusion. Yet, also in the case of rules there is a place for the weighing of reasons. This place is created by distinguishing in the case of rules between the applicability of a rule and the actual application of the rule.

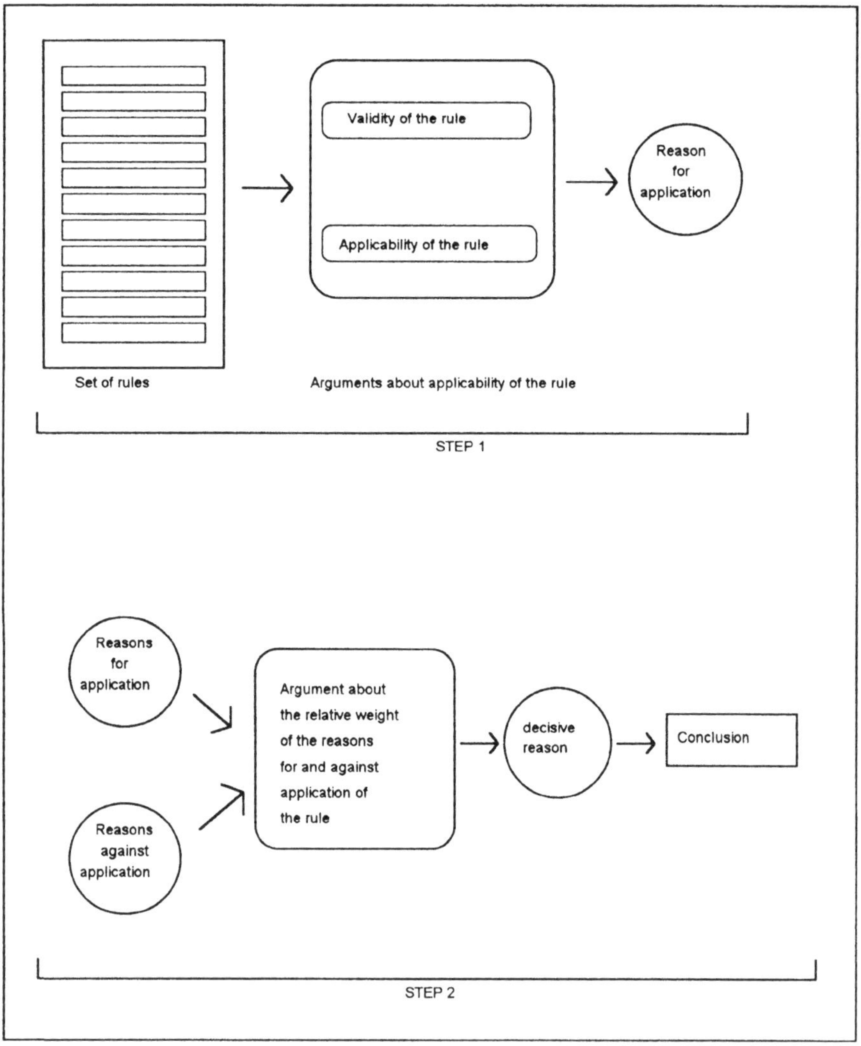

Figure 3: The two step-model of rule application

If a rule is applicable to a case, that is, if its conditions are satisfied and the rule is not excluded, this is only a reason to apply the rule. There may also be reasons not to apply the rule. In that case, the reasons for and against rule application must be weighed. If a rule ought to be applied, it makes the facts that satisfy its conditions into a decisive reason for its conclusion, and this conclusion always follows. Therefore the two-step model of reasoning with rules looks as depicted in figure 3.

In the following sections, I discuss all of the steps involved in the two versions of the model.

5. THE VALIDITY OF RULES, PRINCIPLES AND GOALS

Rules can only generate reasons if they are valid. The fact that I own a personal computer is not a reason for being taxable, because there is no valid rule to the effect that owners of personal computers are taxable. This does of course not detract form the fact that owning property might be a reason for taxability on the basis of some valid rule, but there is no rule that attaches the consequence of being taxable to the mere owning of a personal computer. In this section, I will discuss the validity of rules. This discussion also applies to goals and principles, unless the contrary is clear from the context.

I take the validity of a rule to be the mode of existence of rules (cf. Kelsen 1979, p. 136). The sentence that a rule is valid means that this rule exists and nothing else or more. Actually, this meaning of the term 'validity' can in my opinion be abandoned, and the only reason why I use the term is to adhere to common practice. There is no relation between the notion of validity as the way in which rules and principles exist, and validity as a characteristic of, for instance, arguments, or goals in a soccer match.

That a rule is valid does in my opinion *not* mean that the rule is binding, or that it should be obeyed. The notion of a rule's being binding seems senseless to me, unless it means that the rule should be obeyed. The fact that a rule should be obeyed, or that somebody ought to obey a rule, is a deontic fact like all other ones, based on reasons which in their turn are based on rules. But, again, this is not the same as the validity of the rule. In the sections 5.3 and 15, where I discuss deontic collapse, the relation between the validity of a rule and the reasons why the rule should be obeyed will be addressed.

The insight that a rule must be valid if it is to constitute reasons, leads to a number of complications if we consider the role of points of view and the various modes of existence of rules.

5.1 Points of view

Whether a rule or principle is valid often depends on the point of view. The principle that one should not be impolite is possibly morally valid, but legally it is not. Legal definitions, on the contrary, are only valid from the legal point of view. Somebody may legally be a thief, while morally she is not, or the other way round. The rule of law which precisely defines theft is *legally* valid, but needs not have moral significance.[6]

If the validity of rules is attached to a particular point of view, this attachment also holds for the reasons based on these rules and for the conclusions based on these reasons. The facts that somebody took away somebody else's property with the intention of appropriation are a *legal* reason, and the conclusion based on that reason is that this person is *legally speaking* a thief. The legal classification may or may not coincide with the same classification from other points of view, but this does neither add nor subtract from the connection of the reasons and the conclusions to the point of view of the rule on which they are based.

Practically this means that if we are engaged in a legal discussion and we collect rules to base reasons on, these rules must be *legally* valid. Legal conclusions must be based on legal reasons, which in their turn must be based on legal rules (or legal principles, or legal goals, etc.).

This is a heavy demand, which is relaxed somewhat because intermediate conclusions, most often classifications, need not be based on legal reasons. There are legal rules which deal with classification; they comprise so-called legal definitions and the results from case law. More often, however, the law borrows the conditions of applicability for the terms it uses from common parlance (cf. Valente 1995, p. 57). For instance, usually the law will rely on natural language conventions for the determination whether something counts as a vehicle or not, or whether a particular form of behaviour was negligent or not. There can be special legal rules which deviate from common parlance, and if this is the case, these rules should be used. But in the absence of such rules, the law falls back on other rules. These other rules need not to be legally valid for the legal correctness of the conclusion of the complete argument. Cf. figure 4.

The criteria for the validity of rules will differ from one point of view to the other. To take an extreme example, there are different criteria for physical rules (laws) and for legal rules. A physical law is for instance valid (adopted) if it explains a large number of regularities, if it coheres with other physical laws, if it is not too complex, and if it has not been falsified. A rule of law, on the contrary, need not explain any (behavioural?) regularities to be valid. The most common criterion is whether it was made in accordance with the procedures for making rules of law.

---

[6] Of course it can have indirect moral significance in case morality attaches moral consequences to what is legally the case.

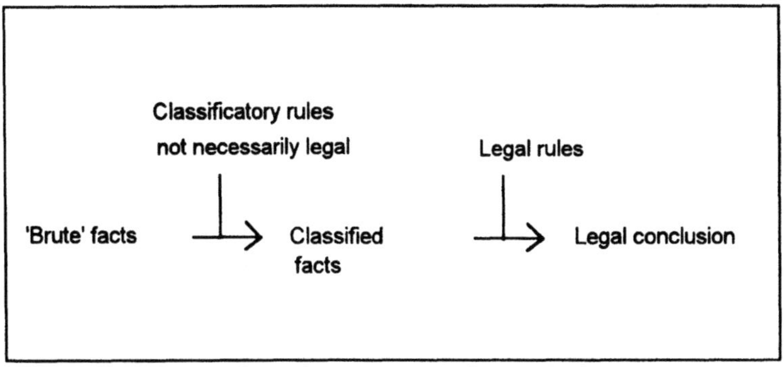

Figure 4: Points of view of rules and their conclusions

This criterion is not a matter of definition, however. If a society has a point of view, the legal point of view for instance, it will also have means to determine what belongs to this point of view and what does not. These means do not have to be precise, but they must exist, for otherwise one point of view can not be distinguished from other points of view and would consequently not exist. So, if there were no means at all to distinguish law from non-law, the legal point of view would not exist.[7] The criterion to distinguish legal rules from other ones is therefore not a matter of stipulative definition, but rather a matter of social practice.

In the case of law, the most burning issue concerning the criteria for the validity of rules is to which extent the validity of rules depends on value judgements, an issue which is often translated into the question whether law and morals can be clearly separated. This issue brings us directly to the second complication concerning the validity of legal rules and principles, that is the mainly institutional nature of the law.

5.2 Validity of legal rules

Until now I have most often used the word 'validity' when talking about the mode of existence of rules. The terms 'valid' and 'invalid' are the customary legal terms for speaking about rule-existence. Rules of law, in particular those based on legislation, exist because they have been made according to the suitable procedure for making them. Their existence is a matter of institutional fact, and this is expressed by using the term *validity* for their mode of existence.

Validity of institutional rules is an all-or-nothing matter. An institutional rule is valid within a particular institution if it has come into existence in ac-

7 It seems that in some primitive societies, the moral, the theological, and the legal point of view could not be distinguished. In my view this means that in those societies these were not three different points of view at all.

cordance with the rules that this institution employs for the creation (coming about) of rules. The conclusion that a rule is valid may be defeasible, but the validity of rules is not a gradual matter.[8] The rule exists - that is, it is valid - or it does not exist, and is invalid.

Validity of institutional rules is also independent of individual acceptation or evaluation. Institutional rules may be good or bad ones, they may be acted upon or not, but all of this is independent of their being valid or invalid. Whether an institutional rule is valid, and whether it is acceptable are two different things. Validity of these rules is a matter of hard institutional fact.[9]

On the one hand, if the law of a society has been institutionalised, if there are legal rules that determine which rules count as legally valid, it does not seem sensible to make the validity of rules also dependent on their acceptance by the citizens or officials to whom they apply. On the other hand, legal rules govern the behaviour of humans, and as a consequence there will be a tendency to adapt the rules to the needs of those humans, even if that adaptation has not (yet) been dealt with in the institutionally prescribed way. That is why there will always be a tendency to treat legal rules, even the institutional ones, as social rules. This means that it may occur that an institutionally valid rule is nevertheless not accepted as a legal rule because of the unacceptability of its contents.[10]

Moreover, an institution may have the terminative rule (cf. section II.4.3) that an institutional rule looses its validity if it has become ineffective. In this way the institution itself takes care of the connection between what is institutionally valid and what is socially accepted. If an institution as a whole becomes ineffective, it does not exist anymore and the validity of the rules that belong to such an institution does not make much sense anymore either (cf. Kelsen 1960, p. 42).

5.3 Validity of social rules

In addition to institutional rules, the law also contains social rules.[11] Most often, these 'rules' will be legal principles or goals. Legal principles exist by their being accepted by the legal community as legally relevant. They are not valid in the sense that they were made according to some procedure, as are

---

8 The gradual nature of some facts is discussed in section VI.5.3.

9 Whether a valid rule should be applied in a particular case is an altogether different matter; cf. section 9.

10 Clearly we encounter here the traditional discussion between natural law theorists and legal positivists.

11 This is the upshot of Dworkin's argument against the 'model of rules'. Cf. Dworkin 1978, chapters 2 and 3. The distinction between the institutional part of the law and the social part will more or less coincide with the distinction between written law and unwritten law.

institutional rules, but they are *accepted*. The conditions of existence of social legal rules will be the same as the conditions for the existence of other social rules (cf. section II.14), with the understanding that social legal rules belong to the legal point of view, which means that they must be employed by the group members as *legal* rules, and not as - say - moral rules.

To make the discussion more uniform, I propose to use the term 'valid' for the acceptation of social rules too, with the understanding that the grounds for this form of validity are different than those for the validity of institutional rules. In civil law countries, the most prevalent reason for the validity of a particular rule of law will be that the law was made by some competent legislative body. The validity of a legal principle can, for instance, be argued by pointing out that the principle has been incorporated in some legal rules (Raz 1972), that it has been mentioned in the legislation[12], or that it has been recognised in case law. The same holds for legal goals (human rights) and for legally protected interests.

An institutional rule can only generate a reason if it is valid. Social rules, on the contrary, can not only generate reasons if they are valid, but also if they *ought to be valid*.[13] This can be illustrated by means of an example about a classificatory rule.

Suppose that there is a legal rule that grants certain rights to persons who are married. To determine the cases to which this rule is to be applied, recourse is made to the common parlance criteria for who counts as married and who not. It may happen (as it has happened in many Western European countries) that many couples consisting of a man and a woman, live lastingly together without being married. Meanwhile the common parlance concerning 'being married' has not changed. As a consequence, the social rule that determines which couples are married, and therefore indirectly also to which couples the rule which grants rights is applicable, does not consider persons who live lastingly together as married.

Still there are lots of reasons to apply the rule about married people also to non-married couples who live lastingly together. One way to achieve this is to apply the rule analogously, but another way would be to use another criterion for determining who count as married in the sense of this particular law. In other words, there are good reasons why the rule that persons who live lastingly together (and possibly satisfy some additional conditions) count as married, should be accepted.

---

[12] The Dutch Penal Code (article 1, section 1) mentions the principle that nobody can be punished except on the basis of a pre-existing penal rule.

[13] If a rule is not valid, but only ought to be valid, this means that the rule does not exist. A non-existing rule can - for trivial reasons - not be a social rule. Therefore it is strictly not correct to say that a social rule can also generate reasons if it only ought to exist.

If this rule only should be valid, that does not mean that the rule is already valid, for the reasons why a social rule should be valid are not the facts which determine that this rule is valid (cf. section II.14). Still the fact that the rule ought to be valid makes that this rule can generate reasons why some unmarried couples count as married for the purpose of the law.

Notice that in this case it is not the factual validity, but rather the deontic 'ought to be valid' of the social rule that enables the classificatory rule to generate reasons. This is an example of the phenomenon of 'deontic collapse' that will be discussed in section 15. Similarly, a social rule that is valid, but should not be valid, sometimes cannot generate reasons (cf. section II.14).

It turns out that it is not only important whether a social rule is valid, but maybe even more whether it ought to be valid. This seems to plead for the thesis that at least in the case of social rules, validity comes down to owing to be obeyed, rather than to the non-deontic criteria which were specified in section II.14. Nevertheless, I do *not* adopt this thesis for two reasons.

First, if a rule that ought to be valid but is not yet valid can also generate reasons, this does not mean that a rule which ought to be valid already exists. Since I defined validity as the mode of existence of rules, this implies that non-valid rules can sometimes generate reasons. But it does not imply that rules which ought to be valid are ipso facto valid.

It might be objected here that this only proves that validity should not be defined as I define it, and that owing to be obeyed is the correct criterion for the validity of rules. If this criterion is used, the objection continues, only valid rules can generate reasons.

This objection brings me to the second reason against adopting the deontic criterion for validity. If a rule is valid if it ought to be obeyed, there need to be reasons why this rule ought to be obeyed, and these reasons need to be based on other valid rules, which must be based on still other reasons, etc. In short, the adoption of the normative criterion for validity leads us to the infinite regress which plagues Kelsen's theory of validity (cf. Peczenik 1989, p. 216 on relative validity).

To avoid this regress, it is necessary to stop somewhere with a rule that is actually valid, rather than with a rule that ought to be valid. This rule should be capable to generate reasons, which means that also rules which are actually valid, and not only those which ought to be valid, can generate reasons. So we still end up with two different foundations for reasons, that is rules which are valid and rules which ought to be valid. This is in accordance with the theory I proposed above.[14]

5.4 Interpretation and classification

If the law is to be applied to a concrete case, we must have a legal rule and a case description, such that the conditions of the rule match the description of the case. For instance, if a rule prescribes that vehicles are to drive on the right hand side of the road, it must be applied to a case described in terms of vehicles, rather than, for instance, cars or bicycles. The conditions of the rule and the facts of the case should be on the same level of abstraction.

Interpretation and classification deal with respectively the rule-side and the case-side of this match. The rule formulation is obtained by the interpretation of *legal sources*, such as statutes, social practice, and case law. The case description is obtained by classifying the most 'brute' description of the case. Cf. figure 5.

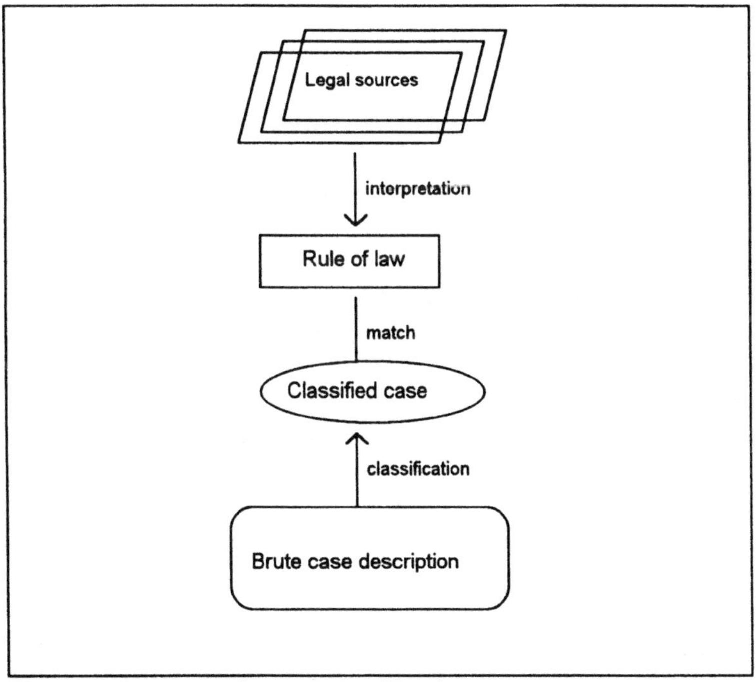

Figure 5: Interpretation and classification

[14] A similar theory was proposed by Von Wright, in his *Norm and Action*, p. 196/7. Von Wright discusses the case where a norm is valid (in a normative sense) relative to another norm on which it is based (a power conferring rule), where that other norm does not need to be valid, but only needs to exist.

To a certain extent, it is immaterial which part of the way from (the texts of) the legal sources to the text of the brute case description is bridged by interpretation, and which part by classification. It does not matter whether the rule is given a rather concrete interpretation, or whether the facts are classified rather abstractly.[15] For the present discussion I propose to cut the knot as follows: Issues concerning the precise conditions and conclusion of a rule are the topic of interpretation; issues concerning the denotations of these conditions and conclusions are a matter of classification.

On this convention, different interpretations of a statute or another source of law, lead to different rules. Arguments for a particular interpretation of a statute can then be considered as arguments why a particular rule, rather than another one is valid on the basis of the source.[16]

Assume, for instance, that we have the following regulation: 'Women and children under sixteen are not allowed to participate in the rodeo.' This sentence is syntactically ambiguous. From the wordings of the regulation it is unclear whether the rule applies to women over fifteen. So there are two possible interpretations:

rule 1: Women and children are not allowed to participate in the rodeo, if they are under sixteen.

rule 2: Children under sixteen, and women are not allowed to participate in the rodeo.

The difference between these two interpretations concerns the precise rule conditions. Therefore, given the convention introduced above, the issue is one of interpretation. If, however, the issue would be whether a person on her sixteenth birthday before the actual hour of being born counts as under sixteen, this would be a matter of classification: Does this particular person count as being under sixteen?

From what is probably the purpose of the regulation, namely to protect women and children against the dangers of a rodeo, and from the senselessness to explicitly name women under sixteen next to children under sixteen, it may be inferred that the second interpretation is to be preferred. These reasons are reasons why rule 2, instead of rule 1, is a valid rule. The fact that

---

[15] Some legal systems allow their Supreme Courts to judge on legal issues only, and not on factual issues. If the distinction between interpretation and classification is (more or less) identified with the distinction between respectively legal and factual issues, it is not immaterial anymore how the borderline between interpretation and classification is drawn. In my opinion, however, the two distinctions should not be identified. Interpretation is always a legal issue, while classification is a legal issue if it is the result of the application of *legal* rules, goals, or principles, which will be the case as soon as these rules, etc. are contested.

[16] Notice that in this view, rules are not the object, but the result of interpretation.

women ought no be discriminated against would be a reason for the validity of rule 1.

It goes without saying that what was written above about legal interpretation of statutory rules, is just as valid when the interpretation of case law is concerned. There may be a difference of opinion about the exact conditions of the rule for which a set of cases provides the authority. The decisions in the cases provide reasons why some interpretation of these cases supports one particular rule or another. Such a discussion can also be conducted as dealing with the validity of a rule.

5.5 Principles of interpretation

Often the sources of law lend themselves to more than one interpretation. This has given rise to extensive methodological discussions, especially concerning the interpretation of statutory texts.[17] In my opinion, the criteria to answer the question which interpretation of a text is to be preferred over another interpretation, are part of the law itself.[18]

Sometimes they are even the object of legislation, which means that there are institutional rules that deal with the interpretation of legal sources. Most often, however, the *principles of interpretation* - because that is what we are talking about - will be social rules. These rules or principles can be applied to generate reasons concerning the validity of (other) legal rules. In that connection, there can be a discussion about the validity (acceptance) of these principles in turn.[19] Cf. figure 6.

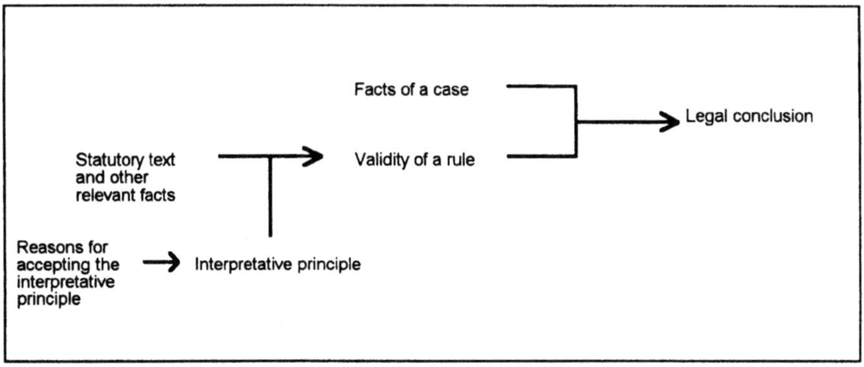

Figure 6: Interpretative principles

---

17 On statutory interpretation, cf. MacCormick and Summers 1991.

18 Cf. Peczenik 1989, pp. 375f. on reasoning norms.

19 In this connection Peczenik 1983, p. 1 speaks of 'deep justification'.

5.6 The recognition of goals

Goal-based reasoning plays an important role in the law (cf. Summers 1978; MacCormick 1978; Alexy 1985). Examples of recognised goals are the goal to treat a suspect as innocent as long as his guilt has not been proven yet, the goals to protect economically weak contract parties and parties who acted in good faith, and most human rights.

Recognition of goals can both be on the institutional and on the social level. Human rights are good examples of goals which have received institutional support. These goals are part of the law, by and large independent of recognition by the members of the legal community. (Of course recognition will have been a factor underlying the institutional support.) Other legal goals are part of the legal culture, although they have never been accepted as such on the institutional level. Protection of economically weak contract parties is a Dutch example of such a goal.

Not all goals that play a role in the law are recognised *from the legal point of view*. For instance, the government may have accepted the goal to further the interests of some minorities by reverse discrimination. This goal may even leave its footprints in a number of statutory rules. Nevertheless, the goal to further the interests of minorities through reverse discrimination is not legally recognised. Rather it is incompatible with the legally recognised goal to treat each person as of equal worth. Goals that play a role in the law, but are nevertheless not legally recognised, cannot *by themselves* generate reasons from a legal point of view. If they are incorporated in legal rules, they can indirectly generate legal reasons through the rules in which they are incorporated.

5.7 Kinds of goals

Not all goals go under that name. Values are also a kind of goals, just as interests. This does not imply that all values underlie reasons from the legal point of view. Only legal values, such as legal security and equality under the law are the basis for legal reasons. However, reasoning with values, whether they belong to the legal point of view or not, works in the same way as reasoning with other goals. If some action contributes to the realisation of a value, this is a reason to perform that action.

The same counts for interests. If I have an interest in, for instance, a rise of the stock markets, and if I am in a position to occasion such a rise, I have a reason to do so. Clearly, interests will normally give rise to personal reasons, although there may also be group interests and even legally recognised interests.[20]

---

[20] There has even be a jurisprudential school called 'interest jurisprudence' (Interessenjurisprudenz). Cf. Larenz 1985, pp. 48f. and Marx 1977.

Actually, Dworkin (1978, pp. 184f; 1981) has defended a theory of rights as legally recognised and specially protected interests, and Alexy (1985) holds that human rights (Grundrechte) are a kind of goals.

All of this means that what is written here about reasoning with goals should, where possible, also be applied to reasoning with values, rights (in the appropriate sense) and interests.

5.8 Goals and principles

According to Alexy (1979, pp. 79f.; 1985, pp. 75f.), legal principles are best considered as what he calls *Optimierungsgebote*, that is as goals that must be realised to as large an extent as is compatible with the realisation of other goals. Because goals are to be realised in a compromise with other goals that also deserve attention and which do not always suggest the same kind of action, legal principles only generate reasons. In this way, Alexy explains the prima facie character of principles.

In my opinion, however, there are at least two differences between goals and principles. The first difference is that while principles can generate reasons for any conclusion whatsoever, goals only generate reasons for acting, and not for e.g. classification. The goal to protect the economically weak, for example, generates reasons to *adopt* particular legal measures. The goal to eat an ice cream generates a reason to *buy* one. No goal, however, can generate a reason why somebody counts as, for example, a thief.[21]

The second difference is that a goal by itself does not make it clear for which conclusions it generates reasons. The nemo plus-principle, for example, will always generate reasons for the conclusion that somebody does not obtain a particular right. The goal to protect the economically weak by itself does indicate for which actions it will generate reasons. This information has to be provided by the facts that will be turned into reasons. For instance, the fact that giving employees permanent positions contributes to the protection of the economically weak becomes a reason for giving employees permanent positions.

Alexy is right with his thesis that legal principles are a kind of goals, to the extent that most so-called 'legal principles' are actually a kind of goals. The principle to protect parties in good faith is a paramount example of a 'principle' which is actually a goal. It generates a reason to do anything that contributes to this protection. However, this does not mean that there are no proper legal principles. The nemo plus-principle is a case in point. It has a

---

21 The phenomenon of deontic collapse makes that goals can indirectly also generate reasons for other things than actions. For the purpose of exposition I will not deal with this phenomenon here; cf. the sections 6.4 and 15.

univocal conclusion, namely that the thing that was transferred without the power to do so, has actually not been acquired by the person to whom the transfer was made. This makes it differ essentially from goals, which generate reasons for anything that contributes to the achievement of the goal. Another example of such a principle with a univocal conclusion is the principle that nobody can be punished without the basis of a pre-existing criminal law (Nulla poena sine lege praevia). So, in my opinion, we should distinguish between proper principles, which have a univocal conclusion, and principles that are actually goals.

That goals do not have univocal conclusions makes that a conflict between two goals is treated differently than a conflict between two proper principles. If two proper principles conflict, their conclusions will be incompatible, and the weighing of the reasons based on these principles will lead to the conclusion of one of the two principles and be incompatible with the conclusion of the other principle.

If two goals 'conflict', this only means that *with regard to some particular solution for a case* the goals point in different directions. For instance, if the interests of the freedom of press conflict with the right of privacy of somebody, this means that the freedom of the press pleads for the permission to publish some stuff, while the right of privacy pleads against this permission. The 'solution' to this conflict is to reformulate the issue so that the conflict disappears. For instance, if the issue becomes whether the publication will be allowed after some date, the involvement of the right of privacy may be removed, and the conflict has disappeared.[22] This way to solve the conflict is not available in the case of conflicting proper principles, because their conclusions are incompatible, and there can be no solution which does not violate at least one of the principles.

Despite the fact that proper principles are certainly not a kind of goals, Alexy is correct in that principles and goals both only generate 'normal' reasons for their conclusions, and not exclusionary reasons. They are also similar in that they 'look' only at one particular aspect of a case, and that they do not attempt to compromise between the different aspects that may be present. For example, in the case of Joyce who transferred the ownership of a book to Casey, the nemo plus-principle only has attention for the fact that Joyce does not own the book, while the goal to protect parties in good faith only looks at the fact that Casey acted in good faith when she bought the book. In short, proper principles and goals have a lot of their logical behaviour in common, but there are also differences.

---

22 This example was inspired by the Lebach-case, which is discussed extensively in Alexy 1985.

5.9 Goals and subgoals

An important type of reason for the validity of a goal is that recognition contributes to the realisation of a 'higher' goal that was already valid. For example, if the interests of lessees are protected, this contributes to the contribution of economically weak contract parties. This fact is a reason to consider the goal to protect the interests of lessees as valid. If this reason makes that the goal to protect lessees ought to be valid, the latter goal can generate reasons for adopting particular measures, such as for instance continuing the rent contract if the property of a rented house is transferred. Cf. figure 7.

Notice that in the case of goals the fact that something *ought to be* a goal suffices to let the goal generate reasons. This is another case of the phenomenon of deontic collapse (cf. section 15).

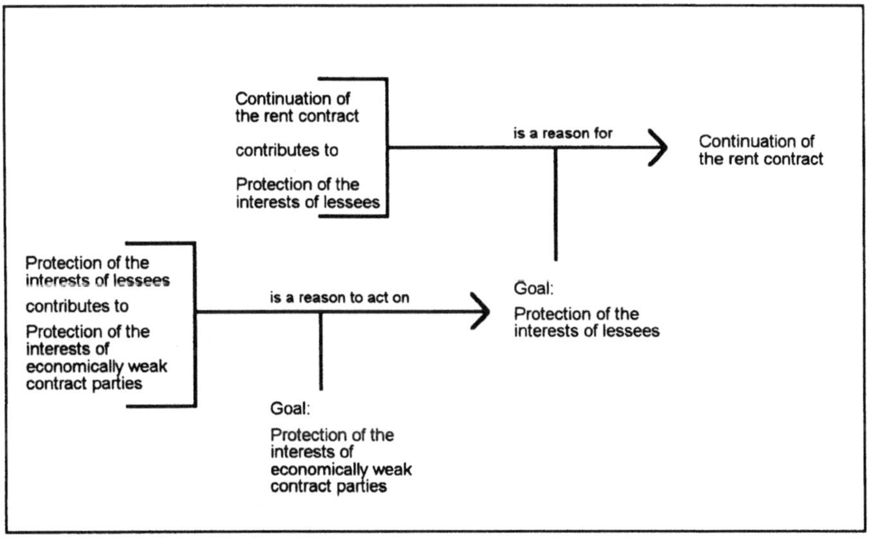

Figure 7: Goals and subgoals

6. THE CONSTITUTION OF REASONS

6.1 The elementary case of reason constitution

The most elementary case of the constitution of a reason is where a rule has one or more conditions which must all be satisfied if the rule is to apply. An example of such an elementary case is provided by the rule that if somebody takes away some good which is owned by another person, while the person who takes the good away intends to appropriate this good, this person is a thief. This is a classificatory legal rule by means of which the conditions for being a thief are specified. This rule has three cumulative conditions, namely

1. that a good G is taken away by a person P,
2. that this good does not belong to P, and
3. that P intended to appropriate G.

Suppose that John took away the car of Ellen, with the intention to appropriate this car. In that case, the facts that

a) John took away the car,
b) the car belonged to Ellen, and
c) John intended to appropriate the car,

together become a reason why John is a thief. Neither one of these facts is by itself a reason.

It might be objected that it is strange that the individual facts are not reasons, while taken together they do constitute a reason. Is it not possible to argue that John is a thief because he took Ellen's car away?

This is certainly possible, and it suggests that not all the facts that match the conditions of a rule need to be present to obtain a reason. To take the edge of this suggestion we must distinguish between reasons and arguments.[23] In an actual discussion, it is often not necessary to state everything that would strictly be necessary to argue a particular thesis. On the contrary, it is common practice not to mention what seems to be obvious. The mere fact of mentioning something even creates the impression that the mentioned facts are not obvious, that something special is the case. Think for example of the old joke of the ship's captain who writes in the log 'The navigating officer was not drunk today'.

Arguments have the function to convince one's auditory; reasons, on the other hand, have a constitutive function. This difference in function explains why facts which can very well serve in arguments for a particular thesis, do not satisfy as reasons for this same thesis. If we can argue that John is a thief because he took Ellen's car, this is because the fact that John wanted to appropriate Ellen's car is presupposed. The argument will tend to convince one's auditory, but this does not show that the mentioned fact constitutes a reason

---

[23] The notion of an argument is ambiguous. In the present context it is used in the sense of something that is actually adduced in some discussion to convince ones auditory. It is therefore a pragmatic notion. An argument is also a chain of reasoning, which leads from one or more premises to a conclusion. I discuss arguments in this sense in section VI.19. Sometimes an argument is also considered as the set of premises from which a conclusion is derived. And finally, an argument may be a quarrel.

for John's being a thief. The facts in a reason must satisfy all the cumulative conditions of the rule on which the reason is based.[24]

6.2 Alternative conditions

If a rule has alternative conditions, it can generate different reasons. Take for instance the rule 'If a person P was either physically incapable to perform his duty, or if P had a justified mental inhibition to do his duty, P acted under force majeure'. This rule has two conditions, but they are alternatives for each other. One can act under force majeure either because of physical impossibility, or because of justified mental inhibition. Both physical impossibility and justified mental inhibition constitute a reason for being under force majeure.

What if somebody was both physically incapable to perform his duty and had a justified mental inhibition? Each of these facts constitutes a reason for being under force majeure. Are there two reasons, if both facts obtain? The answer might be positive: each set of facts that satisfies the conditions of a rule can provide a reason on the basis of that rule, but the combined weight of these reasons is not bigger than the weight of the strongest of the reasons.

The answer might just as well be negative: a rule with alternative conditions can generate only one reason in one case. If one alternative is chosen as a reason, the other alternative does not amount to another reason.

For practical purposes there will be no important difference between the options that there can be more reasons the weights of which do not cumulate, or that there can only be one reason.

6.3 Rules with negative or incompatible conclusions

Next to reasons that plead for a particular conclusion, there are also reasons that plead against a conclusion. If a rule has a negative conclusion, the facts that satisfy the rule's conditions are potential reasons against the fact that is denied in the rule's conclusion.

Suppose that we have the rule that an application for an allowance is invalid if it was not submitted before February 1st of the year in which the allowance is to be granted. This rule makes the fact that the application was not

---

[24] It may seem that if certain facts are usually sufficient to convince the audience, these facts would be a reason. This appearance is correct, but only where these facts are considered as ***epistemic*** reasons. The single fact that you took somebody else's car away may be a good reason to ***assume*** that you are a thief, but it does not ***make*** you a thief in the legal sense. It turns out that parasitic rules of inference need not have precisely the same contents as the constitutive rules on which they are based. In particular those elements of a constitutive reason which normally obtain, may be absent from the corresponding epistemic reason.

submitted before February 1st into a reason *against* the validity of the application.

A more subtle case is where the conclusion of a rule is not the denial of a particular thesis, but is incompatible with it (cf. section VI.3). If we have the rule that somebody is a coward if, as a soldier, he flees at the approach of the enemy, the fact that soldier George flees at the approach of the enemy is a reason against George's being a hero. It is assumed that being a hero and being a coward are incompatible, and therefore a reason for the one fact is ipso facto a reason against the other fact.

6.4 Goals

The basic mechanism by which goals generate deontic reasons is that if an action contributes to the goal, this is a reason why this action ought to be performed. Analogously, if an action detracts from a goal, this is a reason not to perform that action. (Cf. the upper half of figure 8.)

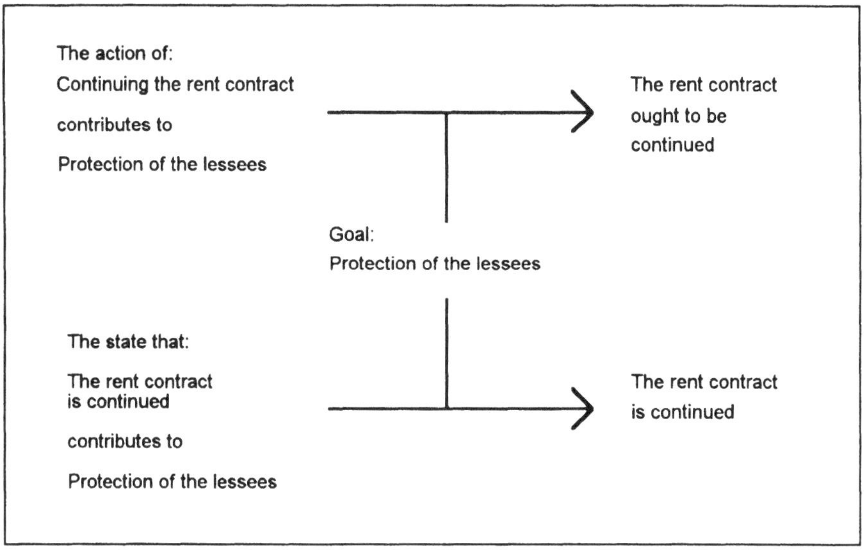

Figure 8: Deontic collapse in the case of goals

This basic mechanism can sometimes be extended from actions to states. For instance, the fact that continuation of a rent contract in case the rented house changes owners, contributes to the protection of the lessees, is a reason to continue the rent contract with the new owner. This is an example of the pure case where an action (continuing the rent contract) contributes to a goal, and should therefore be performed. However, in a legal context we do not only have the question what we should *do*, but also what the legal situation *is*. The fact that we ought to continue the rent contract is not identical to the fact that the rent contract is actually continued. Yet, in a legal context, where we ask the question what the law is, the deontic and the factual sometimes collapse. Sometimes the question what the law is can be answered by saying what the law should be. In the present case, it is possible to conclude from the fact that legally the rent contract ought to be continued to the fact that legally the rent contract is actually continued.

This deontic collapse (cf. section 15) has the consequence that goals cannot only generate deontic reasons for actions, but that they can also generate reasons for the presence of states. In our example, the legal *state* that the rent contract is continued with the new owner contributes to the goal that the interests of the lessees are protected. This fact is a deontic reason why this state ought to be the case. Moreover, because of the collapse of the deontic into the non-deontic, it is even a reason why this state is actually the case. Cf. figure 8.

6.5 Proving and classifying the facts

Often the facts that match the conditions of a rule or principle are not immediately given, but must be derived. In this connection we can distinguish between issues of proof[25] and issues of classification.

Facts need to be proven if they are not immediately given, and if facts that might constitute them are not given either. For instancc, it needs not be proven that somebody is a thief if it is given that this person took away somebody else's property with the intention of appropriation. However, proof is needed if we want the information that somebody is a thief, and we only have the information that this person needed the money, and was the only person known to be in the neighbourhood at the moment of the theft. The step from person P needed the money and was the only person known to be in the neighbourhood, to P is the thief is one of (not necessarily convincing) proof.

Proofs are based on epistemic reasons. The facts by which something is proven are reasons why the conclusion that is to be proven should be believed. Epistemic reasons are in their turn based on epistemic rules (principles), or - which is the same - rules of inference (rules of evidence). The epistemic rules used in the law are usually social rules, based on common sense. The principle that if somebody needed the money, and was the only one who had the occasion to commit the theft, this person may be assumed to be the thief, may be considered as such a social rule of inference.

Some legal rules of evidence are institutional. The Dutch law, for instance, has the rule that an authentic deed made by a notary, definitively proves the

25 The notion of proof is used here in its legal sense of adducing evidence, and not in the logical sense of a sequence of sentences which leads from premises to a conclusion.

declarations described in it. A negative institutional rule of criminal evidence is that the testimony of only one witness does not count as sufficient evidence.

Classification takes place if the argument runs that some facts constitute some other (non-modal) facts. For instance, if two parties say that they want to sell, respectively buy a car, these facts can be classified as engaging into a sales contract. The constituting facts are classificatory reasons for their conclusion.

Classificatory reasons are based on classificatory rules or principles. Just as in the case of epistemic rules, these will most often be social rules. The law makes on a large scale use of the rules of language to determine whether the conditions of legal rules and principles are satisfied.

A special case of classification is evaluation. The conditions of rules are often expressed by means of evaluative terms, such as 'force majeure', 'good faith' and 'reasonable'. The application of these terms is the result of classification which is similar to non-evaluative classification, with the only difference that in the case of classification the standards are not (completely) given by the language.

In special cases there will be institutional legal rules that govern the use of the words in rule conditions. These legal definitions will normally be Leges Speciales with regard to the rules that define the common parlance meaning of words. For example, the Dutch Traffic Law (Wegenverkeerswet) starts with a definition of what counts as a road in the sense of this law. This classificatory rule excludes the application of the normal criteria to classify something as a road. Case law provides us also with many classificatory reasons.

6.6 Summary of the constitution of reasons

We find that the constitution of reasons is based on two kinds of elements. On the one hand there are rules, principles, and goals that can generate reasons. On the other hand, there are facts that somehow satisfy the conditions of these rules, principles, and goals. In order to be able to generate reasons, the rules, goals and principles must be valid. It may demand an additional argument to demonstrate that this is the case. The facts that will become reasons may also be the result of derivation. This 'derivation' may be a proof from other facts that do not constitute the needed facts, or it may be classification, when the input of the derivation consists of constitutive reasons for the conclusion.

7. THE EXCLUSION OF RULES

Normally, if the conditions of a valid rule are satisfied in a particular case, this rule is applicable, which is a reason to apply the rule. Application of a rule makes the facts that satisfy the conditions of the rule into a decisive reason for the rule's conclusion. For instance, if John is a thief, the rule that thieves are punishable is applicable to the case of his theft, and application of this rule makes the fact that John is a thief into a decisive reason why John is punishable.

There are two ways in which this normal course can be interrupted. First, it may be the case that a rule is not applicable, although its conditions are satisfied, and second it may be the case that, although a rule is applicable, it should nevertheless not be applied. In both of these cases, the fact that the conditions of a rule are satisfied does not bring about that the satisfying facts become a reason for the conclusion of the rule. In this section I discuss the cases in which a rule is not applicable although its conditions are satisfied. In such cases, the application of the rule is said to be *excluded*. In section 8 follows a discussion of the replacement of goals and principles by rules, which leads to effects which are similar to the exclusion of rules.

7.1 The scope limitations of rules

Suppose that in the United Kingdom a murder takes place which satisfies all the conditions posed by a rule from the Dutch criminal law for the punishability of the murderer. Suppose moreover, that both the murderer and the victim were inhabitants of the UK and that the case exhibits no connections with the Netherlands or with Dutch law at all. It is clear that the rule from the Dutch criminal law is not applicable to this case, although all of its conditions (the conditions mentioned in section 289 of the Dutch penal law) are satisfied.

This example illustrates that the satisfaction of a rule's conditions does not automatically bring the applicability of the rule along. The reason for the non-applicability of the rule in this example is that the case falls outside the scope of the rule. Next to their conditions for applicability which are stated in the condition part of the rule, rules have scope limitations which limit the application of the rule in, amongst others, time and space.

In connection with physical laws, Toulmin gives the example of laws of physical optics which only hold under particular circumstances (Toulmin 1953, p. 68/9). Similarly, legal provisions are normally only applicable in the territory of the legal system to which they belong. Moreover, the rules that govern the enforcement of legal obligations can, in Dutch law, not be applied to obligations that stem from too long ago. A comparable phenomenon is the prescription of criminal proceedings. Notice that prescription does not occur because of the invalidity of the rule at the time of the crime, but that it is a case of non-applicability of a valid rule.

In general we must distinguish between the span of time in which a rule of law is valid, and the span of time to which it may be applicable. Normally these two time spans (more or less) coincide, but there may be exceptions.

Retroactive laws are a case in point, because they are applicable to cases at a time in which the rules were not yet valid.

Usually scope limitations are not considered as part of the conditions of the rule whose scope they concern. There are several good reasons for that. First because scope limitations in the law often apply to sets of rules. It is more economical to state them in general for the whole set of rules for which they hold, rather than to add the limitations to the conditions of all concerning rules.

Second, and more importantly, the logical role of scope limitations is different from the role of the conditions. Often the satisfaction of the scope limitation is assumed and the non-satisfaction must be proven. The division between rule conditions on the one hand, and scope limitations on the other hand, has a corollary in the division of the burden of proof.[26]

Finally, if a legal rule is not applicable because its scope limitations are exceeded, this leads to a different legal verdict than in case its conditions are not satisfied. In a Dutch criminal case, for instance, transgression of scope limitations leads to the dismissal of the public prosecutor or dismissal of the suspect, while the non-satisfaction of conditions leads to acquittal of the suspect.

Scope limitations are not the only factor that can make a rule not-applicable, even though its conditions are satisfied. Exceptions to a rule have a similar effect. Sometimes, exceptions to legal rules are just negative rule conditions. It must be shown that the exception does not apply to prove that the rule is applicable. Exceptions of this type are normally included in the formulation of the rule in the source from which the rule is derived.

Very often, however, exceptions to rules are formulated outside the provisions on which the rules are based. In these cases exceptions are like scope limitations in that they describe special circumstances under which the rule should not be applied. I will call these exceptions *proper exceptions*. Typical cases in point are situations of force majeure in civil law, and grounds for justification or exculpation in criminal law. Proper exceptions can both be explicitly formulated in rules of law, and be implicit.[27]

For proper exceptions often holds the same as for (other) scope limitations. Their absence is assumed by default, and if they are present, they lead to other verdicts than the mere non-satisfaction of the rule conditions. If a crime is committed under force majeure, for instance, the verdict will be dismissal.

---

[26] Cf. the distinction made in Sartor 1991 between principal and secondary facts in legal language, in particular the distinction between facts to prove and facts to which contrary prove must not be given. Cf. also Baker's views of defeasibility as described in his 1977.

[27] Prakken pointed out to me that sometimes proper exceptions are mentioned in the rule to which they form an exception, as in '...unless the law indicates otherwise'.

Exceptions can apply to categories of rules (e.g. all rules of criminal law, or all law of contract), but they can also apply to individual rules in particular cases.

Scope limitations and exceptions can make a rule inapplicable although the conditions of the rule are satisfied. Their effects are absolute: if a case falls outside the scope of a rule, or if there is a proper exception to the rule, the rule is not applicable anymore, with the consequence that the rule will not be applied. In the terminology of reasons, this means that scope limitations and exceptions give rise to *exclusionary reasons*. If a scope condition is not satisfied, or if an exception applies, the application of the concerning rule is *excluded*.

The exclusion of a rule is to be distinguished form the invalidity of the rule. If a rule is invalid, this means that - in a sense- it does not even exist, and as a consequence it cannot generate any reasons at all. Exclusion, on the contrary, is case-related. A rule can only be excluded if it is valid; exclusion means that the valid rule cannot be applied in the particular case(s) in which its application is excluded.

7.2 Conflict rules

In the law, a particularly important category of scope limitations derives from the phenomenon of rule conflicts. Legal ideology will have it that rules of law do not conflict. If two rules seem to conflict, at least one of them is not applicable. The scopes of conflicting rules are assumed to be disjoint.

This phenomenon can be explained if we take into account that legal rules are meant to identify reasons which replace the original reasons on which the rules are based. The necessary weighing of reasons is considered to be the task of the legislator. The legislator so to speak oversees all conflicting goals and principles, and determines for each possible case what is the outcome of their interaction. This outcome is 'described' in the legal rules that are laid down in legislation (cf. section 2). Since conflicting descriptions of the result of the interacting reasons cannot all be true, conflicting rules cannot all be applicable. That is why conflicting rules should be avoided, or at least made innocent by taking care that at most one of them can be applicable.

Conflict rules have the task to demarcate the scopes of conflicting rules. If, for instance, a more general rule conflicts with a more specific one, the greater specificity of the latter rule is a reason why the case falls outside the scope of the former one. As a consequence, only the more specific rule generates a reason; the conflicting reason which might be generated by the more general rule, is not actually generated.

8. RULES, GOALS AND PRINCIPLES

Suppose that we have a legal issue, for instance whether a particular religious procession is allowed. There are both reasons for and against an allowance. Considerations concerning the free flow of traffic plead against, while considerations concerning the freedom of religion plead for allowing processions. Suppose, moreover, that there is not yet any legislation that explicitly deals with this subject. If a judge has to decide whether a particular procession is allowed or not, he must decide which of the reasons are legally relevant (are reasons from the legal point of view), and he must weigh these reasons to decide whether the procession is allowed or not. In other words, the question whether the procession is allowed is determined on the basis of a subset of all the available reasons for and against allowance, namely those reasons that are legally relevant. These reasons from the legal point of view are divided into reasons for and reasons against allowing the procession, and the final decision is the result of weighing these reasons. Cf. figure 9.

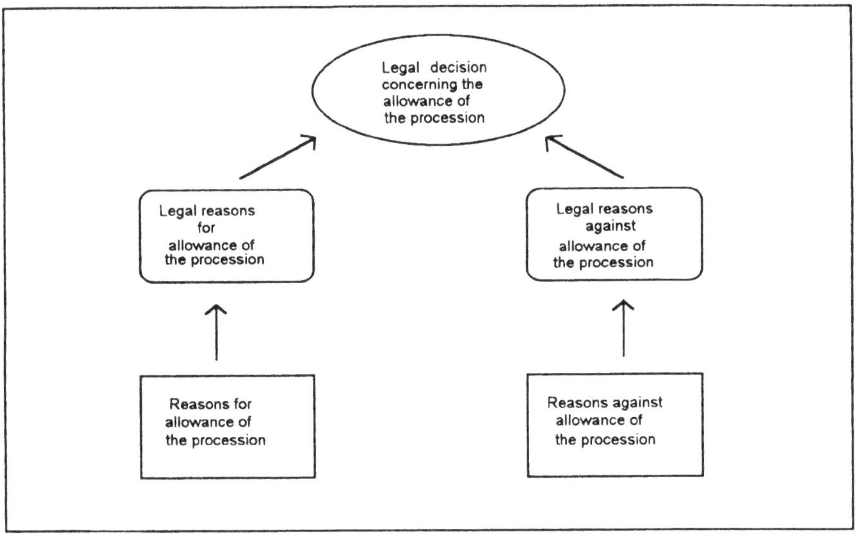

Figure 9: Weighing legal reasons

If the (municipal) legislator wants to regulate the subject matter of religious processions, he will consider all reasons that he deems relevant for making a legislative decision. These reasons will be a subset of all possible reasons, but this subset is not necessarily the same one as the subset of all legally relevant reasons. The legislator is free (subject to some political constraints) to decide which reasons will be taken into account and which will not. On the basis of these reasons, the legislator takes a decision, that will be the result of weighing the reasons that are deemed relevant by the legislator.

The result of this decision making process is laid down in a legal rule, which in its turn identifies the facts that from now on are relevant in determining whether processions are allowed or not (cf. section 2). For instance, processions will only be allowed on Sundays. This condition is the result of weighing the reasons that were involved in the legislative decision making process. Whether this condition is satisfied is now the reason why a particular procession is allowed or not. This reason *replaces* the reasons that originally determined whether a procession was allowed or not, or - better - they replace the reasons that went into the legislative decision making process. The legal rule as the outcome of legislative decision making determines which reasons are from then on legally relevant, and excludes all the reasons that were taken into account in drafting the rule (reasons based on the freedom of religion, and on the interests of the traffic). The reasons based on legal rules may therefore be called *replacing reasons*. Cf. figure 10.

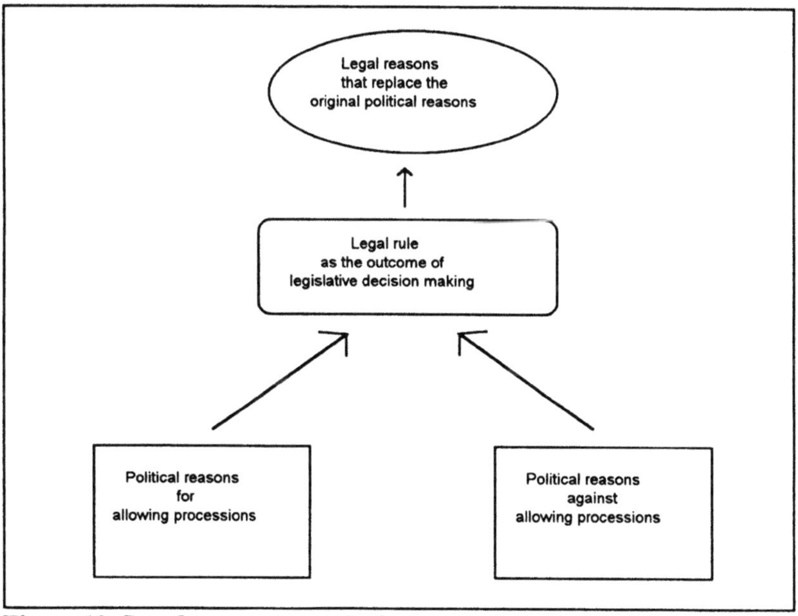

Figure 10: Legal reasons as replacing reasons

What does it mean for legal decision making, if the reasons identified by a rule of law replace the political reasons that were involved in drafting the law? If a rule of law is applied to a particular case, it generates a decisive reason to decide this case in a particular way. But this is not the whole story. If the rule is applied, it also generates exclusionary reasons that prevent other potential reasons to be taken into account. In particular, those principles and goals that were taken into account in drafting the legal rule will now be left out of consideration. Indeed, if the legislator has taken a decision about their role while drafting the legal rule, it is not the task of the judiciary to redo the job of the legislator and give its own opinion about the role of these principles and goals. The reasons identified by the rule replace the reasons that already were involved in drafting the rule. This is completely in accordance with Raz's account of mandatory rules as (generating) exclusionary reasons (cf. section II.1.5).

However, if there still are legally relevant facts that were not taken into account by the legislator, not even in the sense that they were discarded as irrelevant, these facts are not excluded by the reasons generated by the legal rule. A legal decision maker must still take these facts into account as legal reasons next to the reason identified by the legal rule. For instance, if the prohibition on legal processions infringes the right of every citizen to move where he or she wants, and this right was not taken into account in making the rule about processions, this right to move still generates a reason that must be taken into account. (It should be taken into account as a reason not to apply the rule about processions; cf. section 9.)

The Dutch Supreme Court (Hoge Raad) has actually given a decision that seems to confirm the theory about the relation between legal rules and principles as described here (HR 4 april 1989, NJ 1989, 469; Harmonisatiewetarrest). By means of the so-called 'Harmonisatiewet' the Dutch legislator changed (shortened) the period during which a student who started a second study is entitled to financial support. The transitional rules for those who had already started a second study were few. Some of these students claimed in law that the Dutch government would not apply the Harmonisatiewet to them. One of the reasons underlying this claim was based on the principle of legal security: the government should not violate expectations which it had given rise to itself.

To judge the claim of the students, the Dutch Supreme Court addressed, amongst others, the question whether it was possible to review the Harmonisatiewet against the principle of legal security. In this connection, the Supreme Court remarked that two situations must be distinguished. On the one hand there is the situation in which the legislator has taken into account the factors, made relevant by the principle, that plead against the legislation. In this situation, there is no room to review the statutory rule against the principle. On the other hand, there is the situation in which the legislator did not take these factors into account. In that situation, the rule may be left out of application if, in a concrete case, it conflicts with a fundamental legal principle.

Notice that the Supreme Court distinguishes between reasons that were taken into account in making the legislation and reasons that were not taken into account. If the reasons were taken into account, the rule may, in my terminology, be said to replace the principles on which these reasons were based. In that case, there is no room for reviewing the rule against the principle. The applicability of the rule excludes the application of the principle. If the reasons based on the principle were not taken into account, the rule does not replace the principle, and the application of the principle is not excluded. In this case, the rule must be reviewed against the principle. This review is, according to the Dutch Supreme Court, confined to concrete cases. In my terminology this comes down to it that the review concerns the application, not the validity of the rule.

The foregoing account of the relation between legal rules on the one hand, and legal principles and goals on the other hand might evoke the impression that the role of legal principles and goals is confined to that of some kind of proto-law, which is made superfluous by the introduction of legal rules. Such an impression would not be correct. Legal principles and goals do not only play a role in legal reasoning when relevant rules are lacking, but they also provide reasons why regulations are to be interpreted in one way rather than another, and occasionally they generate reasons against the application of an applicable rule. Since this is a text on the logic of rule application and not on legal justification in general, I will refrain from a more thorough discussion of the roles of principles and goals in legal reasoning.

9. REASONS AGAINST APPLICATION OF A RULE

In the context of rule application, the term 'applicable' has been used as a technical term. Applicability of a rule is distinguished from the satisfaction of the rule's conditions. The latter is a necessary, but not a sufficient condition for the former. A rule is applicable to a case, if and only if its conditions are satisfied, and its application is not excluded.

Next to the distinction between the *applicability* of a rule and the *satisfaction* of its conditions, I will distinguish between the applicability and the *application* of a rule. Applicability is a deontic reason for the application of the rule. Unless there are other reasons not to apply the rule, an applicable rule should be applied. Moreover, applicability is the major reason why a rule should be applied. The normal situation is that a rule should be applied if it is applicable, and that it should not be applied if it is not applicable. This distinction between applicability and application only concerns rules, not principles. This does not mean that principles need not to be applied, but only that a principle automatically applies if its conditions are satisfied and its application is not excluded.

The reasons generated by principles are to be weighed against conflicting reasons. In the case of rules, conflicting reasons will not be reasons which conflict with the reasons generated by the rules, but rather reasons not to apply an applicable rule. Since the applicability of a rule is not only a reason to apply the rule, but usually also a reason why competing principles and goals are excluded, there will normally be no reasons against applying an applicable rule.

There are two exceptional cases. One case is when there are goals and/or principles which are not excluded by the rule and which plead for a conclusion that is incompatible with that of the rule. I have already discussed this situation in the previous section in connection with the decision of the Dutch Supreme Court in the case of the 'Harmonisatiewet'. The other case is when application of a rule would be against the rule's purpose.

To understand why the fact that application would be against the rule's purpose is a reason against applying the rule, we should consider the relation between the rule and its purpose. If a rule has a purpose, this means that the rule is a means towards some end. A decision-based rule is the outcome of a process of weighing reasons. The conclusion of this rule contains the choice of specific means to obtain a desired situation and to avoid undesired side-effects. This specific means is estimated to be the best for the particular situation which is described in the rule's conditions.[28]

If application of a rule in a particular case does not contribute to the goals pursued by the rule, or - even worse - detracts from that goal, the application may be said to be *against the purpose* of the rule. Fuller gave an example of a prohibition to sleep in the railway station, which was motivated by the desire to retain tramps from spending their night on the station (Fuller 1958). It would be against the purpose of this rule to apply it to the traveller who dozed away a few minutes while waiting on a late train, because this would not contribute to the goal of retaining tramps from spending their night on the station.

If the application of a rule in a case would be against the rule's purpose, this is a reason not to apply the rule in that case. Such a reason must still be weighed against the reasons for application, the most important of which will be that the rule is applicable. This situation differs from the one in which there is an exclusionary reason against application of the rule, because exclusionary reasons are decisive. The fact that the conditions of a rule are satisfied is not a reason to apply American Federal law to an ordinary Dutch case. The fact that the rule is applicable to the late traveller from Fuller's example

---

[28] I neglect the influences on the legislative process which make it possible that the solution chosen in the rule is not the best one in the eyes of the legislator. The relation between a rule's purpose and the rule itself is an idealised one.

still counts as a reason for applying the rule, although this reason may be outweighed by the reason that application would be against the rule's purpose.

The effects of applying a rule against its purpose are in general undesirable. There may, however, be other reasons why application of a rule is undesirable. Application might, for instance, damage an important political goal, or violate private interests on a large scale. In such cases, there is also a reason not to apply the rule. This does, of course, not mean that the rule will not be applied. It only means that in such cases the applicability of the rule as a reason for applying the rule must be weighed against the reason not to apply the rule. Notice, however, that such conflicting interests and rights will often be excluded by the applicability of the rule, in particular if they were taken into account in making the rule.

10. THE DIFFERENCE BETWEEN LEGAL RULES AND LEGAL PRINCIPLES

Dworkin (1978, p. 25/6) has revived the discussion about the difference between legal rules and legal principles by stating that rules apply in an all-or-nothing fashion, while legal principles state reasons that argue in a direction, but do not necessitate a particular decision.

This way of making the distinction has been subjected to criticism. Alexy, for instance, has argued that legal rules are not exceptionless, unless they are completed with a catch all-clause which makes a general reservation for exceptional circumstances.[29]

Alexy (1979, p. 75) adduces still another argument against Dworkin. Some principles are not even applied, even though their conditions are satisfied. He mentions as an example the principle that the richer party has to bear the damage. This principle conflicts with the principles of the law of contract, but is in concrete cases not weighed against the latter principles, but is instead completely left out of consideration.

Although the criticisms of Alexy seem to be justified, Dworkin has made an important contribution to legal theory by pointing out a logical difference between legal rules and legal principles. The following is an attempt to reconcile the views of Dworkin with the criticisms of Alexy.

The thesis concerning the logical difference is often confined to the difference between legal rules and legal principles, but could just as well be extended to the difference between legal rules and all other generators of legal

---

[29] Cf. the possibility to use explicit exception clauses as discussed in Prakken 1993, chapter 5. The difference with the proposal of Alexy is that Prakken embeds the use of exception clauses in a context of nonmonotonic reasoning, while Alexy seems to stick to the traditional view of rule application.

reasons. Next to legal principles, legally acknowledged goals, interests, and values are also capable to generate legal reasons. As far as the logical difference is concerned, these acknowledged goals, interests, and values can be identified with legal principles.[30] Let us confine ourselves to legal principles, to keep matters relatively simple.

If a legal principle is applied to a case, the principle generates a reason to decide the case in a particular way. This reason (in combination with potential other reasons that plead in the same direction) still has to be weighed against other reasons to solve the case in an incompatible way. Here is where Dworkin's analysis comes in: reasons, and indirectly also principles, have a dimension of weight. They do not decide a case by themselves, but only in combination with all other reasons.

However, the relative 'weight' of a reason may depend on other factors than only the reasons themselves. Weight is case-related, and can therefore not directly be ascribed to the principles on which the reasons are based, because these principles are themselves not case-related. This means that Dworkin is wrong insofar as he attributes the dimension of weight directly to principles instead of to the reasons based on them.

Another characteristic of legal principles is that a legal principle takes only a particular aspect of a case into account. For instance, the nemo plus-principle, if applied to cases where a non-owner transfers the property of some good, only looks at the fact that the transferring party did not have the right that this party attempts to transfer. All other aspects of the case are left out of consideration.

If a legal rule is applicable to a case, it replaces the principles or goals that lead to reasons which were already involved in drafting the rule. Suppose, for instance, that the legislator took the fact into account that allowing religious processions on Sundays hinders the traffic on Sunday. The goal that one should protect the interests of the traffic should therefore not be taken into consideration anymore in determining whether a particular religious procession is allowed or not. The applicability of the rule made by the legislator makes this goal irrelevant for this particular case. The effects on the traffic must be assumed to be incorporated in the conditions under which the legislator allowed processions.

As discussed in the beginning of this chapter, legal rules might be considered as a kind of statements that tell us what is (in the eye of the legislator) the result of the interaction of all relevant reasons, reasons which in their turn are based on principles and goals. Rules have a descriptive element, which is lacking in the case of principles and goals. That is why rules, in contrast to

---

[30] Cf. section 5.8 for the differences between principle- and goal-based reasoning.

principles and goals, aim to take all relevant aspects of a case into account. For example, the rule about the transfer of mutable goods by a non-owner not only looks at the fact that the transferring person was not the owner, but also to the facts that the original owner lost his good through theft, that the receiving party acted in good faith and that he paid a reasonable price for the good. Still, reasoning with rules is defeasible, because rules are necessarily based on the finite number of reasons that were taken into account while making the rule. That is why reasoning with rules can never be the same as reasoning with real statements; reasoning with rules is defeasible, although defeat relatively seldom occurs.

The logical ground for this is twofold: First, the reason generated by the application of a rule is a decisive one. It guarantees the conclusion of the rule. However, this guarantee would only lead to an inconsistency if the principles and goals that plead in a different direction would still generate reasons on the basis of which the opposite conclusion would follow. This inconsistency is avoided because the applicability of a legal rule excludes the application of all principles, goals, values, and interests that were taken into account in making the rule. (It may be difficult to establish, and a matter of serious discussion, to determine which these principles etc. were.) As a consequence, there will not be many competitors for an applicable legal rule. Hence the attractiveness of Dworkin's suggestion that rule application is a matter of all-or-nothing. Reasoning with rules is often very similar to reasoning with statements.

Still, in exceptional cases, there may be some reasons that were not taken into account by the legislator, and are therefore not excluded by the applicability of the legal rule. In that case, there will be reasons not to apply the rule, and if the rule is not applied, its conclusion does not follow. This explains part of Alexy's criticism that sometimes there are exceptions in which the conclusion of a rule does not follow, even though the rule's conditions are satisfied. The criticism that sometimes principles are not applied at all and therefore seem to operate in an all-or-nothing fashion too, can also be explained in the proposed view: the application of a principle or goal can be excluded in a particular case.

Principles which are not excluded by an applicable rule generate reasons not to apply the rule, which should be weighed against the applicability of the rule as a reason for applying the rule. In earlier publications (e.g. Hage and Verheij 1995, and also in Hage Model), I defended the thesis that a rule that is applied only generates a reason for its conclusion, that might have to be weighed against reasons generated by principles and goals that were not excluded. Presently I think that a reason based on a non-excluded principle or goal will always be a reason not to apply the rule, and not an independent reason against the rule's conclusion. If this is correct, a rule needs not to be applied if it is applicable, but if it is applied, its conclusion always follows.

Notice that reasons for and against the application of a rule are deontic reasons, that is reasons why the rule ought, or ought not, to be applied. It is the actual application of a rule, however, that leads to the conclusion of the rule. Somehow, the transition from the conclusion that a rule ought to be applied to the actual application of the rule is made 'automatically'. This, again, is an example of deontic collapse (cf. also the sections 15 and VI.2).

Summarising we can say that Dworkin is correct when he writes that there is a logical difference between legal rules and legal principles (and goals). The former generate exclusionary reasons when they are applicable, the latter do not. Moreover, if a rule is applied to a case, it generates a decisive reason and its conclusion must follow, while principles and goals only generate non-decisive reasons.

11. ANALOGOUS APPLICATION OF A RULE

A rule is applied analogously if it is applied to a case in which the rule conditions are not satisfied, but that sufficiently resembles the cases in which the rule conditions are satisfied, to justify the application of the rule.

Some authors argue that analogous rule application does not actually occur, but that sometimes a more abstract rule is applied to a case that does not satisfy the conditions of the original rule.[31] For example, a Dutch rule of law says that if a house is sold, the existing rent contract is continued with the new owner. This rule appears to be applied analogously to the case where the house is not sold, but the property is transferred on the basis of some other title, e.g. donation. According to the authors that reject analogous rule application, the seeming application of the rule about the sale of a house to other cases in which the property of the house is transferred, only shows that the rule is actually about transfer of houses (or at least also about the donation of

---

[31] This view of analogous rule application is defended in Tammelo and Schreiner 1977, pp. 112f., and Prakken 1993, p. 22. Prakken would say that the analogy is not involved in the application of the rule, but in the suggestion of the rule's new formulation. In this he follows Soeteman 1989, p. 239.

Peczenik 1989, pp. 392f. is not fully clear on its interpretation of statutory analogy. On the one hand Peczenik defines statutory analogy as the case 'that one applies a statutory rule to a case which, viewed from the ordinary linguistic angle, is included in neither the core nor the periphery of the application area of the statute in question, but resembles the cases covered by this statute in essential respects'. This circumscription seems similar to my view. On the other hand, Peczenik gives an example of a logical reconstruction which modifies the rule conditions to make them suit the new case. This is similar to the approach defended by the authors mentioned above.

houses), and not only about the sale of houses. Selling and donating a house are then special cases to which the more abstract rule can be applied in a normal fashion.

The inclination to treat analogous rule application as the application of a more abstract rule is explainable from the tendency to consider rules from a logical point of view as statements. Clearly statements cannot be applied analogously. The only way to deal with analogy in case of statements is to assume that the statements were actually more abstract than they originally seemed to be.

However, rules should be considered as statements, but as a kind of tools, applied by humans to structure the (legal) world. For instance, we use the rule that thieves are punishable to create a connection between the facts that somebody is a thief and that this person is punishable. This rule is normally used if somebody is a thief. Sometimes, however, a tool may even be used if the normal circumstances are not present, but some action is nevertheless necessary. For instance, we encounter a case in which somebody illegally copies software. This is not a real case of theft, but we need a legal tool to deal with it. Analogous rule application might be considered as a situation in which a rule is used under non-ideal circumstances. If a rule is applied analogously, it generates a reason for its conclusion even though its conditions are not satisfied. (However, there are serious objections against applying criminal laws analogously.)

The account of the relation between legal rules and legal principles and goals that was given in the previous sections makes it relatively easy to deal with analogous rule application. Let us reconsider the example about the rule that a rent contract is continued with the new owner if a rented house is sold. This rule is applied analogously to cases in which the property of the house is transferred on the basis of another title than sale.

To obtain an account of what happens, we should consider the legal goal that underlies the rule. This goal is that the persons that rent a house should be protected in their right to live in the house. This goal is elaborated in the conclusion of the rule that if the house is sold, the rent contract is continued with the new owner. Notice that the elaboration is much more specific than the goal itself. Other elaborations with a comparable effect are imaginable, such as that in order to be able to sell a rented house, the owner should offer the inhabitants an equivalent alternative.

If a rented house is sold, the legal rule generates a reason why the rent contract is continued with the new owner and excludes the application of underlying legal principles and goals such as the principle that contracts only are in force between the contracting parties, and the goal that the inhabitants of a rented house should be protected in their right of inhabitation. This principle and this goal were both taken into account in making the rule, and if the rule is applicable, the principle and the goal are excluded.

What happens if a case does not satisfy the conditions of the rule? One possibility is that the rule is not applied to the case. In that case the rule does not give a solution for the case, but neither does it generate exclusionary reasons that prevent the application of the mentioned legal goal and principle. If, for instance, the house is donated, and the rule about sale of the house is not applied, the case must be decided on the basis of the principle that contracts only are in force between the contracting parties, and the goal that the inhabitants of a rented house should be protected in their right of inhabitation. Both the principle and the goal would generate a reason, a reason why the inhabitants should be able to remain in their house, and a reason why they have no rights to remain in the house at all. These reasons must be weighed to obtain a solution for the case. Notice, however, that neither reason explicitly deals with the continuation of the rent contract with the new owner. The principle is much too abstract to generate reasons for or against such a specific solution.

Another possibility is that the principle and the goal generate a reason against, respectively for, application of the rule about sale of the house. The normal reason for applying a rule is that the rule applicable. It is not impossible, however, that there are other reasons for applying a rule, because applying a rule is a kind of acting, and there may be all sorts of reasons to act in a particular way. One reason to apply the rule about selling a house in case the house is donated is that the legal goal of protecting the rights of inhabitants of rented houses is served by applying the rule. Another way to formulate this reason is that application of the rule would serve the rule's purpose. A reason not to apply the rule is that application would be in conflict with the principle that contracts only are in force between the contracting parties. Another reason would be based on the demand for legal security.

Reasons to apply a rule even if its conditions are not satisfied will usually be based on principles or goals that led the legislator to make the rule in the first place. Therefore the cases to which the rule is applied, although the rule conditions are not satisfied, will normally resemble cases to which the rule is applicable. That is why we normally speak of 'analogous application' of a rule if a rule is applied to a case in which it is not applicable.

In the first way of dealing with an inapplicable rule we have direct reasons for and against measures that give the inhabitants the possibility to continue their inhabitation of the house. The conclusion of these reasons is still rather vague. In the second way, on the contrary, we obtain reasons that indirectly (namely via the intermediary of rule application) plead for and against a much more specific solution of the case, namely continuation of the rent contract.

The reasons to apply a rule even if its conditions are not satisfied can also be interpreted as reasons to adopt and apply a more abstract rule which is directly applicable to the case at hand. This option might be preferred by the authors mentioned above, who argue that analogy is not an inference scheme, but rather a heuristic to suggest more abstract rules which can be applied 'normally'. The advantage of this option, that no deviant inference scheme is needed, is balanced by the disadvantage that the more abstract rule will not be legally valid.[32] However, as we have seen in section 5.3, rules can also generate reasons if they are not actually valid, but only ought to be valid.

12. E CONTRARIO 'APPLICATION' OF A RULE

If a rule is not applicable, it may still be applied. Analogous application leads to a reason for the rule's conclusion even if the conditions of the rule are not satisfied. The opposite can, however, also happen. Sometimes it is possible to obtain a reason *against* the rule's conclusion if the rule's conditions are not satisfied. In such cases the rule is said to be used in an argument e *contrario*.

According to the traditional view, an argument e contrario presupposes that the conditions of the rule not (only) state a sufficient condition for the rule's conclusion, but (also) a necessary one (e.g. Soeteman 1989, p. 239). The rule would express an equivalence between its conditions and its conclusion. Such a view would go too far, however. First because it leaves unexplained why of two rules which superficially seem not to differ, one states only a sufficient condition for its conclusion, while the other one states an equivalency between its conditions and its conclusion.

Second, and more important, it would go too far because the conclusion of a rule that is used in an e contrario argument might follow on the basis of some other rule. For instance, the Dutch law has a rule that forbids widows to remarry within 306 days after the dead of their husbands. The ratio of this rule is to avoid confusion about who is the father of a child of which a woman might be pregnant. Clearly this prohibition is not applicable to widowers, but just as clearly it would be wrong to interpret the condition that a widow is involved as a necessary condition for the prohibition of a marriage. A woman may also be prohibited to marry because she is already married. The condi-

32 In Verheij and Hage 1994 a related way to construct analogous rule application is discussed. Cf. also section V.10.

In an actual case, such as the mentioned case of the donation of a rented house, all three constructions may be possible. As was pointed out to me by Prakken, a full argument for the solution of the case would then require both a justification for the analogy however constructed, and a justification of the particular form of analogy which was chosen.

tions of a rule can be a necessary condition for the *application* of the rule, but not for the *conclusion* of the rule.

E contrario' application' of a rule can be explained by looking at the goals and principles that underlie the rule. If in a particular case the conditions of a rule are not satisfied, this can have one of three causes. First, this may be because the rule has nothing to do with this kind of case. For instance, a tax rule has nothing to do with an insurance contract. In such a case the rule should completely be discarded.

A second possible cause is that the legislator overlooked this kind of case. In this situation, the case is to be solved on the basis of the underlying goals and principles, eventually leading to analogous application of the rule.

The third situation is that the kind of case we are dealing with has been considered by the legislator in drafting the rule, and that this consideration has led to a formulation of the rule conditions that made the rule inapplicable to this kind of case. Then we may assume that the legislator did not want the legal consequences of the rule to obtain in this kind of case, and this is a reason to conclude to the opposite of the rule's conclusion. Of course there may still be reasons, on the basis of other rules, which plead for the conclusion of the rule.[33]

An example of this third case would be that the legislator made a law that says that tramps are forbidden to sleep in the railway station. By explicitly referring to tramps, the legislator made it clear that he did not want a general prohibition against sleeping in the railway station. The traveller who dozed away while waiting on a late train is probably not covered by this rule. This means that such travellers are allowed to doze away in the railway station, unless their behaviour falls under another prohibition.

This does not mean that in the last case the rule conditions stated both necessary and sufficient conditions for the rule's conclusion. The legislator did not deal with this kind of case *by means of legislation*. But we still have the underlying principles and goals, and the knowledge that the legislator decided that these principles and goals were no reason to let this kind of case fall under the rule. In combination this may lead us to the conclusion that we should solve this kind of case by denying it the consequence of the rule. In other words, we 'apply' the rule e contrario. In fact, however, we do not apply the rule, but its underlying goals and principles.

---

33 This may even have been intended by the legislator who decided to make the rule inapplicable.

13. DEFEASIBILITY OF REASONING WITH RULES, GOALS AND PRINCIPLES

Rules and principles differ from statements in that they need to be applied. Application of premises does not play a role in traditional logical inferences such as Modus Ponens. If all murderers may be punished and John is a murderer, it logically follows that John may be punished. There is no need to 'apply' the premise that all murderers may be punished. The premise has a certain information content, and given this content it must be the case that John may be punished. In fact, it is not clear at all what application of a factual statement would amount to.[34]

Rules and principles, on the contrary, need to be applied. The principle that murderers may be punished, for example, must be applied if it is to generate a reason to punish John. Most often, the application of this principle will be 'automatic'; it is not given much thought and as a consequence we may overlook the necessity of application. Application will most notably be automatic in the case of institutional rules, because the possibilities to block the application of these rules are limited to those allowed by the institution (e.g. the law). However, it is always possible to adduce reasons why a principle or rule should not be applied in a particular case, and this possibility only makes sense if application of the rule or principle is an issue.

The fact that rules and principles need to be applied explains two characteristics of reasoning with rules that cannot be explained if rules are treated as statements. The first characteristic is that reasoning with rules (and principles) is defeasible; the second one is that rules can be applied analogously.

Analogous rule application was already dealt with in section 11. Reasoning with rules, goals and principles is also defeasible. In connection with rules and principles, defeasibility can be defined as the situation where the conditions of a valid rule or principle are satisfied, but the conclusion nevertheless does not follow.

The first reason for defeasibility is that rules and principles need to be applied in order to contribute to their conclusions. If there are reasons not to apply them (exclusionary reasons in the case of both rules and principles, and in the case of rules also non-decisive reasons), rules and principles do not generate reasons for their conclusions, and these conclusions will not follow.

The second reason is that principles only generate reasons for their conclusions. If there are reasons against the conclusion that balance or even outweigh the reasons generated by the principle, the conclusion does not follow.

---

34 One might argue that application of a statement is the use of this statement in an argument. However, this is only relevant for the *proof* of the conclusion, not for the issue whether the conclusion logically *follows* from the premises.

It turns out that there are two reasons for the defeasibility of reasoning with rules and principles. The first one is the possibility that the application of rules and principles is blocked in concrete cases. The second one is that the reasons generated by principles still have to be weighed against competing reasons.

14. WEIGHING REASONS

Every principle with a particular state of affairs in its conclusion is a potential generator of reasons for that state of affairs. Conversely, every principle with the negation of a particular state of affairs in its conclusion[35] is a potential generator of reasons against that state of affairs. If each of these principles is checked for its applicability to a case, a set of zero or more reasons for, and a set of zero or more reasons against the state of affairs obtain. The reasons from these two sets must be 'weighed', to determine whether the state of affairs, its opposite, or nothing at all follows as a conclusion.

Weighing reasons is a metaphor. The suggestion is that each set of reasons is placed on the scale of a balance and the most heavy set outweighs the other one. In fact there are no such balances which can help weighing reasons. There will be a mental process that leads to a certain outcome in the case that we have both reasons for and reasons against a particular conclusion. However, this process may be unconscious, and even if it is conscious, it need not provide us with *reasons* why one set of reasons outweighs the other set.

If we have no reasons why one set of reasons outweighs another set of reasons, we cannot make a rational decision.[36] Lack of rational means does not withhold us from determining which reasons outweigh the other ones, however. We can make decisions without having reasons (in contrast with causes) to decide either one way. This does not mean that the decisions are fully random. On the contrary, very often different persons will weigh the same reasons in the same way, without being able to give other reasons for it than the conclusion that this one set of reasons clearly outweighs the other set. From a rational point of view, however, such decisions are nothing more than cutting the knot.

Sometimes, however, we are able to argue which sets of reasons outweighs the other set. This is for instance the case if reasons which plead for incompatible behaviour are based on the same goal. In this connection one might think of maintaining different levels of minimum wages, both of which levels

---

[35] Incompatible conclusions will also do the job; contradiction is not necessary. Cf. section 6.3.

[36] Cf. in this connection Raz 1986, pp. 321f. on incommensurability of values and valuables.

may seem to contribute to a larger degree of employment. If both measures seem attractive because of their contribution to this goal, one can rationally adopt the course of action which has the largest contribution to the goal. Another situation where rational comparison is possible, is where incompatible courses of action have the same advantages, but where one course has less disadvantages. Along these lines, one may think of more situations in which rational choices are possible.

Sometimes it is possible to weigh reasons in a rational manner, even if a common standard is lacking. In a legal context, for instance, we can refer to precedent. If we already had an earlier case where the same reasons obtained, and where one set of reasons was assumed (for whatever reason or cause) to outweigh the other set, we can call to the principle that similar cases are to be treated similarly, and make the same weighing as the previous time.[37]

An interesting phenomenon in connection with weighing reasons is that it is possible that reasons which individually are weaker than some other reason, together are stronger. For instance, assume that the fact that somebody is a robber is a reason to punish this person. The same holds for the fact that somebody is a mistreator. That somebody is a minor is a reason against punishing, which outweighs both being a robber and being a mistreator, *as long as these latter reasons are taken separately*. So if somebody is both a minor and a robber, or a minor and a mistreator, he ought, on the balance of reasons, not to be punished. Given these assumptions, it is still possible that if somebody is both a robber, a mistreator and a minor, he ought on the balance of reasons to be punished. This phenomenon, that reasons can in a sense add up, is called the *accrual of reasons*.

In a model for reasoning with principles and rules we should ask for reasons why a set of reasons outweighs another set. If such 'meta'-reasons are lacking, there are no rational means to obtain a conclusion. If such meta-reasons are available, it should be possible to draw the conclusion which is supported by the strongest set of reasons. One meta-reason is very obvious in this connection: If we only have reasons that plead for a conclusion, and no reasons against it, the reasons for outweigh the reasons against. Analogously, if there are only reasons against, they 'outweigh' the (non-existent) reasons for the same conclusion.

---

[37] This approach to weighing reasons is extensively discussed in section V.9.2. Cf. also section VI.1.

15. DEONTIC COLLAPSE, DEONTIC INFLATION, AND THE SHIFTING BOUNDARIES OF RATIONALITY

At several occasions we found that we can replace a deontic sentence with the corresponding non-deontic sentence. We found, for instance, that rules and goals can not only be used in arguments if they are actually valid or recognised, but also when they ought to be valid or recognised (cf. the sections 5.3 and 5.9). An argument based on a goal should ideally lead to the conclusion that some state ought (not) to obtain, but may occasionally lead to the conclusion that this state actually (does not) obtain(s) (cf. section 6.4). And, finally, the reasons for and against the application of a rule or principle lead to the conclusion that the rule ought (not) to be applied, but the effect is that the rule actually applies and leads to its conclusion (cf. section 10).

I propose to call this phenomenon that a deontic sentence can be replaced by its non-deontic counterpart *deontic collapse*, because the deontic content of the sentence as it were collapses. The beginning of an explanation for this phenomenon can, I think, be found if we consider that in all cases of deontic collapse the non-deontic state that is realised because of the collapse is the result of a mental operation. Whether we let a goal, principle or rule generate reasons depends on our mental activities. The same holds when we can obtain a state by performing some mental action. For example, if we conclude that the rent contract must be continued between the new owner of a house and the lessees of the house and we have the legal power to continue the contract, the continuation of the contract is the result of a mental operation (which must of course be made public).

We find that in all the cases of deontic collapse that we encountered, we have reasons to perform some mental action that would lead to a particular result, and these reasons do not only make that we should perform this action, but also to the results of performing this action. The reasons why we should let a goal, principle, or rule generate reasons function as reasons why the goal, principle or rule actually generates reasons, and the reasons for assuming the presence of a state function as reasons why this state is already present.

If deontic collapse is described in this way, it turns out to be a special case of a phenomenon that we encountered in connection with the different functions of constitutive reasons. All constitutive reasons are reasons why something is the case, but also reasons to assume that this is the case. In this connection I distinguished between respectively the ontological and the behavioural level of constitutive reasons (cf. section II.18.6). It seems to that the phenomenon of deontic collapse is just another manifestation of the ontological and the behavioural level of constitutive reasons. The deontic sentence corresponds to the mental behaviour level of the constitutive reason. It says that a particular kind of mental behaviour ought to be performed. The non-deontic counterpart of this sentence corresponds to the ontological level of constitutive reasons. It says that the situation that results from the mental operation actually obtains.

An important function of deontic collapse in legal reasoning is when some rule or principle is used as if it were valid, on the basis that it ought to be valid. Normally, goals cannot underlie reasons for classification, such as the determination that a rule or principle is valid. But a goal can underlie reasons for the presence of deontic states of affairs, such as the state of affairs that some rule or principle ought to be valid. Because of the phenomenon of deontic collapse, this latter state of affairs can, under certain circumstances, underlie the generation of reasons by the rule or principle that ought to be valid.

Alexy (1978, p. 297) discusses this way of arguing for rules. It is interesting to notice that he almost stumbles over the phenomenon of deontic collapse without recognising it. He gives the general argument schema OZ, $\sim M \rightarrow \sim Z$, so OM, where OZ means that Z ought to be achieved, $\sim M \rightarrow \sim Z$ means that M is a necessary means to obtain Z, and where the conclusion OM means that M ought to be the case. Since M functions as the interpretation of a particular regulation, the conclusion of the argument is that some interpretation *ought to be* chosen (ought to be a valid rule). The conclusion which Alexy needs, however, is that this particular interpretation *is* the correct one (is a valid rule). In other words, he needs the transition from OM to M, which is precisely a case of deontic collapse.

Deontic collapse has a counterpart in the phenomenon of *deontic inflation*. Deontic inflation plays a role if we try to find a rock bottom for a process of justification or rationalisation. Notoriously these processes threaten to end in an infinite regress (cf. Albert 1980, p. 13).

Rational behaviour is behaviour that is in accordance with the balance of reasons. It is rational to perform some action if the reasons for that action outweigh the reasons against it. It is irrational to perform an action if the reasons against it outweigh the reasons for it. An action is, finally, a-rational if there are neither reasons for or against it, or if there are no reasons which justify the preference of one set of reasons above another one.

Reasons are not something given to us from a mind-independent reality. They are the result of human assignment of meanings to facts. As such they are dependent on human behaviour, be it individual, group, or institutional behaviour. This behaviour itself can in turn be evaluated as (ir)rational, and such an evaluation again presupposes reasons, which in their turn presuppose the assignment of meanings, ... etc. It is clear that any such chain of evaluations must stop somewhere and that the ultimate verdict of rationality must presuppose some human assignments of meaning which are themselves not evaluated in terms of rationality. In other words, all rationality presupposes an a-rational foundation. Still, no foundation is ultimate in the sense that it cannot be evaluated in terms of rationality. Rationality has shifting boundaries.[38]

Any form of rational behaviour is in accordance with the reasons for and against this behaviour. These reasons are the result of the facts that were actually assumed, of the actual acceptance of rules and principles, and the actual recognition of goals, and on the actual application of these rules, goals and principles. This actual behaviour forms the a-rational boundary for what becomes rational behaviour. However, if the rationality of this boundary is drawn into the discussion, the facts that were actually assumed should be replaced by the facts that rationally ought to be assumed, the rules which were assumed as valid are to be replaced by the rules which rationally should have been assumed as valid, and the rules that were actually applied should be replaced by the rules which rationally should have been applied, etc.

This means that as soon as we start to argue about facts, rules, etc. that underlie reasons, we rationally ought to replace actual acceptance by rational acceptance. That is, we can replace facts that are assumed to obtain by facts we ought to assume, etc. This is the counterpart of deontic collapse, and I propose to call this phenomenon *deontic inflation*.

With these abstract remarks on the bounds of rationality, I want to finish the discussion of reasoning with rules in legal context. Let me summarise the results of the discussion in a fashion that already looks forward to the remainder of this book, that is as the basis for a logic that can deal with rules, principles, and goals and with the reasons that are generated by them.

16. CONCLUSION AND RECOMMENDATIONS

Reasoning with rules, principles and goals turns out to be a lot more complex than simple rule application according to the model of Modus Ponens. On the one hand, rules can be applied (analogously) even though their conditions are not satisfied. On the other hand, even if a rule's or principle's conditions are satisfied, it is not guaranteed that it will be applied: a case that satisfies the conditions may fall outside the rule's or principle's scope or the rule's purpose. And finally, even if a principle or goal is applied to a case, there is no guarantee that its conclusion follows. Weighing reasons may lead to the result that the conclusion is still not drawn.

On the basis of these characteristics of reasoning with rules, we can draw up a list of properties we want in a logic that deals with rules. These proper-

[38] Cf. section 5.3 for an analogous argument against a normative notion of validity.

ties both concern the expressive power of the logical language, and the nature of the rules of inference.

- Although weighing reasons will only play a role in those arguments in which there are both reasons for and against a particular conclusion, a logic for rules, or - even more - goals and principles, should offer facilities to deal with the weighing of reasons. It should contain a rule of inference to the effect that a conclusion follows if the reasons that plead for a conclusion outweigh the reasons against it.
- In this connection, the logic should also offer the possibility to conclude that a particular fact forms a reason for or against a conclusion. As a consequence, it must be possible to refer to facts and reasons. Since it is also necessary to reason about the facts that make up reasons, and to build on these results while arguing with the reasons, the logical connection should be maintained between the sentences that express certain facts and the sentences that refer to these same facts as reasons. For instance, we want to be able to argue that John is a thief, to refer to the fact that John is a thief, and to maintain the logical relationship between the sentence 'John is a thief' and the fact that John is a thief.
- It should also be possible to reason about the relative weight of sets of reasons, and consequently also to refer to such sets.
- A rule or principle can only be applied if it is valid. An important part of legal reasoning deals with the question as to the precise conditions of legal rules, a discussion which can be seen as dealing with the validity or acceptance of rules and principles. A logic for rules should make it possible to deal with arguments about the validity of rules. As a consequence, it should allow reference to rules. Reference to rules is also necessary for arguments about the exclusion, the applicability, and the application of a rule. At the same time it should be possible to use the internal structure of rules and principles to model their application in generating reasons. All of this also holds for goals.
- The rules of inference that deal with rule application should make the application of a rule dependent on the reasons that plead for and against application. The applicability of a rule should be an important reason for application of this rule, but there must be a possibility to have other reasons for (analogous) application of a rule.

In the following chapter, I will describe a logic that meets all of these demands.

IV. REASON-BASED LOGIC

We have seen that a logic based on the semantic notion of validity experiences difficulties in dealing with rules and the reasons that are based on them. In this chapter, I will introduce a logic that was especially developed to deal with the characteristics of rules, principles, goals, and reasons that we encountered in the previous two chapters. Because reasons play a central role in this logic, the logic is called Reason-Based Logic (RBL).[1]

In this chapter, the essentials of RBL are exposed. In an informal introduction, which covers the sections 1 to 5, I describe some characteristics of the logic that result from the demands posed by the nature of reasoning with rules, principles and goals. Moreover, I introduce the elements of the language of RBL. Then follows a formal presentation of the logic, that describes the language (section 6), the 'rules of inference' (section 7), and the derivability relation of RBL (section 8). RBL is an extension of First Order Predicate Logic (FOPL). Therefore the chapter closes with some remarks about the relation between RBL and FOPL. Moreover, this chapter presupposes a reasonable command of FOPL.[2]

The present description of RBL aims to be understandable for lawyers with an interest in logical issues. This aim is reflected in some redundancy in the presentation. Logicians can confine themselves to the sections 1, 2, 6 and 8.

---

1 RBL is the result of gradual development. This development has been laid down in a number of papers that describe different versions of this logic. Cf. Hage 1991, 1993, 1994 and 1995; Hage and Verheij 1994 and 1995. The version described in this book differs from the more recent papers (e.g. Hage 1995 and Hage Model) in four relatively important aspects. First the formalism is simplified. Second, deontic predicates are integrated into the logic to give a better account of rule application and to simplify the discussion of reasoning with goals. Third, goals are not dealt with separately, but are treated as a kind of principles. And, what is perhaps most important, rules and principles are treated differently, because of the considerations mentioned in section III.10.

2 A good introduction to FOPL, which is relatively easy going, can be found in the several editions of Copi's *Introduction to Logic*, e.g. Copi 1978. Summary expositions of FOPL can be found in e.g. Van Dalen 1983, Mendelson 1987 and Lukaszewicz 1990.

1. STATES OF AFFAIRS AND CASES

RBL uses a rich ontology, that includes states of affairs, facts, reasons, rules, and cases.[3] A *state of affairs* is what is expressed by a sentence. For instance, the sentence

```
Thief(john)
```

expresses the state of affairs that John is a thief. The set of well-formed descriptive sentences of a language determines which states of affairs there are.[4]

A *fact* is a state of affairs that is expressed by a *true* sentence. False sentences express states of affairs that do not actually *obtain*; facts are states of affairs that actually *obtain*. Cf. figure 1.

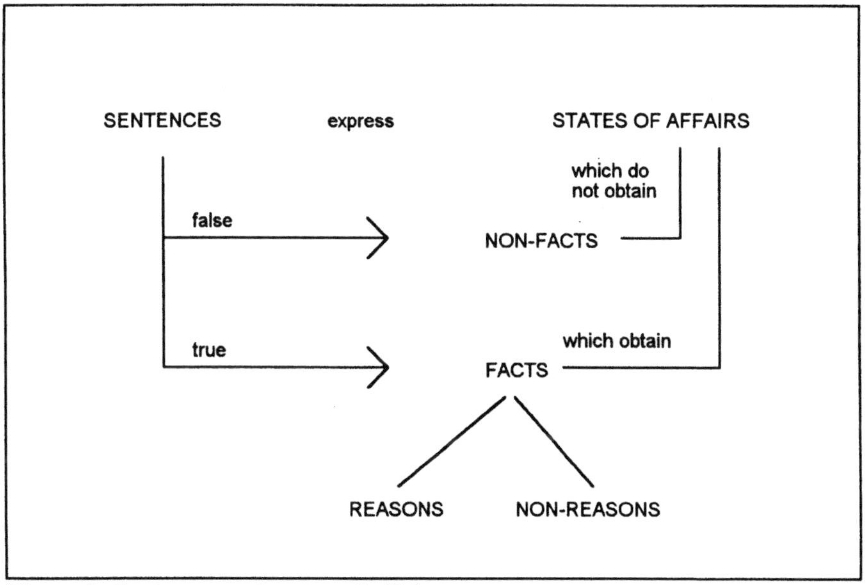

Figure 1: Sentences and states of affairs

A *reason* is a fact that has a particular significance for a(nother) state of affairs, in that it either pleads for or against it. The fact for which a reason pleads is called the reason's conclusion.

From a logical point of view, all states of affairs, including facts and reasons, are individuals, which means that they can be the subject of sentences. Note that this does not involve a mix-up of object- and meta-

3 Those who object against the richness of the ontology are referred to what was written on Occam's razor in section II.6.

4 Cf. also section VI.9.

language, because states of affairs are not linguistic entities, although their presence presupposes language.[5]

RBL provides means to reason with sentences and also to reason about the states of affairs (facts, reasons) that are expressed by those sentences. Moreover, the logical connections between a sentence and the state of affairs expressed by it are maintained. To achieve this, RBL makes use of a special convention to achieve the logical connection between a sentence and the state of affairs that is expressed by it. All RBL-sentences begin with a capital and all expressions that denote individuals begin with a lowercase character. Moreover, if a term is identical to a sentence, with the only difference that the term begins with a lowercase character, this term *denotes* the state of affairs that is *expressed* by that sentence.[6] Cf. figure 2.

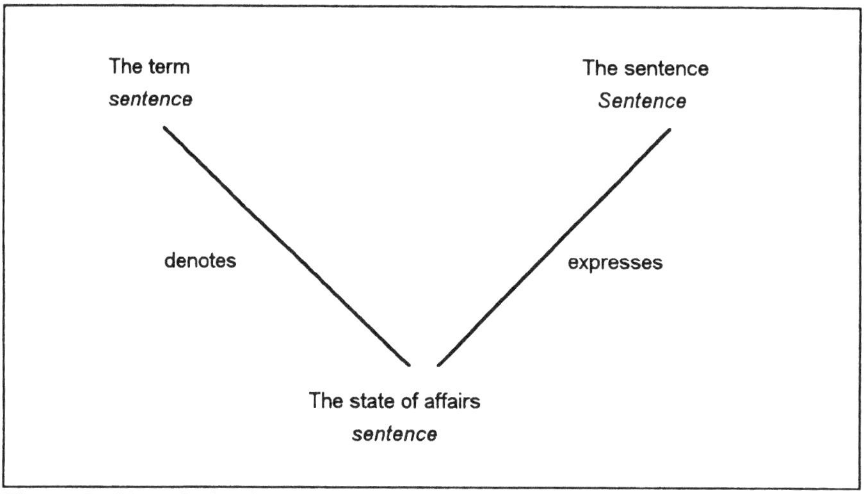

Figure 2: The relation between sentences and terms that deal with the same state of affairs

For instance, the term

```
thief(john)
```

denotes the state of affairs that John is a thief, which is expressed by the sentence

```
Thief(john)
```

---

5 Cf. in this connection Strawson 1971, pp. 193f. on the language-dependence of facts.

6 This convention has the disadvantage that it may be unclear whether a term denotes a state of affairs or not. This disadvantage can, if necessary, be overcome by additional syntactic conventions.

Since facts and reasons are also states of affairs, the convention to denote states of affairs also applies to facts and reasons. This makes it possible to state about a particular fact that it is a reason for the presence of some other state of affairs. I will use the two-place predicate R to express that some fact (the first parameter) is a reason for some state of affairs (the second parameter). Given this convention, the following RBL-sentence expresses that the fact that John is a thief is a reason why John is punishable:

```
R(thief(john), punishable(john))
```

The convention concerning the relationship between sentences and their corresponding terms also applies to logically compound sentences. This means that the term

```
contract(john, geraldine) & defaults(john) &
 damage($3000))
```

denotes the compound state of affairs that there is a contract between John and Geraldine, that John defaulted in this contract, and that the resulting damage is 3000 dollar.

Terms that denote states of affairs may contain free variables. In that case they denote generic states of affairs.[7] An example of a generic state of affairs is the state of affairs that somebody owns a car. This state of affairs is denoted by the term

owns(*x*, car)[8]

Such terms denoting generic states of affairs occur in the formulations of rules, principles, and goals.

If we want to argue that a rule is applicable in a particular case, or that it applies or is excluded in a case, we must often refer to facts that obtain in that case or not. For instance, the fact that John is a thief in a particular case is the reason why the rule that thieves are punishable is applicable *to that case*. That is the reason why RBL needs a way to say that a particular state of affairs obtains in some case.

The RBL-sentences that say that a state of affairs obtains in a particular case have the following form:

Obtains(*state*, *case*)

---

7 My use of the notion of a generic state of affairs has nothing to do with Von Wright's notion of a generic proposition (cf. Von Wright 1963, p. 22/3). A generic proposition in the sense of Von Wright is a proposition the truth of which may vary with time, such as 'It's raining'.

8 Remember the convention that italics in the object language are variables, and that italics in the metalanguage are used for sentence schemes.

In this sentence, `state` stands for the state of affairs that obtains in the case denoted by `case`. Suppose that we have a particular case, `john's_theft`, in which John is a thief. The fact that John is a thief in this case is expressed by the sentence:

```
Obtains(thief(john), john's_theft)
```

Normally when a case is described, it will be clear to which case the facts belong. Then the description of facts as belonging to a particular case is rather cumbersome. That is why the case-related notation is only used when necessary. Normally facts are described by means of the sentences that express these facts without mentioning the case. For instance,

```
Obtains(thief(john), john's_theft)
```

will normally be replaced by

```
Thief(john)
```

2. RULES AND PRINCIPLES AS STRUCTURED LOGICAL INDIVIDUALS

There are many kinds of arguments in which rules are involved, and rules play several roles in them. Most often a rule is just applied, and leads to its conclusion. However, there are also arguments about the validity of rules, and about the application of rules to particular cases. In these arguments, a rule is the topic of the argument. To formalise arguments in which rules are the topic, there should be a possibility to refer to rules.

RULES

RBL treats rules as logical individuals because it is necessary to refer to rules. This has the consequence that it is not possible to use a rule as a complete sentence in RBL. Rules can only be introduced into an RBL-theory by making statements about them, e.g. the statement that a rule is valid.

Traditionally, individuals are represented in formal logics by means of an unstructured character or string. For instance, in the FOPL-sentence

```
Is_bald(the_king_of_france)
```

the string 'the_king_of_france' has no structure or meaning whatsoever that can be recognised by the rules of inference of predicate logic. The meaning of this string is there only to help human readers remind which individual is denoted.

The representation of rules as logical individuals in RBL is different, however. The rules of inference of RBL must be able to distinguish between the conditions and the conclusion of an RBL-rule, and therefore the representation of these logical individuals exhibits a structure.

A rule contains two elements, that are kept together by the function symbol $\Rightarrow$. These elements are - on the left hand-side - the condition-part of the rule, and - on the right hand-side - the conclusion of the rule. They are both terms denoting states of affairs. Notice that $\Rightarrow$ is a function symbol that operates on terms, and not a logical operator which operates on sentences. Since rules are from a logical point of view individuals, it is possible to quantify over rules, or to have rules about rules.

Both the condition-part and the conclusion-part of a rule consist of one RBL-term which denotes a state of affairs. If the natural language version of the rule has more than one condition, the term that denotes the conditions will be logically compound. Cumulating conditions are expressed by a conjunction, while alternatives are expressed by a disjunction. Rule conclusions are atomic states of affairs or their negations.

An example of a rule (which happens to be about rules) would be:

```
made_by_legislator(rule) & ~abolished(rule) ⇒
 valid(rule)
```

This rule says that a rule is valid if it has been made by the legislator and has not been abolished. The use of variables for rules indicates that this rule can be applied to any rule.

Remember that a rule constant is not a well-formed RBL sentence, just as `the_king_of_france` would not be a well-formed sentence in predicate logic. Well-formed sentences are for instance statements about rules. In theory, any kind of statement can be made about a rule. A well-formed sentence would for instance be:

```
Made_by_legislator(thief(x) ⇒ punishable(x))
```

(The rule that thieves are punishable was made by legislator.)

If a rule is often referred to in an argument, it is useful to have a short name for the rule. I will introduce the name, followed by a colon and the formulation of the rule. E.g.

```
punishable: thief(x) ⇒ punishable(x)
```

It is then possible to refer to the rule by means of its name:

```
Made_by_legislator(punishable)
```

PRINCIPLES

Since principles exhibit a somewhat different logical behaviour than rules, they are in RBL also represented somewhat differently. The difference is that the functor $\Rightarrow$ which is used for rules, is replaced by the functor $\supset$ in the case of principles. So the term

```
vehicle(x) & four_wheel(x) ⊃ car(x)
```

denotes the classificatory principle that vehicles with four wheels normally are cars. Principles can be given names too, in the same way as rules:

```
definition_cars: vehicle(x) & four_wheel(x) ⊃ car(x)
```

GOALS

In theory, goals are to be distinguished from proper principles (cf. section III.5.8). To represent goals, RBL has the predicate `Goal`, which has a state of affairs as its parameter. This state of affairs is to be pursued as the goal.

To simplify the present version of RBL, goals are for logical purposes treated as a special kind of principles.[9] In this connection there are deontic principles of two different kinds. A goal may be represented as the principle that if an action contributes to the goal, this action ought to be performed. A goal may also be represented as the principle that if a state of affairs contributes to the goal, this state of affairs ought to be the case. Technically this will be done by special inference rules (section 7), a special part in the definition of extensions (section 8), and by means of the definition of RBL-possible worlds (section VI.14).

These two representation forms of goals correspond to the distinction between ought-to-do and ought-to-be deontic modalities (cf. Castañeda 1970). Amongst others to represent goals, I introduce a number of deontic predicates in the language of RBL, two of which are `Ob` and `Od`.

Ob operates on states of affairs and the resulting sentence expresses that a particular state of affairs ought to obtain. For instance, the sentence

```
Ob(locked(door))
```

expresses that the door ought to be locked. `Ob` can be interpreted as a predicate for ought-to-be.

`Od` can be interpreted as a predicate for ought-to-do. It is a predicate with two parameters. The first denotes an actor, and the second an action type. For instance, the sentence

---

9 Hage 1995 and Model illustrate how goals can be given a separate treatment.

```
Od(mary, pay_taxes)
```

expresses that Mary ought to pay taxes.

Obligations that hold for unspecified actors, such as 'It is forbidden to kill', have an unbound variable on the place of the actor-parameter:

```
Od(x, ¬kill(y))
```

Given these deontic predicates, it is possible to represent goals as principles. For instance the principle

```
contributes_to(action, goalstate) ⊃ od(x, action)
```

expresses the effects of a goal for what ought to be done. Literally the term denotes the principle that if some type of action contributes to `state`, everybody ought (in principle) to perform an action of this type. This principle is valid for every state such that `Goal(goalstate)`.

Notice that in the conclusion part of this principle the deontic 'predicate' starts with a small letter, because the sentence `Od(x, action)` has been transformed in a term.

Analogously the principle

```
contributes_to(state, goalstate) ⊃ ob(state)
```

expresses the effects of a goal for what ought to be the case. Also this deontic principle is valid for every state such that `Goal(goalstate)`.

3. DERIVING REASONS FROM PRINCIPLES

The derivation of a conclusion on the basis of one or more principles (including goals) takes two steps. In the first step, the sets of all reasons for, respectively against the hypothetical conclusion are collected. In the second step, the reasons in these sets are weighed against each other (cf. the model exposed in section III.4).

A reason for a conclusion is based on a valid principle with this particular conclusion. If the conditions of this principle are satisfied, and if it cannot be derived that the principle is excluded in the relevant case, the instantiated conditions of the principle are a reason for its instantiated conclusion. Let us have a closer look at these conditions.

VALIDITY

If a principle is to be used in making a derivation, it should be valid. The statement that a principle is valid has the following form:

```
Valid(conditions ⊃ conclusion)
```

Instead of a valid principle, a principle that ought to be valid will also do the job. The statement that a principle ought to be valid has the following form:

```
Ob(valid(conditions ⊃ conclusion))
```

Suppose that *facts* is an instantiation of the conditions of the principle, and that *iconcl* is the corresponding instantiation of the conclusion. In that case it is derivable that *facts* is a reason for *iconcl*, assuming that is not derivable that the principle is excluded. That *facts* is a reason for *iconcl* is represented by means of the predicate R.

```
R(facts, iconcl)
```

EXCLUSION

If a principle is excluded in a particular case, this is represented by means of the predicate Excluded. This predicate has two parameters. The first one denotes the principle that is excluded, and the second one denotes the case in which it is excluded. For instance:

```
Excluded(principle, case)
```

Let us look at an example. If it is not derivable that

```
Excluded(thief(x) ⊃ punishable(x), john's_theft)
```

it is possible to derive from

```
Valid(thief(x) ⊃ punishable(x))
Obtains(thief(john), john's_theft)
```

that

```
R( thief(john), punishable(john))
```

This argument boils down to that if it is not *derivable* that the rule that thieves are punishable is excluded in the case of John's theft, it can be derived, from the fact that John is a thief, and the validity of the principle that thieves are punishable, that the fact that John is a thief is a reason why John is punishable.

The first condition for the derivation is weaker than the last two in that it is satisfied in case nothing is known about the exclusion of the rule. This reference to what is not derivable, rather than to what is given or derivable, makes the logic nonmonotonic[10]: If the set of premises is extended, so that it

---

[10] A logic is monotonic if the sentences that can be derived from a superset of a theory are a superset of the sentences that can be derived from the theory. So if S can be derived from T, then S can be derived from T, P. A logic that is not monotonic is nonmonotonic.

becomes derivable that the principle is excluded, reason why John is punishable is invalidated.

Often there can be no confusion about the case in which a principle is excluded. Then it is possible to omit the reference to the case, and `Excluded` functions as a one-place predicate. E.g.

```
Excluded(definition_car)
```

REASONS AGAINST A CONCLUSION

Not only can there be reasons for a conclusion, there can also be reasons against it. To keep the formalism of RBL relatively simple, reasons against a conclusion are represented as reasons for the negation of the conclusion. So if the fact that John is a minor is a reason why John is not punishable, this is formalised as:

```
R(minor(john), ~punishable(john))
```

4. WEIGHING REASONS

If there are both reasons for and against a conclusion, these reasons need to be 'weighed' to determine whether the conclusion, its negation, or nothing at all follows. This weighing of reasons is done on the basis of explicit 'weighing knowledge', which refers to the sets of reasons which plead for and against the conclusion.

To facilitate the discussion about the reasons for and against a conclusion, we need terms that refer to these sets of reasons. In this connection the following convention is used:

reasons(*state*)

denotes the set of *derivable* reasons that plead for *state*. Analogously

reasons(~*state*)

denotes the set of *derivable* reasons that plead against *state*.

In case of the theory

```
Valid(thief(x) ⊃ punishable(x))
Valid(juvenile(x) ⊃ ~punishable(x))
Thief(john) & Juvenile(john)
```

it holds that

```
reasons(punishable(john)) = {thief(john)}
```

and

```
reasons(~punishable(john)) = {juvenile(john)}
```

To decide on the basis of reasons which conclusion is to be drawn, explicit *weighing-knowledge* is needed. This weighing-knowledge indicates which set of reasons outweighs which other set.

It is not impossible that the same two sets of reasons are relevant for different conclusions, but that their relative weight differs for these different conclusions. Therefore weighing-knowledge is relativised to a conclusion. In the present example, the relevant weighing-knowledge is laid down in the following RBL sentence:

$$\texttt{\{juvenile(john)\} > \{thief(john)\}}_{\texttt{punishable(john)}}$$

which means that, regarding the conclusion that John is punishable, (the set of reasons containing) the fact that John is a juvenile outweighs (the set of reasons containing) the fact that John is a thief.

This sentence illustrates the general form of weighing-knowledge. Weighing-knowledge is described in a sentence formed by the infix-predicate >. This predicate has three parameters which denote the sets of reasons, and the conclusion for and against which these reasons plead. The weighing-knowledge expresses that the first set of reasons outweighs the second set.

In actual arguments it almost never occurs that the same sets of reasons play a role with regard to different conclusions. This makes it possible to simplify the formalism of RBL by omitting the reference to the conclusion for and against which the reasons plead, with the following result:

```
{juvenile(john)} > {thief(john)}
```

Notice that the parameters do not have a fixed order in the sense that either the reasons for, or the reasons against are mentioned first. On the contrary, the order of the sets of reasons indicates whether the reasons for outweigh the reasons against, or the other way round. If the first parameter refers to the reasons that plead for the conclusion, the reasons for outweigh the reasons against, and the conclusion follows. If, on the contrary, the first parameter refers to the reasons that plead against the conclusion, the reasons against outweigh the reasons for. In that case, the negation of the conclusion follows. So, if we have that

```
{thief(john)} > {juvenile(john)}
```

it may be derived that

```
Punishable(john)
```

However, if we have

```
{juvenile(john)} > {thief(john)}
```

then it may be derived that

`~Punishable(john)`

Notice that `reasons(`*`state`*`)` and `reasons(~`*`state`*`)` denote all the reasons for, respectively against *`state`* that are *derivable* from the theory. Here again we have a factor that makes RBL nonmonotonic. If a theory is extended, this can make it possible to derive more reasons both for and against a conclusion.[11] As a consequence, conclusions that are derivable from a theory T need not be derivable anymore from the theory T', that results from extending T with some additional sentences. The new sentences might make it possible to derive new reasons against these conclusions, reasons that can tip the balance.

To derive a conclusion on the basis of reasons, it is always necessary to have weighing-knowledge that indicates which set of reasons outweighs the other set. Normally, this weighing-knowledge is not provided by RBL, but should be incorporated in the theory from which the derivations are made.

For instance, it is not the task of RBL to indicate whether the fact that John is a thief outweighs the fact that John is a juvenile as a reason concerning the punishability of John. This information should be specified by the domain theory from which the derivations are to be made.

There is, however, one important exception. RBL provides the weighing-knowledge for weighing a non-empty set of reasons against an empty set. If there are only reasons for a conclusion, or only reasons against, it is possible to derive the conclusion, respectively its negation, even if the theory does not say anything about the relative weight of the reasons. In RBL any non-empty set of reasons outweighs an empty set.

So, if there is only a reason for a conclusion, and no reason against it, this conclusion can be derived. The other way round the same holds: if there is only a reason against a conclusion, and no reason for it, the negation of this conclusion can be derived. In practice this situation, where there is one reason that pleads for a conclusion, and no reason that pleads against it, is very important. In fact, it is the situation that is classically dealt with by arguments of the form Modus Ponens (cf. the example in section V.1).

5. THE APPLICATION OF RULES

A rule can be used in making a derivation if it is valid, or if it ought to be valid. The statements that a rule is, respectively ought to be, valid have the same form as the corresponding statements concerning a principle:

---

11 If extension of the theory leads to more exclusions, this leads to less reasons.

```
Valid(rule_conditions ⇒ rule_conclusion)
Ob(valid(rule_conditions ⇒ rule_conclusion))
```

If the conditions of a rule are satisfied in a particular case, and if the rule is not excluded in that case, the rule is said to be *applicable* to that case. To state that, RBL has a special predicate `Applicable`, that has two parameters. The first parameter is meant for the rule that is applicable, with its condition- and its conclusion-part instantiated by the facts of the case to which the rule is applicable. The second parameter indicates the case to which the rule is applicable.

For instance, if we have:

```
default:
  contract(x, y) & defaults(x) & damage(z) ⇒
    owes(x, y, z))
Valid(default)
Obtains(
  contract(john, geraldine) & defaults(john) &
     damage($3000),
    contract)
```

(The rule is valid that if *x* has a contract with *y*, *x* defaults, and the resulting damage amounts to *z*, then *x* owes *y* the amount of *z*, and: In the case contract, the facts obtain that there is a contract between John and Geraldine, that John defaulted, and that the damage amounted to $3000.)

then, if it is not derivable that

```
Excluded(default, contract),
```

it is derivable that

```
Applicable(
  contract(john, geraldine) & defaults(john) &
        damage($3000) ⇒
     owes(john, geraldine, $3000),
    contract)
```

Very often, reference to the case in which the rule is applicable is not essential for understanding the argument. Then it is possible to omit reference to a case in the statement that a rule is applicable:

```
Applicable(
  contract(john, geraldine) & defaults(john) &
     damage($3000) ⇒
    owes(john, geraldine, $3000))
```

If an applicable rule contains alternative conditions, the condition part of the instantiated rule only contains those conditions that were actually satisfied in the case at hand, or - if more than one alternative is satisfied - only one of the alternatives.

Suppose that we have

```
Valid(minor(person) v mentally_ill(person) ⇒
 ~accountable(person))
Mentally_ill(john)
```

it will normally be possible to derive that

```
Applicable(mentally_ill(john) ⇒ ~accountable(john))
```

Because only one of the alternatives of the rule conditions was satisfied, the sentence that expresses the applicability of the rule only mentions this one alternative in the first parameter.

Let us consider another example, which deals with the exclusion of rules.

```
Valid(
 criminal_law(rule) & actor(c, actor) &
    ~accountable(actor, c) ⇒
  excluded(rule, c)
```

This valid rule boils down to that a criminal law is excluded in a case `c`, if the actor in that case was not accountable. Suppose that we have a case, called `bonny's_case`, which is characterised by the following facts:

```
punishable: thief(x) ⇒ punishable(x)
Valid(punishable)
Criminal_law(punishable)& Actor(bonny's_case, bonny)
Thief(bonny) & ~Accountable(bonny, bonny's_case)
```

In this case, it will normally, that is, if the rule about accountability is not excluded, be true that

```
Applicable(
 criminal_law(punishable) & actor(bonny's_case, bonny) &
   ~accountable(bonny, bonny's_case) ⇒
  excluded(punishable))
```

In other words, the rule

```
criminal_law(rule) & actor(c, actor) &
  ~accountable(actor, c)) ⇒
 excluded(rule, c)
```

is applicable to a case where the rule that thieves are punishable was a criminal law, where the actor was Bonny, and where Bonny was not accountable. The instantiated conclusion becomes that in this case, the application of the rule `punishable` (to the case of Bonny) is excluded.

Given the applicability of the rule about accountability, the application of the rule that thieves are punishable will normally be excluded. So this latter rule will not be applicable and the fact that Bonny is a thief does not lead to the conclusion that Bonny is punishable.

If a rule is applicable, this is a reason to apply this rule (why the rule ought to be applied). From

```
Applicable(thief(john) ⇒ punishable(john))
```

it may be derived that

```
R(applicable(thief(john) ⇒ punishable(john)),
 ob(applies(thief(john) ⇒ punishable(john))))
```

(The fact that the rule `thief(x) ⇒ punishable(x)` is applicable, with its condition-part instantiated to `thief(john)` and its conclusion-part instantiated to `punishable(john)`, is a reason why this same rule, with the same instantiations, ought to be applied.)

Whether the rule in the end ought to be applied depends on whether there are also reasons against its application. Normally this will not be the case, and then it is possible to derive that

```
Ob(applies(thief(john) ⇒ punishable(john)))
```

In that case it immediately follows that

```
Punishable(john)
```

without the necessity of weighing reasons.

The predicate `Applies` goes in principle with two parameters. The first one denotes the instantiated rule that applies, the second one the case to which the rule applies. Where the case is clear from the context, the second parameter can (and will) be omitted, as in:

```
Ob(applies(thief(john) ⇒ punishable(john)))
```

This discussion of the `Applies`-predicate closes the informal part of the treatment of RBL. In the following sections, the language, the 'rules of inference', and the derivability-relation of RBL will be discussed.

6. THE LANGUAGE OF REASON-BASED LOGIC

RBL is based on FOPL in the sense that the language of RBL is the language of FOPL, and that the theorems of FOPL are all true in RBL.

Before discussing the extensions to the language of FOPL, I want to introduce some conventions.

Predicate constants, or *predicates* are strings of one or more characters, numerals, apostrophes and/or underscores that start with an uppercase character. Each predicate has an arity of zero or more. The arity stands for the number of parameters of the predicate.

A predicate with all of its parameters instantiated is called an *atom* of the language. A *literal* is either an atom or a negated atom.

Function constants, or *functions* are non-italicised strings of one or more characters, numerals, apostrophes and/or underscores that start with a lowercase character. Each function has an arity of zero or more. The arity stands for the number of parameters of the function. Functions with a zero-arity are *individual constants*.

Individual variables are italicised strings of one or more characters, numerals, and/or underscores that start with a lowercase character, or functions with one or more of their variables uninstantiated.

Action types and *act tokens* are denoted by functions, such as `steal`, `chopping_the_tree`, or `imprison(john)`.

Individual constants and individual variables of the language are called *terms* of the language. To obtain the term that denotes the state of affairs that is expressed by a sentence, the first (uppercase) letter of each predicate symbol in the sentence is replaced by the same letter in lowercase.[12]

All well-formed formulas of FOPL are well-formed *formulas* of RBL. A *sentence* of RBL is an RBL-formula without free variables.

The language of RBL contains a number of special function and predicate symbols which are discussed below. The number following the slash / in predicate and function symbols indicates the arity.

- `¬/1`

  ¬ is a function that operates on action types and act tokens. If `action` denotes an action type, `¬action` denotes the refraining from `action`. The same holds for acts.

---

[12] The connectives of FOPL, e.g. → and &, are treated as if they are also function symbols. By overloading the notation, the translation of sentences to terms is as simple as described in the text.

- `⇒/2`

  In RBL rules are denoted by *terms* of the language. A term denoting a rule has the form:[13]

  condition ⇒ *conclusion*

  where *condition* is a formula of RBL and *conclusion* is a literal of RBL.

  It is possible to give rules a name. This is done by giving the name, followed by a colon and the rule formulation. E.g.

  name: *condition* ⇒ *conclusion*

- `⊃/2`

  Just like rules, principles are denoted by terms. A term denoting a principle has the form:

  condition ⊃ *conclusion*

  where *condition* is a formula of RBL and *conclusion* is a literal of RBL.

  It is possible to give principles a name. This is done by giving the name, followed by a colon and the principle formulation. E.g.

  name: *condition* ⊃ *conclusion*

- `{ ., ., ..., . }/n (for n = 0, 1, 2, ...)`

  These symbols are used to refer to sets of states of affairs, most often states of affairs which are reasons.

- `reasons(`*literal*`) = {`*r* `|` it is derivable that `R(`*r*`, `*literal*`)}`

  The function expression `reasons(`*literal*`)` has as its value the sets of all *derivable* reasons that plead for *literal*, where *literal* is a literal.

---

[13] Metavariables for sentences are denoted by strings of italic characters beginning with an upper case character, e.g., *Atom*. Metavariables for terms are denoted by strings of italic lower case characters, e.g., *atom*. I use the convention that matching metavariables, such as *Atom* and *atom*, represent a sentence and its corresponding term.

- `Od/2`

  `Od` is a deontic predicate for ought-to-do. `Od(`*`actor, action`*`)` means that *`actor`* ought perform *`action`*. `Od(`*`actor,`*` ¬`*`action`*`)` means that *`actor`* ought to refrain from *`action`* .

- `Ob/1`

  `Ob/1` is a deontic predicate for ought-to-be. `Ob(`*`state`*`)` means that the state of affairs *`state`* ought to be the case. `Ob(~`*`state`*`)` means that the state of affairs *`state`* ought not to be the case.

- `Valid/1`

  The sentence `Valid(`*`conditions`*` ⇒ `*`conclusion`*`)` means that the rule *`conditions`*` ⇒ `*`conclusion`* is valid. The predicate `Valid` can also be applied to principles.

- `Goal/1`

  Goals are states of affairs. That a particular state of affairs is a goal is indicated by means of the `Goal`-predicate.

  E.g. `Goal(freedom_of_press)`, means that `freedom_of_press` is a state that is to be pursued as a goal. The `Goal`-predicate has a function which is somewhat similar to that of the `Valid`-predicate.

  Reasoning with goals is dealt with by means of a number of principles which are assumed to be valid if some state of affairs is a goal. The condition part of these principles denotes the state of affairs that some state or action contributes to or detracts from the goal-state. The conclusion part denotes that this first state ought (not) to be the case, respectively this action ought (not) to be performed by anybody. So if we have `Goal(`*`state_2`*`)`, the following principles will be valid:

```
contributes_to(state_1, state_2) ⊃ Ob(state_1)
contributes_to(state_1, ~state_2) ⊃ Ob(~state_1)
contributes_to(action, state_2) ⊃ Od(x, action)
contributes_to(action, ~state_2) ⊃ Od(x, ¬action)
```

- `Excluded/n (n = 1,2)`

  The sentence `Excluded(`*`rule, case`*`)` means that application of the rule *`rule`* is excluded in the case *`case`*.

  Reference to the case will usually be omitted if there is no risk of confusion, e.g. `Excluded(`*`rule`*`)`. The predicate `Excluded` can similarly be applied to principles.

- `Applicable/n (n = 1,2)`

  The sentence

  `Applicable(`*`facts`* ⇒ *`concl`*`,` *`case`*`)`

  means that the instantiated rule *`facts`* ⇒ *`concl`* is applicable to the case `case`. E.g.

  ```
  Applicable(thief(john) ⇒ ob(punished(john)),
    john's_theft)
  ```

  By means of abbreviation, reference to the case will usually be omitted. E.g. `Applicable(thief(john) ⇒ ob(punished(john)))`

- `Applies/n (n = 1,2)`

  The sentence

  `Applies(`*`facts`* ⇒ *`concl`*`,` *`case`*`)`

  means that the instantiated rule *`facts`* ⇒ *`concl`* applies to the case *`case`*. E.g.

  ```
  Applies(thief(john) ⇒ ob(punished(john)),
   john's_theft)
  ```

  By means of abbreviation, reference to the case will usually be omitted. E.g.

  `Applies(thief(john) ⇒ ob(punished(john)))`

- `R/3`

  The sentence `R(`*`facts`*`,` *`atom`*`)` means that the facts denoted by the term *`facts`* are a reason for the conclusion denoted by the term *`atom`*.

  The sentence `R(`*`facts`*`,` *`~atom`*`)` means that the facts denoted by the term *`facts`* are a reason against the conclusion denoted by the term *`atom`*.

- `>/n (n = 2,3)`

  The sentence $(\mathit{reasons1} > \mathit{reasons2})_{\mathit{atom}}$ means that the reasons in the set denoted by the term *`reasons1`* outweigh the reasons in the set denoted by the term *`reasons2`* as reasons concerning *`atom`*.

The terms `reasons1` and `reasons2` must both have the form
`{`$facts_1$`,` $facts_2$`, ...,` $facts_n$ `},` with $n \geq 0$.

Normally the reference to the conclusion for and against which the reasons plead will be omitted, because the conclusion will be clear from the context. E.g. `reasons1 > reasons2`.

7. RULES OF INFERENCE

7.1 A reservation

RBL has extra 'rules of inference' next to those of FOPL. The following section deals with nine rules that characterise inference in RBL. I want to point out on beforehand, however, that these rules are not constructive in the sense that they can be applied to an RBL-theory to obtain derivable sentences. Some rules of inference refer to sentences that cannot, and to reasons that can be derived. These sentences and reasons are only available if the complete set of derivable sentences and reasons is given. In other words, to determine what can be derived, one already needs the set of derivable sentences. That is why the rules are not constructive, and why I placed quotation marks around the phrase 'rules of inference'.

Moreover, for some theories, the 'rules of inference' do not provide an unambiguous answer to the question whether some sentence follows from a theory or not. These theories are the ones which have multiple extensions (cf. section 8.2f.), and for them it is necessary to refer to the 'official' definition of derivable sentences in section 8.1. Nevertheless, description of the 'rules of inference' gives an intuitive account of the derivational power of RBL.

7.2 Minimal entailment

The rules described in the following section make use of the notion of *minimal entailment*. Minimal entailment is a relation between sentences.

A sentence S1 *entails* a(nother) sentence S2, if and only if S2 is true in all RBL-possible worlds in which S1 is true.[14]

A sentence S1 *minimally* entails a(nother) sentence S2, if and only if:

1. S1 entails S2;
2. There is no sentence S3 such that:
   a. S1 entails S3;
   b. S3 does not entail S1;
   c. S3 entails S2.

---

[14] The notion of an RBL-possible is elaborated in section VI.14. For the present purposes the intuitive understanding of possible worlds in general suffices.

For instance, the sentence `A` minimally entails `A ∨ C`, while the sentence `A & B` does not entail `A ∨ C` minimally, because `A & B` entails `A`, which does not entail `A & B`, but does entail `A ∨ C`.

7.3 The rules

An RBL-theory is a set of RBL sentences without free variables (except in the conditions and the conclusions of rules and principles). Let T be an RBL-theory.

R1 a Any sentence that can be derived from T in FOPL can be derived from T.[15]

b Any sentence that can be derived in FOPL from sentences that can be derived from T can be derived from T.

This rule comes down to it that the consequences of an RBL-theory are closed under deduction.[16]

R2 Let

a. the sentence *`Facts`* minimally entail the sentence *`Condition`* under some substitution σ, and let

b. the term *`iconcl`* be the instance of the term *`conclusion`* under σ, then if

```
Valid(conditions ⊃ conclusion) ∨
 Ob(valid(conditions ⊃ conclusion))
```

and

```
Obtains(facts, case)
```

can be derived, and

```
Excluded(conditions ⊃ conclusion, case)
```

cannot be derived, then it is possible to derive

```
R(facts, iconcl)
```

Intuitively, this means that if the conditions of a principle that is valid, or ought to be valid, are satisfied in a case, and if the principle is not

---

[15] If not indicated otherwise, 'can be derived' means 'can be derived on the basis of RBL'.

[16] The deductive closure of a set of sentences S is the infinite set of sentences that can be deduced from S. A set of sentences T is closed under deduction if it is identical to its own deductive closure. Such a set will always be infinite, unless it is the deductive closure of the empty set.

excluded in this case, the facts that satisfy the conditions of the principle are a reason for the conclusion of the principle.

R3a If `Goal(state)` is derivable, then the following sentences are also derivable:

```
Valid(contributes_to(new_state, state) ⊃
 ob(new_state))
Valid(contributes_to(new_state, ~state) ⊃
 ob(~new_state))
Valid(contributes_to(action, state) ⊃
 od(x, action))
Valid(contributes_to(action, ~state) ⊃
 od(x, ¬action))
```

R3b If `Ob(goal(state))` is derivable, then the following sentences are also derivable:

```
Ob(valid(contributes_to(new_state, state) ⊃
 ob(new_state)))
Ob(valid(contributes_to(new_state, ~state) ⊃
 ob(~new_state)))
Ob(valid(contributes_to(action, state) ⊃
 od(x, action)))
Ob(valid(contributes_to(action, ~state) ⊃
 od(x, ¬action)))
```

Intuitively these rules mean that if something is or ought to be a goal, principles are, respectively ought to be valid, which specify that states or actions which contribute to, or detract from this goal, ought (not) to be the case, c.q. ought (not) to be performed.

R4 Let

a. the sentence *Facts* minimally entail the sentence *Condition* under some substitution σ, and
b. the term *iconcl* be the instance of the term *conclusion* under σ, then if

```
Valid(conditions ⇒ conclusion) ∨
 Ob(valid(conditions ⇒ conclusion))
```

and

`Obtains(facts, case)` can be derived, and if

`Excluded(conditions ⇒ conclusion, case)`

cannot be derived, then it is possible to derive

`Applicable(facts ⇒ iconcl, case)`

Intuitively, this means that if the conditions of a rule which is valid, or ought to be valid, are satisfied in a case, and if the rule is not excluded in this case, the rule is applicable in this case.

R5 If

`Applicable(instantiated_rule, case)`

can be derived, then it is possible to derive

```
R( applicable(instantiated_rule, case),
  ob(applies(instantiated_rule, case)))
```

Intuitively this rule can be understood as saying that if a rule is applicable, this is a reason to apply the rule (why it ought to be the case that the rule is applied).

R6 Let `State` be an literal of RBL. If

`Ob(applies(conds ⇒ state, case))`

can be derived, then it is possible to derive `state`.

Intuitively this means that if a rule ought to be applied, its conclusion can be derived.

R7 Let `State` be an atom of RBL, and let `reasons(state)` denote the sets of facts *f*, such that it can be derived that `R(f, state)`, then if

$(\texttt{reasons}(state) > \texttt{reasons}(\sim state))_{state}$

can be derived, then `State` can be derived.
Intuitively this rule says that a conclusion can be derived if the derivable reasons that plead for it outweigh the derivable reasons that plead against it.

R8 Let `State` be a variable that ranges over atoms of RBL, and let *reasonset* be a variable that ranges over sets of conjunctions of zero or more literals. Then it is possible to derive

$$(\forall reasonset)(\forall state)$$
$$(reasonset \neq \emptyset) \rightarrow (reasonset > \emptyset)_{state}$$

This rule means that for any non-empty set of reasons it is given that it outweighs the empty set of reasons, no matter which conclusion is involved.

R9 If `(∃case)Obtains(state, case)` can be derived, then it is possible to derive `State`.

Intuitively this means that if a state of affairs obtains in connection with a case, this state of affairs obtains.

Notice that the rules R1 to R9 above cannot easily be turned into an inductive construction of the set of sentences that can be derived from a theory T, because the rules R2 and R4 mention a sentence that cannot be derived and therefore indirectly refer to the *whole* set of sentences that can be derived. R7 makes use of *all* the reasons for and against a conclusion that can be derived from a theory T. As a consequence, these rules can only be applied if its on beforehand known what can be derived and what cannot be derived (cf. also section 8.2). To overcome this drawback, I will in section 8 define which sentences are valid conclusions from an RBL-theory by means of extensions of an RBL-theory.

8. VALID CONCLUSIONS

It is possible to define the valid conclusions of an RBL-theory by means of extensions of an RBL-theory.[17]

8.1 Extensions of a Reason Based Logic-theory

Let T be an RBL-theory, let Th(T) be the deductive closure of T, let E be a set of sentences, and let $T_0 \ldots T_\infty$ be a sequence of sets of sentences such that:

1. $T_0 = Th(T) \cup$

```
{
  (∀reasonset)(∀state)
    (reasonset ≠ ∅) → (reasonset > ∅)state)),
  (∃case)(∀state) Obtains(state, case) → State
  Valid(applicable(r, c) ⊃ ob(applies(r, c))) }
```

   Intuitively T_0 is the original theory with the additional information that:
   - every non-empty set of reasons outweighs the empty set,
   - if a state of affairs obtains in some case, this state of affairs obtains,
   - the principle is valid that if a rule is applicable, this is a reason why this rule ought to be applied

17 The following definition of extensions is based on Reiter 1980.

and everything which can be deduced from this.

2. $T_{m+1} = Th(T_m \cup \Delta(T_m))$, where $\Delta(T_m)$ is *exhaustively* defined by:
Assume that the sentence *Facts* minimally entails the sentence *Condition* under some substitution σ, and that the term *iconcl* is the instance of the term *conclusion* under σ. Then it holds that:

a. If

Valid(*cond* ⊃ *concl*) ∨ Ob(valid(*cond* ⊃ *concl*)) ∈ Tm,

and

Obtains(*facts*, *case*) ∈ Tm, and
Excluded(*cond* ⊃ *concl*, *case*) ∉ E, then

R(*facts*, *iconcl*) ∈ Δ(Tm).

b. If

Valid(*cond* ⇒ *concl*) ∨ Ob(valid(*cond* ⇒ *concl*)) ∈ Tm,

and

Obtains(*facts*, *case*) ∈ Tm, and
Excluded(*cond* ⇒ *concl*, *case*) ∉ E, then

Applicable(*facts* ⇒ *iconcl*, *case*) ∈ Δ(Tm).

c. If Goal(*state*) ∈ Tm, then the sentences

Valid(contributes_to(*new_state*, *state*) ⊃ ob(*new_state*))
Valid(contributes_to(*new_state*, ~*state*) ⊃ ob(~*new_state*))
Valid(contributes_to(*action*, *state*) ⊃ od(*x*, *action*))
Valid(contributes_to(*action*, ~*state*) ⊃ od(*x*, ¬*action*))

are elements of Δ(Tm).

d. If Ob(goal(*state*)) ∈ Tm, then the sentences

Ob(valid(contributes_to(*new_state*, *state*) ⊃ ob(*new_state*)))
Ob(valid(contributes_to(*new_state*, ~*state*) ⊃ ob(~*new_state*)))

```
Ob(valid(contributes_to(action, state) ⊃
 od(x, action)))
Ob(valid(contributes_to(action, ~state) ⊃
 od(x, ¬action)))
```

are elements of Δ(Tm).

e. If `Ob(applies(facts ⇒ iconcl, case)) ε Tm`, then `iconcl ∈ Δ(Tm)`.

Let `reasons(atom)` be {s: `R(s, atom) ∈ E`}

f. If `(reasons(literal) > reasons(~literal))`$_{literal}$ `∈ Tm`, then `Literal ∈ Δ(Tm)`.

3. E is an extension of T iff $E = \bigcup_{i=0}^{\infty} T_i$

Intuitively this definition of an extension of the theory T comes down to the following. Starting with a set of sentences that consists of the original theory T and the axioms that any non-empty set of reasons outweighs the empty set, that facts which obtain in some case, obtain, and that the principle is valid that an applicable rule ought to be applied (T_0), a series of ever increasing sets of sentences (T_0 ... T_∞) is defined. Every set contains the sentences of the previous set plus what 'immediately follows' from that set (Δ(Tm)). Normally, at some moment there are no new conclusions possible anymore ($T_{m+1} = T_m$) The set which is achieved at that moment is an extension of T.

A *valid conclusion* of an RBL-theory T is a sentence which occurs in the intersection of all extensions of T.

8.2 The number of extensions of a theory

A complication in the definition of extensions of an RBL-theory is that the sentences that can be added to a set to obtain the new set (Δ(Tm)) do not only depend on the first set (T_m), but also on the final set that will be achieved (E). That this is the case follows from the conditions sub a, b, and f, which refer to the exclusions or the reasons which are present in the final extension of the theory (E).

This complication has at least two consequences. The first consequence is that it is not possible to generate the series of sets of sentences just by starting with the original theory. Next to the original theory, an 'hypothesis' concerning the final extension is needed to generate the series of sets. An hypothesis concerning the extension of a theory is correct if the series of sets based on the original theory and the hypothetical extension ends with the hypothetical extension. Cf. figure 3.

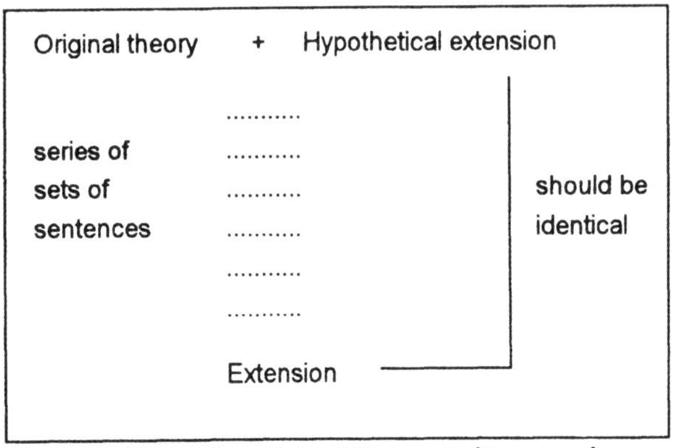

Figure 3: From the original theory to its extension

The second consequence is that a theory can at least in theory have more than one extension. That is because there may be more than one combination of the original theory and a hypothetical extension that fulfils the demand that the resulting series of sets of sentences ends up with the hypothetical extension on which the series was based. Cf. figure 4.

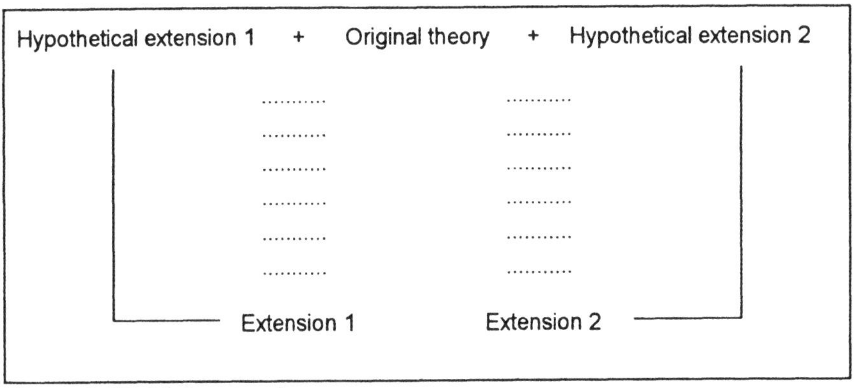

Figure 4: Multiple extensions

Let me give an example of a theory which has no extension.

```
rule_0: a ⇒ excluded(rule_0)
Valid(rule_0)
A
```

This theory has no extension, because if an extension contains the sentence

```
Excluded(a ⇒ excluded(rule_0))
```

it should for this very reason not contain that sentence, and the other way round. (If `rule_0` is not excluded, it can be derived that it is excluded. If it is excluded, the very reason why it should be excluded, that is derivation on the basis of the rule itself, does not obtain anymore.)

The following theory has two extensions:

```
A
rule_1: a ⇒ excluded(rule_2)
Valid(rule_1)
rule_2: a ⇒ excluded(rule_1)
Valid(rule_2)
```

The one extension contains, amongst others, the sentences

```
Applicable(a ⇒ excluded(rule_2))
Excluded(rule_2)
```

and not the sentences

```
Applicable(a ⇒ excluded(rule_1))
Excluded(rule_1)
```

The other extension contains, amongst others, the sentences

```
Applicable(a ⇒ excluded(rule_1))
Excluded(rule_1)
```

and not the sentences

```
Applicable(a ⇒ excluded(rule_2))
Excluded(rule_2)
```

It seems that the occurrence of multiple extensions or the lack of any extension is the consequence of circularities in a theory.[18] As may be seen in the first example, if a rule directly refers to itself, this may block the existence of extensions. If the self-reference is indirect (one rule refers to another rule and vice versa), the result is that there are multiple extensions (cf. the second example).

If this hypothesis is correct, the intuitively correct conclusions from a theory can be obtained by not applying the rules which are involved in the self-reference. In the case of multiple extensions, the present definition of

---

[18] It is not the consequence of the possibility to use several subsets of the premises to obtain an extension, as in other nonmonotonic logics. (Cf. section VI.16.2) RBL always takes all sentences of a theory into account in defining an extension. Moreover, it already has a cautious notion of consequence, because in case of a conflict of reasons, nothing can be derived unless on the basis of explicit weighing knowledge.

valid conclusions obtains this result by using the intersection of all extensions to define valid conclusions. In this way, any rule that cannot be applied in some extension does not lead to conclusions in that extension. Its conclusion will therefore not be an element of the intersection of all extensions of the theory, and consequently also not be derivable from the theory.

If a theory contains a rule that rules out its own application, the theory has no extensions, and nothing can be derived from it. This problem can be solved by disallowing such rules.

9. THE RELATION BETWEEN FIRST ORDER PREDICATE LOGIC AND REASON-BASED LOGIC

In one sense, RBL is no more than an extension of FOPL. All deductive arguments are valid in RBL. Moreover every well-formed sentence of FOPL is a well-formed sentence of RBL and the other way round. RBL 'only' adds a number of inferential possibilities to those of FOPL.

Nevertheless, the 'spirit' of RBL is completely different from that of FOPL. RBL is a nonmonotonic logic, because the part that is added to FOPL is nonmonotonic. Moreover, the central notions in RBL-inferences are those of a reason and of the weighing of reasons, not that of a deductive argument.

The difference between the two logics is most prominent where the use of the material implication is concerned. Most real life-arguments will be represented in FOPL as arguments of the form Modus Ponens. In RBL, most of these arguments will be represented as the application of a rule or principle. As a consequence, almost all real life-arguments will be dealt with by the part of RBL that is built on top of FOPL. Where RBL is from a technical point of view only an extension of FOPL, it is for practical purposes an alternative.

The following chapter contains numerous illustrations of how arguments are dealt with by RBL and - implicitly - how this differs from the way in which such arguments would be dealt with by FOPL.

V. APPLICATIONS OF REASON-BASED LOGIC

In this chapter I will illustrate how RBL can be used for legal applications. This involves:

1. a demonstration of the facilities offered by the language and the inference mechanism of RBL, and
2. a series of examples of how legal arguments can be cast in the form of reasons for and against particular conclusions.

These examples are particularly relevant for those who read this text from the point of view of legal knowledge representation.

First I will show how the standard cases such as simple rule application and the weighing of reasons for and against a particular classification are handled (sections 1- 4). Then follows a number of examples that show how RBL deals with complex legal reasoning. These complex cases include the use of conflict rules and possible conflicts between conflict rules, the relation between legal rules and the principles and goals on which they are based, reasoning by analogy, and arguments about the interpretation of legal sources.

1. RULE APPLICATION

Most often, when we apply a rule, there are no complications. The conditions of the rule are satisfied and the rule conclusion follows. A theory about reasoning with rules should be able to handle this situation without problems. This section deals with normal rule application and illustrates how RBL works if there are no special circumstances.

1.1 The theory and its conclusion

Suppose we have the rule that thieves are punishable, and the fact that John is a thief. From this theory we want to derive that John is punishable. The information can be represented by the following RBL-sentences:

```
punishable: thief(x) ⇒ punishable(x)
Valid(punishable)
Thief(john)
∴ Punishable(john)
```

After the definition of the rule `punishable`, the first two sentences are an RBL-theory, and the third sentence is a conclusion from this theory. I will elaborately discuss the steps that lead from the two premises to the conclusion.

By application of rule R4 it is possible to derive that the rule `punishable` is applicable, with its condition-part instantiated to `thief(john)`, and its conclusion-part `punishable(john)`:

```
Applicable(thief(john) ⇒ punishable(john))
```

1.2 The non-constructiveness of rule R4

The step that leads to the conclusion that the rule `punishable` is applicable makes use of rule R4 and is only possible if it cannot be derived that `punishable` is excluded. Here we encounter for the first time the non-constructive nature of the rules of inference. It is not possible to show that `punishable` is not excluded by applying one or more rules of inference to sentences that were given or have already been derived.

The question arises how we can continue our derivation, if we do not know whether it can be derived that the rule is excluded. I will show that it is possible to prove by meta-level reasoning that some extension of the theory does not contain the sentence `Excluded(punishable)`. As a consequence we know that the exclusion of `punishable` is not derivable, and we can derive that this rule is applicable.

By following the definition of an extension of an RBL-theory in section IV.8.1, it can be seen that the deductive closure of the following sentences is an extension of the theory given above:

```
Valid(punishable)
Thief(john)
(∃case)(∀state) Obtains(state, case) → State
Valid(applicable(rule, case) ⊃ ob(applies(rule, case)))
(∀reasonset)(∀state_of_affairs)
  (reasonset ≠ ∅) → (reasonset > ∅)state_of_affairs
Applicable(thief(john) ⇒ punishable(john))
R( applicable(thief(john) ⇒ punishable(john)),
  ob(applies(thief(john) ⇒ punishable(john))))
Ob(applies(thief(john) ⇒ punishable(john)))
Punishable(john)
```

This extension does not include the sentence

```
Excluded(punishable)
```

Therefore the intersection of all extensions does not include this sentence either, and the sentence is not derivable from the theory.

We can also resort to a more sloppy type of meta-level reasoning. By inspecting the theory that consists of the two premises, it can easily be seen that there is no information from which it might be possible to derive that the rule is excluded. In fact, the predicate `Excluded` does not even occur in the theory. Moreover, there is no rule of inference which allows the introduction of the `Excluded`-predicate. Therefore, we can be sure that it is not derivable that the rule is excluded.

For practical purposes, this second way to deal with the non-constructiveness of the RBL rules of inference will be the most adequate. The reliability of this approach depends, however, on the ingenuity of one's reasoning, and the outcome does not guarantee the correctness of its result.

From now on, I will skip the proofs that the non-constructive rules can be applied.

1.3 The derivation that a rule applies

If we have derived that `thief(john) ⇒ punishable(john)` is applicable, it is possible to derive by means of R5 that this applicability is a reason for applying the rule with the same instantiations:

```
R( applicable(thief(john) ⇒ punishable(john)),
  ob(applies(thief(john) ⇒ punishable(john))))
```

We have derived a reason to apply the rule

```
thief(john) ⇒ punishable(john)
```

and on the basis of this reason we want to derive that this rule ought to be applied. To make this step, we must weigh the reasons that plead for application against the reasons that plead against it. For that purpose we need to have the premise that the reasons for application of this rule outweigh the reasons against application. Formally this premise is:

$$(\texttt{reasons(ob(applies(thief(john)} \Rightarrow \texttt{punishable(john))))} > \texttt{reasons(\~{}ob(applies(thief(john)} \Rightarrow \texttt{punishable(john)))))}_{\texttt{punishable(john)}}$$

Moreover, we need to know exactly which reasons plead for and against punishing John. In other words, we need the values of the functions

```
reasons(ob(applies(thief(john) ⇒ punishable(john))))
```

and

```
reasons(~ob(applies(thief(john) ⇒ punishable(john))))
```

Again we knock against the non-constructive nature of the RBL inference rules. We need all the derivable reasons for and against application of the rule `thief(john) ⇒ punishable(john)`, while presently we have only derived one reason for application. Somehow we must establish whether there are still other reasons for or against application of the rule.

In practice it is easiest to observe that there is only one rule that might lead to a reason, and only one fact to which this rule can be applied, and that therefore there cannot be other reasons than the one we have already found. By using this informal procedure, we find that there is precisely one reason for the application of the rule `theft` and that there are no reasons against the application of this rule. Formally:

```
reasons(ob(applies(thief(john) ⇒ punishable(john)))) =
 {thief(john)}
```

and

```
reasons(~ob(applies(thief(john) ⇒ punishable(john)))) =
 ∅
```

By means of R8 it follows that the set of reasons for application, that contains the reason that John is a thief, outweighs the empty set of reasons against application of the rule `theft`:

$(\{\texttt{thief(john)}\} > \varnothing)_{\texttt{ob(applies(thief(john)} \Rightarrow \texttt{punishable(john)))}}$

By means of R7 follows that the rule `theft` ought to be applied:

```
Ob(applies(thief(john) ⇒ punishable(john)))
```

From the fact that the rule ought to be applied, it is possible to derive by means of R6 the rule's instantiated conclusion:

```
Punishable(john)
```

1.4 Observations on normal rule application

A logic for reasoning with rules should at least be capable to deal adequately with normal rule application. We found that the RBL-procedure for normal rule application is not very simple. Is this procedure an adequate way to deal with something as simple as normal rule application?

The answer is shadedly affirmative. It is shaded, because the procedure is by far not as simple as normal rule application seems to be. Still it is affirmative, because simple rule application is not as simple as might seem at first sight. Reasoning with rules is defeasible. Any account of reasoning with rules should take this defeasibility into consideration. Even if a rule is simply applied, and its conclusion follows from the facts that satisfy the rule conditions, there is the *possibility* that the connection between the facts of the rule conditions and the rule's conclusion is interrupted. A logic that deals with rule application must check whether there is a ground for defeat. In real life situations, this check is skipped and the absence of exceptions is assumed by default. The logic should, however, make room for this check in its rules of inference. The complexity of the RBL -procedure for 'normal' rule application reflects the complexity that is hidden under the surface of real life rule application.

2. WEIGHING REASONS

In legal reasoning, weighing reasons most often occurs when there are no legal rules (in the narrow sense; cf. section III.2) to apply. Classification springs to mind as a field that is not always governed by rules of law and where reasons for and against a particular classification have to be weighed. Another situation where weighing reasons is important, is where legal decision makers have discretion. In the Netherlands, determining the measure of punishment (within certain limits) belongs to this field.

2.1 An example

I will adapt an earlier example to show how weighing reasons in the field of criminal law can be represented in RBL. We have already met with the case of John the thief. There is a principle that thieves ought to be punished, and on the basis of this principle the fact that he is a thief is a reason why John ought to be punished. Suppose, however, that John is a child of thirteen. This is a reason not to punish him on the basis of the principle that minors ought not to be punished. In some legal systems the age of John may even block the application of the normal principle about the punishment of thieves. In that case it should be represented by means of an exclusionary reason. If the age does not completely block the application of the principle, and if the judge has discretion to determine whether the crime will be punished, the age of John will at least form an reason against punishing him. The situation can then be represented as follows:

```
Valid(thief(x) ⊃ ob(punished(x)))
Valid(minor(x) ⊃ ~ob(punished(x)))[1]
Thief(john) & Minor(john)
```

Since it cannot be derived that either one of the two principles is excluded, the following sentences can be derived:

---

[1] To simplify the example, I let the conclusion of the principle run that it is not the case that the minor ought to be punished, rather than that it is the case that the minor ought not to be punished.

```
R(thief(john), ob(punished(john)))
R(minor(john), ~ob(punished(john)))
```

Since there are no other reasons, we have:

```
reasons(ob(punished(john))) = {thief(john)}
reasons(~ob(punished(john))) = {minor(john)}
```

To derive a conclusion regarding whether John ought to be punished, we need to know which set of reasons outweighs the other set. On the basis of the present theory, which contains no information concerning the relative weight of the reasons, it is not possible to derive whether John ought to be punished or not. Suppose, however, that the information is added that being a minor outweighs being a thief:

```
(∀x){minor(x)} > {thief(x)}
```

This makes it possible to apply rule R7 and to derive that it is not the case that John ought to be punished:

```
~Ob(punished(john))
```

2.2 Accrual of reasons

Suppose, now, that instead of the principle that thieves ought to be punished, we have the principle that mistreators ought to be punished, and that John is a mistreator, but also a minor. Given the weighing knowledge

```
(∀x){minor(x)} > {mistreator(x)}
```

the conclusion would still be that John ought not to be punished. If, however, the principle that thieves ought to be punished is added again, and if John is both a mistreator, a thief and a minor, the situation may become different:

```
reasons(ob(punished(john))) =
  {mistreator(john), thief(john)}
reasons(~ob(punished(john))) = {minor(john)}
(∀x){mistreator(x), thief(x)} > {minor(x)}
```

Given these reasons and the new weighing knowledge that the combination of being a thief and a mistreator outweighs being a minor, it becomes derivable that John ought to be punished:

```
Ob(punished(john))
```

This new conclusion demonstrates the phenomenon of the accrual of reasons, which is essential for RBL. The accrual of reasons is based on the possibility that reasons for or against a conclusion can add up to a combined weight which is bigger than the weight of each of them by itself. This presumes a certain independence of the reasons in a set.[2]

3. ELEMENTARY GOAL-BASED REASONING

An important legal goal in most Western countries is to protect the possibility for every citizen to express his or her opinion. Let us call this goal Freedom of Expression. Clearly having a free press contributes to this goal. As a consequence of the goal Freedom of Expression, there should be a free press.

This simple argument, based on the application of a goal, would be expressed in RBL as follows:

```
Goal(freedom_of_expression)
Contributes_to(free_press, freedom_of_expression)
∴ Ob(free_press)
```

The intermediate steps of this argument are the 'derivation' on the basis of rule R3a of:

```
Valid(contributes_to(state, freedom_of_expression) ⊃
 ob(state))
```

Because it cannot be derived that this principle is excluded, it is possible to derive by means of R2 that

```
R(contributes_to(free_press, freedom_to_express),
 ob(free_press))
```

and consequently also

```
Ob(free_press)
```

Imagine, however, that a particular country is at war, and that there are serious reasons to assume that the freedom of expression can be misused for spreading unnecessary anxiety. Under these circumstances there is reason to restrict the goal to have freedom of expression. The goal is not completely abandoned; its effects are only temporarily suspended. Under these circumstances, application of the goal Freedom of Expression would be excluded:

```
Excluded(
 contributes_to(state, freedom_of_expression) ⊃
  ob(state))
```

and the derivation of `Ob(free_press)` would be blocked.

---

2 Cf. the sections III.14, and VI.1.

4. THE EXCLUSION OF RULES

RBL uses the mechanism of exclusionary reasons to model exceptions that block the application of a rule. The law knows several situations in which exceptions occur. Sometimes an exception only makes it impossible to apply a rule. At other occasions the exception not only blocks the application of a rule, but also leads to an incompatible conclusion. In the following two subsections I will discuss the prescription of punishable facts as an example of the first situation, and the rule that governs force majeure in contract law as an example of the second situation.

Important cases where exclusionary reasons play a role are when rules of law conflict with legal principles or goals, and when rules of law are in conflict without one rule being meant as an exception to the other rule. These more complex situations are discussed in the sections 6-8.

4.1 Undercutters and the scope of rules

Reasons that only block the application of a rule, without having any other impact are sometimes called *undercutters*.[3] In the terminology introduced in chapter II (section 1.5), undercutters are exclusionary reasons.

The scope limitations of legal rules form the basis for several kinds of undercutters. One of them concerns the scope of legal rules in time. A criminal law, for instance, may not be applicable anymore if the crime occurred sufficiently long ago. This can be illustrated by an adaptation of our old example about John, the thief. Although John is a thief, he is not punishable, because his crime is prescribed. Let us formulate the relevant data in an RBL-theory:

```
Valid(punishable)
Thief(john)
Criminal_law(punishable)
Crime_type(punishable, stealing)
Type(theft, stealing)
Prescribed(theft)
prescription:
  criminal_law(rule) & crime_type(rule, crime_type) &
     type(crime_token, crime_type) &
      prescribed(crime_token) ⇒
   excluded(rule)
Valid(prescription)
```

3 The term stems from Pollock 1987, and was also adopted in Prakken 1993.

The rule `prescription` means that if a particular rule is a rule of criminal law, if it is about a particular type of crime, and if a crime of this type is prescribed, then the application of this rule is excluded.

The facts of the case make that the rule `prescription` ought to be applied to the theft of John, with the consequences that

`Excluded(punishable)`

can be derived and that is not possible to derive that

`Applicable(thief(john) ⇒ punishable(john))`

nor that

`Punishable(john)`

The facts that `punishable` is a rule of criminal law, and that the crime was prescribed are together an undercutter or an exclusionary reason. They only block the application of the rule `punishable`, and have no other implication for the punishability of John whatsoever.

4.2 Rebutters

Some exceptions to rules do not only block the application of the rule, but also provide the case with a legal consequence that is incompatible with the conclusion of the rule. Such exceptions are called *rebutters*.[4]

One example of a rebutter is based on the rule that in the case of force majeure, one needs not compensate for the damages that one's contract partner suffers as a consequence of ones default.[5] Let us see how RBL handles this rebutter by means of an example. The facts are the following: Jones defaulted his contractual obligations towards a computer firm, and this firm suffered damages of $ 10,000. However, Jones' default was a consequence of force majeure. The relevant rules are that one must pay for the damages which one's contract party suffers as a result of ones default, but that in case of force majeure, one needs not pay for the damages. The relevant RBL-theory is[6]:

---

4 Pollock 1987. Sartor 1991 distinguishes between exceptions to norms and exceptions to effects, where the former are undercutters, and the latter rebutters.

5 From a legal point of view, it is defensible that force majeure leads to an undercutter rather than to a rebutter. For the purpose of the present example, however, I will assume that force majeure leads to a rebutter.

6 To make the example more readable, I leave reference to the case away, although the formulations of the rules loose some credibility thereby.

```
contractual_default:
 contractual_default(x, y) & damages(y, amount) ⇒
  od(x, pay(y, amount))

force_majeure1:
 force_majeure(p) & damages(q, amount) ⇒
  ~od(p, pay(q, amount))
```
[7]

```
force_majeure2:
 force_majeure(x) ⇒ excluded(contractual_default)

Contractual_default(jones, computer_firm)
Force_majeure(jones)
Damages(computer_firm, $10000)
Valid(contractual_default)
Valid(force_majeure1)
Valid(force_majeure2)
```

The issue at stake is whether it is possible to derive

```
Od(jones, pay(computer_firm, $10000))
```

or its negation.

Let us start with the latter sentence. The conditions of `force_majeure1` are satisfied, and since there are no special circumstances, the rule's instantiated conclusion can be derived:

```
~Od(jones, pay(computer_firm, $10000))
```

Similarly `force_majeure2` can be applied, with the conclusion that

```
Excluded(contractual_default)
```

As a consequence, it cannot anymore be derived that

```
Applicable(
 contractual_default(jones, computer_firm) &
   damages(computer_firm, $10000) ⇒
  od(jones, pay(computer_firm, $10000)) )
```

Therefore there is no reason to conclude that

```
Od(jones, pay(computer_firm, $10000))
```

and this sentence is therefore not derivable.

---

7 A better formalisation would be to limit the scope of the negation in the rule conclusion, so as to exclude the deontic predicate from it. This would make the example more complex, however. In the next section I will present a deontic extension of RBL to deal with this type of situation.

Notice that the original rule that in the case of force majeure, one need not pay for the damages, has been translated into two RBL-rules. The reason for this is that the application of this rule has two effects. First that the application of the rule for contractual default is blocked, and second that there is no obligation to pay for the damages. RBL-rules can only have one conclusion, and therefore two rules are needed to express the two effects of force majeure.[8]

With this example, the part on elementary applications of RBL is closed. It will probably be clear how the most frequent cases of legal reasoning are handled in RBL. In the following sections, that contain more complex applications, it should become clear that RBL is also capable to deal with relatively complex forms of legal reasoning, and also how the formalism of RBL suggests particular ways of modelling those forms of reasoning.

5. A DEONTIC EXTENSION OF REASON-BASED LOGIC

The examples of the following sections need for their formalisation more deontic predicates than the ones defined for RBL proper. To accommodate for this need, I will give in this section a deontic extension of RBL. The reader should not expect a full-blown deontic logic here, however. The extension of RBL that is presented here was devised primarily to make the examples in the following sections 'work'.

First I want to introduce the predicates `Fd` and `Pd`, which have an actor and an action type as their parameters, and stand for forbidden-to-do, respectively permitted-to-do. These predicates are defined as follows:

$$(\forall actor)(\forall action)\mathrm{Fd}(actor,\ action) \equiv \mathrm{Od}(actor,\ \neg action)$$
$$(\forall actor)(\forall action)\mathrm{Pd}(actor,\ action) \equiv {\sim}\mathrm{Fd}(actor,\ \neg action)$$

Second, I want to introduce characteristics of action types. If `action` stands for an action type, then `action[char]` stands for the same action type characterised in a particular way. For instance, `killing[gently]` stands for gently killing, and `killing[gently](suzy_mae)` stands for killing Suzy Mae gently.

If some concrete act belongs to a characterised action type, it also belongs to the corresponding uncharacterised action type. So, if some concrete act belongs to the type of gently killing, this act also belongs to the type killing:

[8] In section VI.14 I implicitly defend the view that something only ought to be done on the basis of reasons. For the present example this means that if the application of the rule `contractual_default` is blocked by application of `force_majeure2`, this suffices for the conclusion that prima facie Jones does not have to pay. Application of `force_majeure1` would then be superfluous.

```
(∀act)(∀action)(∀char)Type(act, action[char]) →
 Type(act, action)
```

Moreover, if some uncharacterised action type has a deontic classification (obligated, forbidden, permitted), this same classification holds in principle also for characterised versions of this type:

```
Valid(Od(x, action) ⊃ Od(x, action[char])
```

Finally, I want to introduce the predicates `O`, `F` and `P`, which have action *tokens* as their parameter, and which stand for respectively ought-, forbidden- and permitted-to-do. These predicates, which are the counterparts of the `Od`, `Fd`, and `Pd` predicates for action *types*, cannot fully be defined in terms of the other deontic predicates. Yet, there are some connections, indicated by the following sentences, which might be added to RBL as deontic axioms:

```
od(x, action) → valid(type(act, action) ⊃ o(act))
fd(x, action) → valid(type(act, action) ⊃ f(act))
pd(x, action) → valid(type(act, action) ⊃ p(act))
```

If a concrete act belongs to an action type that ought (is permitted, forbidden) to be done, (this is a reason why) this act is (was) obligated (permitted, forbidden).

Moreover, the following classical relations hold:

```
P(act) ≡ ~F(act) ≡ ~O(¬act)
```

6. LEGAL RULES, GOALS AND PRINCIPLES

In the following subsections, a number of examples concerning the mutual relations between rules, goals and principles is discussed.

6.1 Replacing reasons

Rules of law are often the result of a legislative decision making process, in which a number of reasons, based on policies, goals, values, interests, principles, etc. are weighed to achieve a balanced result. In many of the cases to which these rules of law can be applied, the underlying goals, principles, etc. would also be relevant for the legal consequences of the case, had their application not been excluded by the applicability of the legal rule. The reasons generated by the rule replace the reasons generated by the goals and principles that underlie that rule. The role of the goals and principles was confined to their influence on the drafting of the rule. That is why I called the reasons, generated by a rule, *replacing reasons*. Similarly, the legal rule can be said to replace its underlying goals and principles (cf. section III.8).

To show how RBL formalises the consequences of when some rule replaces a principle, I need some additional logical tools. Let the functions `iconds(rule, case)` and `ic(rule, case)` have as their values respectively the states of affairs denoted by the instantiation of the conditions and the conclusion of the principle or rule `rule` on the basis of the facts of the case `case`. For instance, if the rule is

```
thief(x) ⇒ ob(punished(x))
```

and the only fact of the case `theft_peter` is

```
Thief(peter)
```

it holds that

```
iconds(thief(x) ⇒ ob(punished(x)), theft_peter) =
  thief(peter)
ic(thief(x) ⇒ ob(punished(x)), theft_peter) =
  ob(punished(peter))
```

Using these functions, the effects of replacing rules can be formalised by the following principle:

```
principle_replacement:
  replaces(rule, principle) &
      applicable(
        iconds(rule, case) ⇒ ic(rule, case), case) ⊃
    excluded(principle, case)
```

This means that if a rule replaces a principle, the applicability of the rule to a case excludes the application of the principle to this case.

6.2 Example 1: The procession

Suppose that a municipality has prohibited religious processions in the city centre on all weekdays except Sunday. In this way the municipality has tried to balance the interest in a free flow of traffic, which pleads against all religious processions, and the value of a free exercise of religion which pleads for unrestricted allowance of religious processions. The question arises whether a particular religious procession, that is planned for a Saturday afternoon, is permitted.

Given the deontic predicates which were introduced in section 5, this situation can be formalised as follows:

```
procession_on_sunday:
 true ⇒ ~pd(x, procession[~on_sunday])
Valid(procession_on_sunday)
```

(Processions which are not on a Sunday, are not allowed.)

```
expression_of_religion:
 expression_of_religion(action) ⊃ pd(x, action)
Valid(expression_of_religion)
```

(Expressions of one's religion are permitted.)

```
traffic_flow:
 harms_free_flow_of_traffic(action) ⊃ ~pd(x, action)
Valid(traffic_flow)
```

(Actions which harm the free flow of traffic are not allowed.)

```
Expression_of_religion(religious_procession[~on_sunday])
Harms_free_flow_of_traffic(
 religious_procession[~on_sunday])
Type(procession, religious_procession[~on_sunday])
```

(Respectively: Religious processions which are not on a Sunday are expressions of religion, they harm the free flow of traffic. The concrete procession of our case is a religious processions which is not on a Sunday.)

Is it possible to derive from this theory that a particular religious procession (`procession`) which is not on a Sunday is allowed? First notice that we have both a prohibition and a permission:

```
~pd(x, procession[~on_sunday])
pd(x, procession[~on_sunday])
```
[9]

If this is all the information there is, nothing can be derived. We find two reasons that deal with the question whether `procession` is permitted:

```
R(type(procession, procession[~on_sunday]),
 p(procession))
R(type(procession, procession[~on_sunday]),
 ~p(procession))
```

[9] Notice that the prohibition of processions not on Sunday occurs for two reasons, because it is both based on `procession_on_sunday` and on `traffic_flow`. This raises the interesting question how such a double foundation should be taken into account in the weighing of reasons. This situation seems related to that where more than one alternative of a rule with alternative conditions is satisfied. Cf. section III.6.2. I will leave these issues for later research.

There is no weighing information that deals with this set of reasons, so nothing can be derived.

The situation becomes much different, however, if the rule `principle_replacement` is taken into account. Given the information that:

```
Replaces(procession_on_sunday, expression_of_religion)
Replaces(procession_on_sunday, traffic_flow)
```

it can be derived that

```
Excluded(expression_of_religion)
Excluded(traffic_flow)
```

As a consequence, only the reason

```
R(type(procession, procession[~on_sunday]),
 ~p(procession))
```

is derivable, and on the basis of this single reason it can be derived that

```
~P(planned_procession)
```

However, many will consider the freedom of religion to be a human right that cannot be set aside by a mere municipal regulation, even if that by-law somehow takes the human right into account (cf. Dworkin 1978, pp. 184 f.). A way to express this objection in RBL is to let the rule that guarantees freedom of religion generate reasons that exclude the application of most rules that infringe this freedom.

How is it possible to indicate in advance all rules the application of which will be excluded because they infringe the freedom of religion? The answer is that it is not necessary to specify all these rules in advance. All that is needed is that if the application of a rule infringes the freedom of religion, this is *a reason* why application of this rule is excluded. The following principle will do the job:

```
contributes_to(
 applies(conds ⇒ concl), ~freedom_of_religion) ⊃
  excluded(conds ⇒ concl)[10]
```

(If the application of some rule detracts from the freedom of religion, this is a reason why the application of this rule is excluded.)

Notice that this principle is actually a kind of right, that is, the freedom of religion.

---

[10] To keep the example relatively simple, I left the instantiation of the rule conditions and conclusion away in the clause about the application of the rule.

6.3 Example 2: The transfer of the stolen book

The example of the planned procession dealt with two conflicting principles. It is also possible that a principle and a goal conflict, and the conflict is resolved by a replacing rule. Take the case of Joyce, who has stolen a book that belonged to Alice, and who sells this book to Casey, who did not know that the book was stolen. In this case, the following sentences are important:

```
Stole(joyce, book)
Transfers(joyce, book, casey)
In_good_faith(casey)
Valid(stole(x, y) ⇒ ~owner(x, y))
```

(If somebody stole something, he is not the owner.)

```
nemo_plus:
 ~owns(x, y) & transfers(x, y, z) ⊃ ~owns(z, y)
Valid(nemo_plus)
```

(If somebody who is not the owner transfers something to somebody else, this latter person does not become the owner. The nemo plus principle)

```
good_faith:
 contributes_to(state,
    protection_parties_in_good_faith) ⊃
   ob(state)
Valid(good_faith)
```

(Parties in good faith ought to be protected.)

```
Contributes_to(owner(casey, book),
 protection_parties_in_good_faith)
```

(If Casey is (becomes) the (new) owner of the book, this contributes to the protection of parties in good faith.)

On the basis of the rule that thieves do not become the owners of what they stole, and the fact `stole(joyce, book)`, we obtain:

```
~Owner(joyce, book)
```

If the nemo plus-principle is applied to this fact, we obtain the reason:

```
R( ~owner(joyce, book) & transfers(joyce, book, casey),
 ~owner(casey, book))
```

The case can, however, also be approached from another direction. By means of the principle that persons in good faith are to be protected and the fact that if Casey becomes the owner of the book, this contributes to her protection as a party in good faith, we obtain the reason:

```
R( contributes_to(owner(casey, book),
   protection_parties_in_good_faith),
  ob(owner(casey, book)))
```

INTERMEZZO: DEONTIC COLLAPSE

This latter reason is not a reason why Casey is the owner of the book, but rather a reason why it ought to be the case that Casey is the owner of the book. To obtain the former reason, we need an additional principle which takes care of the necessary deontic collapse (cf. section III.15):

```
deontic_collapse:
  r(reason, ob(state)) & legal_point_of_view(state) ⊃
   r(reason, state))
Valid(deontic_collapse)
```

(If some set of facts is a reason why a particular state of affairs ought to obtain, and this state of affairs belongs to the legal point of view, then this set of facts is normally also a reason why this state of affairs actually obtains.)

By means of the additional information

```
legal_point_of_view(owner(casey, book))
```

the principle for deontic collapse allows us to derive:

```
R(
  r( contributes_to(owner(casey, book),
      protection_parties_in_good_faith),
     ob(owner(casey, book)) &
    legal_point_of_view(owner(casey, book))),
  r( contributes_to(owner(casey, book),
     protection_parties_in_good_faith),
    owner(casey, book))
  )
```

(The facts which are a reason why Casey *ought to be* the owner of the book are also a reason why Casey *is* the owner of the book.)

As a consequence we can also derive:

```
R( contributes_to(owner(casey, book),
   protection_parties_in_good_faith),
  owner(casey, book))
```

CONTINUATION OF EXAMPLE 2

As a result of the foregoing, we have:

```
reasons(owner(casey, book)) =
  {contributes_to(owner(casey, book),
   protection_parties_in_good_faith)}
reasons(~owner(casey, book)) =
  {~owner(joyce, book) & transfers(joyce, book, casey)}
```

To determine whether Casey is the owner of the book, these two (sets of) reasons must be weighed. The theory presented above does not contain any weighing information, and as a consequence, it cannot be derived whether Casey has become the new owner of the book.

This legal dilemma has been solved by the legislator by making a rule that deals with this type of cases. The following RBL-rules formalise a strongly simplified version of that rule[11]:

```
1:  transfers(x, z, y) & ~owner(x, z) & bought(y, z) &
      in_good_faith(y) & ~stolen(z) ⇒  owner(y, z)
2:  transfers(x, z, y) & ~owner(x, z) & ~bought(y, z) ⇒
      ~owner(y, z)
3:  transfers(x, z, y) & ~owner(x, z) & bought(y, z) &
       in_good_faith(y) & stolen(z) &
        time_since_theft < 3 ⇒
      ~owner(y, z)
4:  transfers(x, z, y) & ~owner(x, z) & bought(y, z) &
       in_good_faith(y) & stolen(z) &
        time_since_theft ≥ 3 ⇒
      owner(y, z)
```

These rules boil down to that if the party to whom the good was transferred acted in good faith, bought the good, and if the good was not stolen from the original owner, the third party becomes the new owner (rule 1). If the party in good faith did not buy the good (or paid no reasonable price for it for some other reason), this party does not become the owner (rule 2). If the good was stolen, the original owner retains his ownership during a period of three years sine the moment of the theft (rules 3 and 4).

These four rules replace the nemo plus-principle and the goal to protect parties in good faith:

[11] In the next section I will elaborate this example and then it will turn out that the present formalisation is not very realistic. For my present purposes, it suffices, however. To facilitate the discussion of the rules and principles, I gave them a number.

```
Replaces(1, nemo_plus) & Replaces(2, nemo_plus) &
Replaces(3, nemo_plus) & Replaces(4, nemo_plus) &
Replaces(1, good_faith) & Replaces(2, good_faith) &
Replaces(3, good_faith) & Replaces(4, good_faith)
```

Let us change our case so that the book was not stolen, and that Casey bought the book from Joyce:

```
~Stolen(book)
Bought(casey, book)
```

With this additional information, it becomes possible to derive that

```
Applicable(1)
```

Because rule 1 is applicable, and this rule replaces both the nemo plus-principle and the goal to protect parties in good faith, we have:

`R(applicable(1),excluded(nemo_plus))`, and
`R(applicable(1),excluded(good_faith))`

Since there are no conflicting reasons, it can be derived that:

`Excluded(nemo_plus)`, and
`Excluded(good_faith)`

Because rule 1 is applicable and there are no reasons not to apply it, its conclusion follows:

```
Owner(casey, book)
```

This example shows how a legal principle and a goal can be replaced by a legal rule. This legal rule is represented by means of four RBL-rules, each of which replaces the original principle and goal. If one of these rules is applicable, it answers the question whether the party in good faith has become the new owner of the good. This answer will be decisive, because the application of the nemo plus-principle and the goal to protect parties in good faith is excluded.

Another aspect of this example is that it illustrates how goals generate reasons why particular legal situations *ought* to obtain, and that by deontic collapse these reasons also become reasons why this state *actually* obtains.

7. A COMPLEX CASE OF UNDERCUTTERS

The replacement of goals and principles by rules is a special case of the use of undercutters: if a rule is applicable to a case, this excludes the application of its underlying principles and goals. Insofar the conclusion of the rule is incompatible with that of the principle or goal, application of the rule even rebuts the principle or goal.

A more complex example of the use of undercutters that concerns the mutual relation between legal rules, can be found if we analyse more closely the situation in which a right is transferred by a non-owner. The Dutch regulation of this subject consists of a number of increasingly more specific rules with alternating conclusions.

The main rule for the transfer of a right (including the right of property) can be found in article 3:84 section 1 BW.

```
a1: right(r) & transfer(act, r, x, y) ⇒ ~has(x, r)
Valid(a1)

a2: right(r) & transfer(act, r, x, y) ⇒ has(y, r)
Valid(a2)
```

If there is some transfer between *x* and *y* of a right *r*, *x* loses this right (rule a1), and *y* obtains it (rule 1b).

There are, however, necessary conditions for a valid transfer:

```
b1:
 right(r) & transfer(act, r, x, y) &
   ((~∃t)title_for(t, act) ∨
    (title_for(t, act) & ~valid(t))) ⇒
  excluded(a1)
Valid(b1)

b2:
 right(r) & transfer(act, r, x, y) &
   ((~∃t)title_for(t, act) ∨
   (title_for(t, act) & ~valid(t))) ⇒
 excluded(a2)
Valid(b2)
```

If some right is transferred, but there is no title for the transfer, or the title is invalid, then the rules `a1` and `a2` are excluded.

```
c1:
 right(r) & transfer(act, r, x, y) &
  ~has_power(x, act) ⇒ excluded(a1)
Valid(c1)
```

```
c2:
 right(r) & transfer(act, r, x, y) &
  ~has_power(x, act) ⇒ excluded(a2)
Valid(c2)
```

If the transferring person did not have the power to transfer the right, then the rules a1 and a2 are excluded.

```
d1:
 right(r) & transfer(act, r, x, y) &
  ~formalities(act) ⇒ excluded(a1)
Valid(d1)
```

```
d2:
 right(r) & transfer(act, r, x, y) &
  ~formalities(act) ⇒ excluded(a2)
Valid(d2)
```

If the necessary formalities were not performed, then the rules a1 and a2 are excluded.

The necessary conditions for a valid transfer are expressed by means of exclusionary reasons that can block the rule that a transfer implies the transition of the right from the transferring to the receiving party.

However, there can be an exception to one of these exceptions, with as its effect that the receiving party still does obtain the right. As we have already seen (section 6), this exception occurs if the transferring party did not have the power to transfer, and if the rights concerns a mutable good, the receiving party was in good faith, and paid a reasonable price for the right:

```
1_improved:
 right(r) & transfer(act, r, x, y) &
   ~has_power(x, act) & mutable(r) &
   in_good_faith(y) & paid_for(y, r) ⇒
  excluded(c2)
Valid(1_improved)
```

However, if the right concerned a stolen good, the receiving party only becomes owner after three years:

```
3_improved:
 right(r) & transfer(act, r, x, y) &
  ~has_power(x, act) & stolen(r) &
  time_since_theft < 3 ⇒ excluded(1_ improved)
Valid(3_improved)
```

If the rule `3_improved` is applicable to a case, this means that the rule `1_improved` is not applicable to that case anymore, with as a consequence that the rule `c2` becomes applicable again, with as a final consequence that the rule `a2` is not applicable anymore and that the receiving party does not obtain the right. Here we encounter a long sequence of exceptions to exceptions where application of the primary rule (`a2`) is alternatively excluded and reinstated. Cf. figure 1.

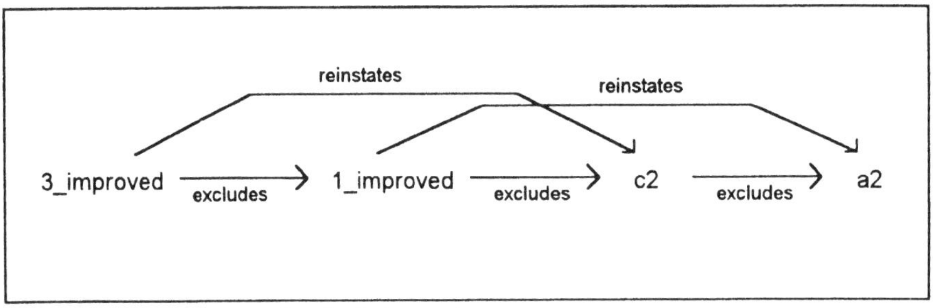

Figure 1: Exclusions and reinstatements

The reader may be interested to learn that in the real Dutch law the chain of exceptions actually contains even two additional links, and that there are more exceptions to the main rule.

8. CONFLICT RULES

A well-known problem in the law occurs when two legal rules conflict. The conflict of principles can be solved by weighing the resulting reasons, but legal rules are esteemed not to conflict because they embody - at least in theory - the result of all conflicting goals and principles (cf. section III.8). If rules nevertheless conflict, this is a problem that is handled by so-called *conflict rules*. Conflict rules indicate which of two legal rules is to apply to a case, if the case satisfies the conditions of both rules, and if the legal consequences of the two rules are incompatible.

Conflict rules can be dedicated to the conflict of particular rules. An example from the Dutch law is the rule of article 7A:1637c of the Civil Code, that says that if a contract has both the characteristics of a labour contract and of another contract, and if the regulations of these two kinds of contracts conflict, the labour regulations prevail over the other ones (cf. Prakken 1993, p. 164).

Better known are general conflict rules, such as Lex Superior (the higher rule prevails over the lower), Lex Specialis (the more specific rule prevails over the less specific), and Lex Posterior (the later rule prevails over the earlier one).

8.1 The formalisation of conflict rules

Let us see how RBL can deal with conflict rules.[12] If two rules of law are in conflict in a particular case, and one of the two prevails over the other, application of the latter rule is excluded:

```
Valid(prevails_over(rule1, rule2, case) &
   in_conflict(rule1, rule2, case) ⊃
  excluded(rule2, case))
```

Conflict rules determine which rule prevails over another one. The rule of article 7A:1637c of the Civil Code can, for instance, be formalised as:

```
Valid(labourcase(case) &
   is_about(rule1, labourcontract) &
   ~is_about(rule2, labourcontract) ⊃
  prevails_over(rule1, rule2, case))
```

(In case of a labour contract, the rules about labour-contracts prevail over the rules that govern contracts of the other type.)

The general conflict rules Lex Specialis, Lex Superior and Lex Posterior, can be formalised as:

```
more_specific(rule1, rule2) ⊃
  prevails_over(rule1, rule2, case)
superior(rule1, rule2) ⊃
  prevails_over(rule1, rule2, case)
more_recent(rule1, rule2) ⊃
  prevails_over(rule1, rule2, case)
```

8.2 When are two rules in conflict?

It remains to be specified when two rules are in conflict. One reason why rules might be in conflict is that they have logically incompatible conclusions, but it is also possible to introduce other notions of rule conflict.

By means the function `ic/2` (cf. section 6.1) it is possible to formulate the following definition of one case of rule conflict:

```
Incompatible(ic(rule1, case), ic(rule2, case)) ⊃
  in_conflict(rule1, rule2, case))
```

[12] Given the logical behaviour of conflict rules, they would better be called conflict principles. Therefore I will formalise conflict rules by means of RBL-principles. Concerning the terminology, however, I will stick to the traditional usage.

That is, two rules are in conflict in a particular case, if the instantiations of their conclusions on the basis of the facts of this case are incompatible. The notion of incompatibility has to be specified by the domain theory (but cf. section VI.3).

8.3 Conflicting conflict rules (1)

Since the conflict rules as formalised are RBL-principles, they generate reasons why one rule prevails over another rule. This means that if two conflict rules have incompatible conclusions, they generate reasons that must be weighed. (Unless, of course, one of the two is excluded by the application of the other one.) Consider the following example about the case `chopping`:

```
exercise_right:
 right(r) & exercise(action, r) ⇒ pd(x, action))
Valid(exercise_right)
```

(If some action type is an exercise of a right, this action type is permitted. This rule formulates the strong permission to exercise ones rights. Cf. section II.18.5))

```
tree_chopping: true ⇒ ~pd(x, chop_tree))
Valid(tree_chopping)
```

(It is forbidden to chop trees.)

```
Right(ownership(tree)) &
 Exercise(chop_tree, ownership(tree))
```

(The ownership of a tree is a right, and the chopping of this tree is an exercise of this right.)

The rule `exercise_right` is superior to the rule `tree_chopping`, which is presumably based on a by-law. On the other hand `tree_chopping` is more specific than `exercise_right`:

```
Superior(exercise_right, tree_chopping)
More_specific(tree_chopping, exercise_right)
```

As a consequence we have both a reason why the rule `exercise_right` prevails over the rule `tree_chopping`, and a reason why it is exactly the other way round:

```
R(more_specific(tree_chopping, exercise_right),
 prevails_over(tree_chopping, exercise_right, chopping))
R(superior(exercise_right, tree_chopping),
 prevails_over(exercise_right, tree_chopping, chopping))
```

Presently we have two reasons that intuitively are in conflict, but which seem logically independent, that is a reason why the rule `exercise_right` prevails over the rule `tree_chopping`, and a reason why the latter rule prevails over the former. To make the implicit conflict explicit, I propose to adopt the principle that if two states of affairs are incompatible, a reason for the one state of affairs is a reason against the other (cf. also section VI.3):

```
Valid(incompatible(state1, state2) ⊃
 r(reason, state1) → r(reason, ~state2))
```

Let us also add the intuitively attractive information that the states of affairs that in a particular case both one rule prevails over another and also the other way round, are incompatible:

```
(∀r1)(∀r2)(∀c)Incompatible(
 prevails_over(r1, r2, c) & prevails_over(r2, r1, c))
```

On the basis of this principle and this information, we have:

```
R(more_specific(tree_chopping, exercise_right),
 ~prevails_over(
    exercise_right, tree_chopping, chopping))
```

(That the rule `tree_chopping` is more specific than the rule `exercise_right`, is a reason why the latter rule does not prevail over the former.)

The relevant sets of reasons concerning the issue which rule prevails over which rule then become:

```
reasons(
 prevails_over(exercise_right, tree_chopping,
    chopping)) =
 {superior(exercise_right, tree_chopping)}
reasons(~ prevails_over(exercise_right, tree_chopping,
    chopping)) =
 {more_specific(tree_chopping, exercise_right)}
```

Given these sets of reasons, the following weighing knowledge may cut the knot:

```
(∀r1)(∀r2){superior(r1, r2)} > {more_specific(r2, r1)}
```

(Superiority of a rule is more important than specificity.)

Given this weighing knowledge, we find that the rule `exercise_right` prevails over the rule `tree_chopping`. The action of John is therefore allowed.

8.4 Conflicting conflict rules (2)

We have seen that it is possible to deal with a conflict of conflict rules by adding weighing knowledge that deals with the conflict of reasons that were generated by the conflict rules. Another possibility is that the application of one of the conflict rules generates a reason that excludes the application of the other conflict rule. It is for instance possible to have the rule that a human right not only excludes all conflicting rules, but also all conflict rules that theoretically might override it. Such a rule would in RBL be represented by the following two principles:

```
Valid(human_right(r1) & ~human_right(r2) ⊃
 prevails_over(r1, r2, case))
Valid(human_right(r1) & ~human_right(r2) &
   ic(r3, case) = prevails_over(r2, r1, case) ⊃
 excluded(r3, case))
```

The first of these two principles says that a rule (or principle) that expresses a human right normally prevails over a rule (or principle) that does not express a human right. The second principle says that if a conflict rule in some case dictates another prevalence relation, this conflict rule is in that case excluded.

These last examples show how the mechanisms of RBL to deal with conflicts, weighing reasons and the exclusion of rules, are not only available on the bottom level of 'normal' rules, but also on the 'meta-level' of conflict rules. In theory, the number of argument levels can be extended infinitely, and the same mechanisms of RBL will do their jobs on all of these levels.

9. REASONING ABOUT WEIGHTS

Whether one set of reasons outweighs the other set, or just the other way round, needs not solely depend on the reasons and the conclusion for or against which they plead. It is also possible that there are other facts which, although they are not reasons for or against a particular conclusion themselves, influence the relative weight of the concerned sets of reasons.

9.1 An example

Such a situation is illustrated by the following real life example (Kantongerecht Rotterdam, June 12th, 1985). A small supermarket had to dismiss one of its employees for financial reasons. For this dismissal, the allowance of a judge was necessary. One of the employees, called Mary, has been longer in service, and this is a reason for the judge not to permit to dismiss her.

```
R(longer_in_service(mary), ~pd(employer, dismiss(mary)))
```

The other employee, called Richard, has better papers for the job, and this is a reason not to dismiss him.

```
R(better_papers(richard),
 ~pd(employer, dismiss(richard)))
```

Since it is clear that one of the employees has to be dismissed for financial reasons, a reason against permitting the dismissal of Richard is also a reason for permitting the dismissal of Mary. This leads to the following sets of reasons:

```
reasons(pd(employer, dismiss(mary))) =
 {better_papers(richard)}
reasons(~pd(employer, dismiss(mary))) =
 {longer_in_service(mary)}
```

The judge decided that, although Richard had better papers for the job, Mary was still sufficiently qualified, so that the better papers did not count for much. The fact that Mary had been longer in service should therefore tip the balance of reasons:

```
R( suitable_for_job(mary),
 {longer_in_service(mary)} > {better_papers(richard)})
```

and therefore:

```
~Pd(employer, dismiss(mary))
```

Notice that the fact that Mary was suitable for the job was not considered as a reason no to dismiss her, but only as a reason why the seniority of Mary outweighs the better papers of Richard.

9.2 Case-based reasoning as a way to reason about relative weights

One important function of case law is to indicate how sets of reasons are to be weighed against each other. A case that has already been decided can be seen as containing both a set of reasons that pleads for a particular decision, a set of reasons that pleads against this decision, and the decision about the issue, which is also a decision about which set of reasons outweighs the other set.[13] In this connection the following functions may be used:

```
reasons_for(decision, case) =def.
 {f: obtains(f, case) & r(f, decision)}
reasons_against(decision, case) =def.
 {f: obtains(f, case) & r(f, ~decision)}
```

[13] In section 11.2, I will use a similar line of reasoning to determine on the basis of legislative history whether a case falls under the purpose of a rule.

`decision(issue, case)` stands for the decision in the case `case` on the issue `issue`, that is either `issue`, or `~issue`.

If we can find a case in which some decision was taken, this is a reason why the reasons in that case that pleaded for this decision, outweigh the reasons in that case that pleaded against that decision. In this connection we can distinguish five situations. In all of them I assume that the issue at stake is the same for the case that was already decided, and for the new case.[14] Let `old` stand for the case that was already decided, and let `new` stand for the case at hand. Given these abbreviations, the following situations and their consequences can be distinguished[15] [16]:

SITUATION 1

```
reasons_for(issue, old) = reasons_for(issue, new)
reasons_against(issue, old) =
 reasons_against(issue, new)
decision(issue, old) =  issue
```

In this situation there is a reason why

```
decision(issue, new) = issue
```

because the situations are completely identical insofar as the reasons are concerned.

SITUATION 2

```
reasons_for(issue, old) ⊂ reasons_for(issue, new)
reasons_against(issue, old) ⊇
 reasons_against(issue, new)
decision(issue, old) =  issue
```

In this situation there is a reason why

```
decision(issue, new) = issue
```

because in the new case there are only more reasons that plead for `issue`.

---

14 A sub-decision in a case can in this connection be considered as a case by itself. Cf. Branting 1991.

15 The situations 3 and 4, and 2 and 5 are each others mirrors. Notice, moreover, that the symbol ⊃ in the description of these situations stands for the superset-relation, and not for a principle.

16 The distinctions between the situations and the consequences attached to the distinctions were inspired by the HYPO-system for case-based reasoning. Cf. Ashley 1991.

SITUATION 3

```
reasons_for(issue, old) ⊆ reasons_for(issue, new)
reasons_against(issue, old) ⊃
 reasons_against(issue, new)
decision(issue, old) =  issue
```

In this situation there is a reason why

```
decision(issue, new) = issue
```

because in the new case there are only less reasons that plead against `issue`.

SITUATION 4

```
reasons_for(issue, old) ⊃ reasons_for(issue, new)
reasons_against(issue, old) ⊆
 reasons_against(issue, new)
decision(issue, old) =  ~issue
```

In this situation there is a reason why

```
decision(issue, new) = ~issue
```

because in the new case there are only less reasons that plead for `issue`.

SITUATION 5

```
reasons_for(issue, old) ⊇ reasons_for(issue, new)
reasons_against(issue, old) ⊂
 reasons_against(issue, new)
decision(issue, old) =  issue
```

In this situation there is a reason why

```
decision(issue, new) = ~issue
```

because in the new case there are only more reasons that plead against `issue`.

These different situations are based on an underlying style of reasoning concerning the accrual of reasons. I will return to this style of reasoning in section VI.1.

10. REASONS AGAINST THE APPLICATION OF A RULE

RBL considers the application of a rule as a kind of action and as a consequence makes it possible to adduce reasons for and against this action (cf. the sections III.9 and 10). It is up to the domain theory to specify what counts as a reason to apply a rule, and what as a reason against applying a rule. The only exception is that RBL has the principle (embodied in R5) that if it can be derived that a rule is applicable, this applicability is a reason for applying the rule.

The sentence that a rule is to be applied `Ob(applies(rule))` is a 'normal' sentence that can be the result of a derivation. This makes it possible to derive that a rule is not to be applied, even if its conditions are satisfied, and that a rule is to be applied, even if its conditions are not (all) satisfied. The first case will normally be one where application would be against the rule's purpose. The second case, where a rule is to be applied even though not all of its conditions are satisfied, will normally be a case of analogous rule application. I will start my discussion with the first case.

In the law, the fact that application of a rule is against its purpose is a reason not to apply the rule. A theory might therefore contain the sentence:

```
Valid(against_purpose(rule, applies(rule)) ⊃
 ob(~applies(rule)))
```

Let me illustrate the use of this principle by means of an example borrowed from Fuller (1958). There is a rule that forbids to sleep in the railway station. This rule has the purpose to prevent tramps from occupying the station as a place to spend the night. An old lady that wants to meet a friend at the station dozes off when the evening trains turns out to be retarded. Should the prohibition apply to this lady?

The following sentences summarily describe the situation:

```
sleep_prohibition:
 true ⇒ ~pd(x, sleep_in_railway_station)
Valid(sleep_prohibition)
Against_purpose(sleep_prohibition,
 applies(sleep_prohibition))
```

In this situation we can derive:

```
R(applicable(sleep_prohibition),
 ob(applies(sleep_prohibition)))
R(against_purpose(sleep_prohibition,
   applies(sleep_prohibition)),
  ob(~applies(sleep_prohibition)))
```

(The fact that the rule `sleep-prohibition` is applicable, is a reason to apply it, while the fact that application would be against the rule's purpose is a reason not to apply it.)

Let us, moreover, assume that it is incompatible that some state of affairs both ought and ought not to be the case (cf. section VI.3):

```
(∀state)Incompatible(ob(state), ob(~state))
```

So a reason why a rule ought to be applied is ipso fact a reason against the conclusion that this rule ought not to be applied, and the other way round.

As a consequence we have:

```
reasons(ob(applies(sleep_prohibition))) =
  {applicable(sleep_prohibition)}
reasons(~ob(applies(sleep_prohibition))) =
  {against_purpose(sleep_prohibition,
    applies(sleep_prohibition))}
```

On the basis of the additional information:

```
{against_purpose(sleep_prohibition,
   applies(sleep_prohibition))} >
  {applicable(sleep_prohibition)}
```

we can derive

```
~Ob(applies(sleep_prohibition))
```

Because it is not the case that the rule `sleeping_prohibition` ought to be applied, there is no reason why the old lady's sleeping was forbidden.

11. REASONING BY ANALOGY AND THE E CONTRARIO ARGUMENT

RBL makes it possible that there are other reasons to apply a rule than the applicability of the rule. In practice, this possibility will only be used to realise rule application by analogy. However, not all cases of reasoning by analogy turn out to be cases in which a rule is applied even though its conditions are not satisfied. In fact, I will distinguish three different ways of constructing reasoning by analogy (cf. also section III.11 and Verheij and Hage 1994).

The first way of constructing reasoning by analogy is to say that instead of the non-applicable rule an underlying principle is applied. The second way is to say that the original rule is applied, even though its conditions are not all satisfied. And the third way, finally, is to say that a new, more concrete principle is applied, the use of which is justified on the basis of the goals and principles that underlie the non-applicable rule. I will discuss these three constructions in turn. To finish the discussion of analogous rule application, I will also briefly discuss the opposite of analogous rule application, that is the argument e contrario.

Let us reconsider the example of the rented house that was donated, rather than sold. Can the rule about the sale of rented house rule be applied analogously to the donation of a rented house?

11.1 Applying an underlying principle

The first step in considering the analogous application of a rule is to ascertain that the rule cannot be applied normally, for instance by extensive interpretation. I will assume that in the case at hand the original rule

```
sale: sold(rented_house) ⇒ binds(contract, new_owner)
```

is not applicable, because its conditions are not satisfied. Instead of `Sold(rented_house)` we have `Donated(rented_house)`.

The non-applicability of the rule brings with it that its underlying goal and principle are not excluded. These are that renters are to be protected, and that contracts bind only the parties involved[17]:

```
rent_protection:
 contributes_to(state, rent_protection) ⊃ ob(state)
limited_scope_contracts:
 ~party(x, contract) ⊃ ob(~binds(contract, x))
```

Since these principles are not excluded, they give rise to both a reason for and against continuation of the rent contract:

```
R(contributes_to(
   binds(contract, new_owner), rent_protection),
  ob(binds(contract, new_owner)))
R(~party(new_owner, contract),
  ob(~binds(contract, new_owner)))
```

These same reasons have probably also been taken into account by the legislator when he made the rule `sale`. The fact that this rule protected the renters of the house at the cost of the new owner, is a reason why the reason for continuation of the rent contract outweighs the reason against. So we may assume that:

```
{contributes_to(
   binds(contract, new_owner), rent_protection)} >
 {~party(new_owner, rent_contract)}
```

On the basis of this weighing knowledge and the principle `deontic_collapse` (cf. the intermezzo in section 6.3):

---

17 In case of the goal, I only mention the principle that is based on it. Cf. the sections IV.6 and 7.

```
deontic_collapse:
 r(reason, ob(state)) &
   legal_point_of_view(state) ⊃
  r(reason, state)
```

we can also conclude for the new case, in which the house was donated, that:

```
Binds(contract, new_owner)
```

So the conclusion of the original rule also holds for the new case in which the house was not sold, but rather donated. However, this conclusion was not based on the rule, but on its underlying principle and goal.

11.2 Applying a non-applicable rule

We have seen that if a rule is not applicable, its underlying goals and principles gain force again. As a consequence, the reasons that the legislator had to adopt the rule play their role again, but now in a different setting. For the legislator, these reasons were reasons to adopt a particular legal rule, because the way for the legislator to achieve his goals and to do what he has reason to do is by means of legislation.

In a context of legal decision making for a concrete case, these very same reasons become reasons for a different kind of behaviour, namely for making a particular legal decision. However, the import of the reasons is still the same. The limited scope of contracts is still a valid principle, and the interests of house renters are still to be protected.

One means to follow this principle and to pursue this goal is to take a decision that is in line with the balance of reasons that was originally struck by the legislator. If one thinks that this balance is also right for a (slightly) different case, one can take the same course of action, at least to the extent that this is possible. If the decision maker is of the opinion that in a particular concrete case, the balance of reasons is essentially the same as when the legislator drafted the rule, he may decide to apply the rule made by the legislator, even if its conditions are not all satisfied.

Of course, if the balance of reasons is approximately the same, the facts of the case will probably approximately satisfy the rule conditions, and the case will be 'similar' to the ones in which the rule is applicable. That is why we speak of 'analogous application' of the rule. It is, however, not the analogy that justifies the application of the rule, but the balance of reasons that are involved in the case at hand, and its essential identity to the balance of reasons that lead the legislator to making the rule.

This same balance of reasons is why the present case falls under the purpose of the rule, which is to protect the interest of house renters, despite the fact that a contract is made to bind a non-party. That the case falls under the purpose of the rule is in its turn a reason to apply the rule to that case.

This leads us to the formulation of a new principle about rule application:

```
purpose_rule:
 within_purpose(rule, case) ⊃ ob(applies(rule, case))
```
[18]

If in a case the same reasons are involved that were also taken into consideration in making a rule, this is a reason to assume that this case falls under the purpose of that rule. In fact, the weighing of reasons by the legislator can be compared to the weighing of reasons in an earlier court decision. Our findings of section 9.2 can therefore be applied analogously, with the conclusion that a case falls within the purpose of a rule.

Let `rule_conclusion` be the instantiated conclusion of the rule that might be applied analogously, and let

```
reasons_for(rule_conclusion, legislation)
```

stand for the set of reasons considered during legislation that pleaded for the thesis `rule_conclusion`.

Let

```
reasons_against(rule_conclusion, legislation)
```

stand for the set of reasons considered during legislation that pleaded against the thesis `rule_conclusion`.

Let

```
reasons_for(rule_conclusion, case)
```

stand for the set of reasons in the present case that plead for the thesis `rule_conclusion`.

Let

```
reasons_against(rule_conclusion, case)
```

stand for the set of reasons in the present case that plead against the thesis `rule_conclusion`.

---

[18] Theoretically it is the instantiated rule that ought to be applied. This can be formalised by means of the functions `iconds/2` and `ic/2` (cf. section 6.1). I skip this complication to keep the example relatively simple.

Then it holds that if

```
reasons_for(rule_conclusion, legislation) ⊆
 reasons_for(rule_conclusion, case)
```

(The reasons for the conclusion of the rule as considered during the legislative process are a subset of the reasons for this same conclusion which obtain in the present case)

and

```
reasons_against(rule_conclusion, case) ⊆
 reasons_against(rule_conclusion, legislation)
```

(The reasons against the conclusion of the rule which obtain in the present case are a subset of the reasons for this same conclusion as considered during the legislative process)

this is a reason why the case falls within the purpose of the rule.

In our example it holds that:

```
reasons_for(binds(contract, new_owner), legislation) =
 reasons_for(binds(contract, new_owner), present_case) =
 {contributes_to(
   binds(contract, new_owner), rent_protection}

reasons_against(binds(contract, new_owner),legislation)=
 reasons_against(
  binds(contract, new_owner), present_case) =
 {~party(new_owner, contract)}
```

Because the sets of reasons are identical, it holds that:

```
Within_purpose(present_case, sale)
R(within_purpose(present_case, sale),
 ob(applies(sale, present_case)))
Ob(applies(sale, present_case))
Binds(contract, new_owner)
```

This illustrates how a rule can be applied to a case, even though it is not applicable.

11.3 Reasoning for a new rule

Application of the rule `sale`, which was originally written for the sale of rented houses, to all transfers of rented houses has the effect that in all cases where a rented house is transferred, the rent contract is continued with the new owner. The same effect can also be obtained by adopting a new rule to the effect that if a rented house is transferred, the rent contract is continued with the new owner. That this effect can be obtained by adopting this new rule may be considered as a reason why this new rule ought to be valid.

Let us call this new rule `transfer`. The crucial argument leading to the conclusion that this rule ought to be valid can be represented as follows:

```
R(contributes_to(binds(contract, new_owner),
  rent_protection),
 ob(binds(contract, new_owner)))
R(~party(new_owner, contract),
 ob(~binds(contract, new_owner))
{contributes_to(binds(contract, new_owner),
 rent_protection)} >
 {~party(new_owner, rent_contract)}
```

therefore

```
Ob(binds(contract, new_owner))
```

To derive from this intermediary conclusion that the rule ought to be valid that if a rented house is transferred, the rent contract is continued with the new owner, an additional principle is needed:

```
Valid(ob(state1) & contributes_to(state2, state1) ⊃
 ob(state2))
```

(If some state of affairs ought to be the case, and some other state of affairs contributes to the first state of affairs, then this is a reason why the second state of affairs also ought to be the case.)[19]

Given this additional principle and the information that

```
Contributes_to(
 valid(transferred(rented_house) ⇒
  binds(contract, new_owner)),
 binds(contract, new_owner))
```

the conclusion

```
Ob(valid(transferred(rented_house) ⇒
 binds(contract, new_owner)))
```

(The rule that if a rented house is transferred, the rent contract binds the new owner ought to be valid)

can be derived.

This conclusion is sufficient to base reasons on the 'new' rule (cf. R4)

---

19 Cf. also section III.5.9 on the relation of goals and subgoals.

```
Ob(applies(transferred(rented_house) ⇒
 binds(contract, new_owner)))
```

In combination with

```
Donated(rented_house) → Transferred(rented_house)
```

it can be derived that also in the case of donation of the house, the rent contract will be continued with the new owner.

This example ends the discussion of the analogous application of rules. We have seen that the interplay between legal rules and the principles and goals on which they are based provides the possibility for at least three different reconstructions of reasoning by analogy. Only in one of these cases, the rule is applied analogously. In the other two cases, the solution is either found by the direct application of the underlying goals and principles, or by the 'derivation' of a new rule that is tailor-made for the case at hand.

11.4 The e contrario argument

Sometimes, if a rule is not applicable, this is used as a reason why the legal consequences of this rule do not take effect. Suppose, for instance, that there would not be a rule about the sale of rented houses, but rather a rule about the donation of rented houses:

```
donation:
 donated(rented_house) ⇒ binds(contract, new_owner)
Valid(donation)
```

If we would then encounter a case in which a rented house is sold, it would not be bad reasoning to conclude that the rent contract is not continued with the new owner. This line of reasoning, where from the non-satisfaction of the rule conditions is concluded to the denial of the rule conclusion, is called an *e contrario* argument.

How can the occurrence of this type of reasoning be explained? One possible explanation would be that if a rule is not applicable in a case, this is a reason against having the legal consequences of the rule. With this I do not only mean that the consequences of the rule do not take effect, but also that the opposite conclusion 'takes effect'. So in the case of `donation` it is not only concluded that the legal consequence that the rent contract is continued does not take effect, but also that the continuation does *not* take place. In the formalism of RBL this would amount to:

```
R(~applicable(
   icond(rule, case) ⇒ ic(rule, case), case),
 ~ ic(rule, case))
```

The principle underlying such a reason would certainly be too strong, because in many cases the non-applicability of a rule does not provide a reason against the conclusion of that rule. For instance, the fact that a rule concerning punishability for theft is not applicable in a case of murder, is not a reason against the punishability of the murderer on the basis of some other rule.

To explain the argument e contrario, we must, I think, refer to the principles and goals that underlie the non-applicable rule (cf. section III.12). If a rented house is sold, the non-applicability of the rule `donation` makes that the goal `rent_protection`, and the principle `limited_scope_contracts` regain their relevance. They generate respectively a reason for and a reason against continuation of the rent contract.

However, if a rented house has been sold, there are more reasons to protect the new owner than if it had been donated.[20] As a consequence, the balance of reasons in case the house was sold may be different than the balance in case the house was donated. In fact, the balance may now be in the advantage of the new owner, so that the conclusion follows that the rent contract is not continued. This is precisely the outcome of the e contrario argument. In this view, however, the argument e contrario is not a special kind of rule application, but rather the application of the rule's underlying principles and goals.

12. REASONING ABOUT THE VALIDITY OF RULES

Since, from an RBL-point of view, rules are individuals, and not sentences, they cannot stand on their own in a theory of RBL. Moreover, only a valid rule (or one which ought to be valid) can be used in a derivation. These two facts together are the reason why rules are introduced into arguments by means of the statement that they are, or ought to be, valid. This has the additional advantage that it becomes possible to 'derive rules', because to derive a rule it is only necessary to derive the statement that it is, or ought to be, valid.

RBL does not specify from which premises it can be derived that a rule is valid. In fact, it completely depends on the domain which criteria are used to determine the validity of rules (cf. Toulmin 1958, pp. 36f. and 104 on the field dependence of backings). In the following subsections, I will discuss a number of examples.

---

20 This is why I changed the example to have the rule `donation`, rather than `sale`.

12.1 Rules of recognition

According to Hart, a rule is a valid rule of law, if it is identified as such by a rule of recognition (Hart 1961, pp. 92f.). An example of such a rule of recognition would be that a rule is a valid rule of law if it was made by the legislator. In RBL such a rule of recognition is expressed as follows:

```
Valid(adopted_by_legislator(rule) ⇒ valid(rule))
Adopted_by_legislator(statutory_rule)
```

From these two sentences it is possible to derive (the validity of) `statutory_rule`:

```
Valid(statutory_rule)
```

12.2 Interpretation

Another way to argue about the validity of a rule has to do with the interpretation of a legal source. Take for instance the rule that women and children under sixteen are not allowed to partake in the rodeo (cf. section III.5.4). This rule formulation is syntactically ambiguous, because at first sight it is not clear whether women over fifteen are allowed to partake. There are two possible interpretations of the rule formulation, only one of which expresses a valid rule:

```
rodeo1:
  woman(x) ∨ (child(x) & under_sixteen(x)) ⇒
   ~pd(x, partake_in_rodeo))
rodeo2:
  (woman(x) ∨ child(x)) & under_sixteen(x) ⇒
    ~pd(x, partake_in_rodeo))
```

Clearly the second interpretation (`rodeo2`) does not make much sense, because on this interpretation the condition that somebody is a woman is completely superfluous. This is a reason why the second interpretation does not expresses a valid rule.

```
R( superfluous(condition_woman, rodeo2), ~valid(rodeo2))
```

On the basis of this reason it can be derived that the rule `rodeo2` is not valid. Moreover if there are only two seemingly acceptable interpretations, the rejection of interpretation 2 forms a reason to accept interpretation 1:

```
R( ~valid(rodeo2), valid(rodeo1))
```

This leads to the final conclusion that the rule expressed in the first interpretation (`rodeo1`) is a valid one:

```
Valid(rodeo1)
```

12.3 Principles of interpretation

The law knows a number of traditional reasons that can be adduced in arguments about the interpretation of statutory rules (cf. MacCormick and Summers 1991). These reasons are connected to 'maxims of interpretation', such as that the law should be interpreted according the normal meaning of its wordings, according to the historical intention of the legislator, according to the interests of society, or according to the system of the law. These maxims can in RBL be represented as principles that generate reasons why particular rules are valid ones. Take, for instance, the following principle that says that a rule is correctly interpreted if the interpretation is in accordance with the intentions of the legislator as they become clear from the preparatory works:

```
genetic_interpretation:
 interpretation_of(text, rule) &
   in_accordance_with(rule, intention_legislator) ⊃
  correct_interpretation_of(text, rule)
```

Moreover, the correct interpretation of a legal source is in principle a valid rule:

```
source_validity:
 legal_source(text) &
   correct_interpretation_of(text, rule) ⊃
  valid(rule)
```

Historical, grammatical and systematic interpretation can be dealt with by similar principles of interpretation:

```
historical_interpretation:
 interpretation_of(text, rule) &
   in_accordance_with(rule, history_of_the_law) ⊃
  correct_interpretation_of(text, rule)

grammatical_interpretation:
 interpretation_of(text, rule) &
   in_accordance_with(rule, literal_meaning_of(text)) ⊃
  correct_interpretation_of(text, rule)
```

```
systematic_interpretation:
 interpretation_of(text, rule) &
   in_accordance_with(rule, system_of_the_law) ⊃
  correct_interpretation_of(text, rule)
```

It is well-known that different maxims of interpretation can lead to different interpretations. Suppose that a particular text `statutory_text` has two reasonable interpretations, `rule_1` and `rule_2`, and that the first interpretation is supported by grammatical interpretation of the text, while the second interpretation is supported by genetic interpretation:

```
R( interpretation_of(statutory_text, rule_1) &
    in_accordance_with(rule_1,
     literal_meaning_of(statutory_text)),
  correct_interpretation_of(statutory_text, rule_1))
R( interpretation_of(statutory_text, rule_2) &
    in_accordance_with(rule_2, intention_legislator),
  correct_interpretation_of(statutory_text, rule_2))
```

Moreover, two different interpretations of one text are incompatible. Therefore a reason for one interpretation is a reason against the other interpretation. So if we have

```
Incompatible(
 correct_interpretation_of(statutory_text, rule_1),
 correct_interpretation_of(statutory_text, rule_2))
```

we can derive that:

```
reasons(
   correct_interpretation_of(statutory_text, rule_1)) =
 {interpretation_of(statutory_text, rule_1) &
  in_accordance_with(rule_1,
   literal_meaning_of(statutory_text))}

reasons(
   ~correct_interpretation_of(statutory_text, rule_1)) =
 {interpretation_of(statutory_text, rule_2) &
  in_accordance_with(rule_2, intention_legislator)}
```

To solve this conflict of reasons, we can use the weighing knowledge that in the case of old statutes the literal meaning of the text is more important than the intention of the legislator:

```
Valid(old_statute(text) ⊃
 {interpretation_of(text, rule) &
   in_accordance_with(rule, literal_meaning_of(text))} >
 {interpretation_of(text, rule) &
  in_accordance_with(rule, intention_legislator)}
 )
```

On the basis of this weighing knowledge, we can derive that

```
Correct_interpretation_of(statutory_text, rule_1)
```

If `statutory_text` is a legal source, the conclusion that directly follows from this on the basis of `source_validity` is:

```
Valid(rule_1)
```

12.4 Case-based interpretations

Case law is an important source of reasons for and against interpretations of legal texts. If in a case a particular interpretation of a statutory regulation has been adopted, this is a reason why this interpretation is the 'correct' one. Analogously, the rejection of an interpretation is a reason against this interpretation. So we have the principle of legal precedent:

```
legal_precedent:
 (∃c)case(c) & content(decision(c)) =
    correct_interpretation_of(source, rule) ⊃
  correct_interpretation_of(source, rule))
Valid(legal_precedent)
```

(If there is a case in which it is decided that the correct interpretation of a particular source is some rule, this is a reason why this rule is the correct interpretation of that source.)

Remember that this is no more than a principle that generates reasons which may be outweighed by other reasons. If there is only one relevant case, it leads to only one reason concerning the interpretation of the legal source, and this one reason will probably be decisive in the sense that the interpretation of the previous case is a sufficient reason to adopt this interpretation for future cases. However, it is possible that in different cases, different interpretations of a source have been adopted:

```
content(decision(new_case)) =
 correct_interpretation_of(source, rule_1)
content(decision(old_case)) =
 correct_interpretation_of(source, rule_2)
```

If we also have

```
(∀source)(∀rule_1)(∀rule_2)
 rule_1 ≠ rule_2 →
  Incompatible(
   correct_interpretation_of(source, rule_1),
   correct_interpretation_of(source, rule_2))
```

we must make a decision which court decision concerning the interpretation of `source` is to be preferred. One good reason in this connection is that recent cases prevail over old ones:

```
Valid(
 recent(decision(c1)) & old(decision(c2)) ⊃
  prevails_over(decision(c1), decision(c2)))
```

If the contents of two decisions are incompatible, and one of the decisions prevails over the other, this is a reason why the reason based on the prevailing decision outweighs the reason based on the other decision:

```
Valid(
 Incompatible(
     content(decision(c1)), content(decision(c2))) &
    prevails_over(decision(c1), decision(c2)) ⊃
   {case(c1) & content(decision(c1)) = a} >
    {case(c2) & content(decision(c2)) = b} )
```

Another good reason why a decision prevails over another one is that decisions of superior courts prevail over decisions of inferior courts:

```
Valid(
  superior_to(
   court_of(decision(c2)),
   court_of(decision(c1))) ⊃
  prevails_over(decision(c1), decision(c2)) )
```

If only one of these (or other) reasons is present to prefer a particular court decision above another one, this decision will provide us with the reason to prefer a particular interpretation of the source. For instance, if one court is superior, while both decisions are approximately equally recent, the decision of the superior court will be preferred and the interpretation of this court will be chosen.

If, however, one court is superior, while the decision of the other court is more recent, we must weigh reasons about which court decision to adopt. Suppose that if there have been changes in society that are relevant for the issue at stake, the most recent decision is to be preferred, while if there were no such changes, the superiority is decisive. In that case, we will have the following reasons:

```
R( relevant_changes,
  {recent(decision(new_case)) &
    old(decision(old_case))} >
  {superior_to(
     court_of(decision(old_case)),
     court_of(decision(new_case))
   )})
```

(If there have been relevant changes in society, the fact that one decision is more recent than another outweighs the hierarchical relation between the courts.)

```
R( ~relevant_changes,
  {superior_to(
     court_of(decision(old_case)),
     court_of(decision(new_case))
   )} >
  {recent(decision(new_case)) & old(decision(old_case))})
```

(If, however, there have been no relevant changes in society, the hierarchical relation between the courts outweighs the fact that one decision is more recent than another.)

Suppose that there have been relevant changes. In that case, the more recent case will be adopted as authoritative for the interpretation:

```
Prevails_over(decision(new_case), decision(old_case))
```

This leads us to the conclusion that the interpretation of the more recent decision `(decision(new_case))` is the correct one:

```
Correct_interpretation_of(source, rule_1)
```

and that the rule that was decided for in that case is valid:

```
Valid(rule_1)
```

This extended example not only shows how cases can serve as the justification for preferring one interpretation above another one, but also how it is possible to weigh reasons about the issue how reasons (for some other conclusion) ought to be weighed. With this example the chapter on applications of RBL is closed.

VI. CONCLUDING OBSERVATIONS

The first three chapters of this book introduced the issue of reasoning with rules and provided a jurisprudential analysis of it. In the chapters IV and V, RBL was introduced and its facilities for dealing with the several aspects of legal reasoning were illustrated. In this concluding chapter I will attempt to tie some remaining strings together.

The chapter is divided into four parts. Part A deals with some possible amendments to RBL. Part B returns to the difference between rules and statements through a discussion of directions of fit and a proposal for a special semantics for rules and principles. Part C compares RBL with some of its alternatives. The comparison focuses on topics which are in particular relevant for reasoning with rules. And finally, part D returns to the semantic notion of validity and its unsuitability for rules. It proposes an alternative in the form of the pragmatic notion of validity. Both notions of validity are connected to an underlying metaphor of valid reasoning.

A. POSSIBLE AMENDMENTS TO REASON-BASED LOGIC

RBL as described in the previous two chapters is a logic that can deal with the demands that are imposed by the characteristics of reasoning with rules (cf. section III.16). These demands do not dictate RBL; it would have been possible to develop a different - although I think, related - logic that would also do the job. In part A of this chapter I want to discuss some possible changes to RBL.

1. THE ACCRUAL OF REASONS

If we know that a set of reasons outweighs another set, and the stronger set is only strengthened by adding new reasons, it seems reasonable that the result will also outweigh its unchanged (or even weakened) rival. And analogously, if a set of reasons is outweighed by another set, and this set is weakened by deleting one or more reasons from it, the resulting set will also be outweighed by the other set that remained the same or was even strengthened.

Formally these principles look as follows:

strengthening_of_reasons:
$(\texttt{reasons1} > \texttt{reasons2})_{\texttt{conclusion}}$ & $\texttt{reasons1} \subseteq \texttt{reasons3} \supset$
  $(\texttt{reasons3} > \texttt{reasons2})_{\texttt{conclusion}}$

(If a set of reasons outweighs another set, this is a reason why a superset of the first set will also outweigh the last set.)

```
weakening_of_reasons:
(reasons1 > reasons2)conclusion & reasons3 ⊆ reasons2 ⊃
  (reasons1 > reasons3)conclusion
```

(If a set of reasons outweighs another set, this is a reason why a subset of the last set will also be outweighed by the first set.)

It may be questioned whether these principles hold unconditionally. Take for instance the following case: If it is raining this is a reason not to go out jogging. If the weather is hot, this is also a reason not to go out jogging. But if it is both hot and raining, this is a reason to go out jogging.[1] As this example shows, the facts that it is hot and that it is raining together provide less support for the conclusion that I should not go out jogging than each of the facts taken individually would have provided. It seems that the accrual of reasons does not hold in this situation.

This appearance is in my opinion deceptive. If it is raining, the normal connection between the temperature and going out jogging does not hold. And if it is hot, the normal connection between rain and jogging does not hold either. Therefore the fact that it is raining should be considered as an exclusionary reason against application of the principle that if it is hot, one should not go out jogging. And analogously, the fact that it is hot is an exclusionary reason against application of the principle that if it is raining, one should not go out jogging. And finally, the principle holds that if it is both hot and raining, one should go out jogging. Formally the case looks as follows:

```
Valid(raining ⊃ ob(~jogging))
Valid(hot ⊃ ob(~jogging))
Valid(raining ⊃ excluded(hot ⊃ ob(~jogging)))
Valid(hot ⊃ excluded(raining ⊃ ob(~jogging)))
Valid(hot & raining ⊃ ob(jogging))
Hot & Raining
```

In this case there is only one reason regarding the issue of jogging:

```
R(hot & raining ⊃ ob(jogging))
```

and the case provides no counter-example to the accrual of reasons.

Nevertheless it may be doubted whether the accrual of reasons holds unconditionally. Since the accrual of reasons is formulated as a set of principles the application of which can be excluded, it remains possible to formulate explicit exceptions to the accrual of reasons in a domain theory. Therefore, it seems perfectly possible to add `strengthening_of_reasons` and `weakening_of_reasons` to RBL.

---

1 This example was suggested to me by Prakken.

2. DEONTIC COLLAPSE AND DEONTIC INFLATION

There are three rules of derivation in RBL that deal with deontic collapse. R2 and R4 allow the use of principles, respectively rules in making derivations, not only if they are valid, but also if they *ought to be* valid. R6 allows the derivation of a rule's conclusion, not if the rule is applied, but if it *ought to be* applied. All three rules might have been different.[2]

From a logical perspective, it would have been more attractive to use only rules and principles which are actually valid. However, we have seen in the sections III.5.3 and 5.9 that also rules, principles and goals which ought to be accepted (valid), can be used in arguments. It would have been possible to consider this as domain knowledge and leave it out of the logic. Since the phenomenon is so wide-spread, however, I decided to incorporate it in the logic.

Where the step from a rule's application to its conclusion is concerned, my motivation was a little different. Ideally there would be three steps from the reasons to apply a rule to the rule's conclusion. First from the reasons for and against application to the conclusion whether the rule ought to be applied. Then from the conclusion that the rule ought to be applied to the conclusion that the rule applies. (This is the step which is skipped through the phenomenon of deontic collapse.) And then from this last conclusion to the conclusion of the rule. However, if the reasons for applying a rule outweigh the reasons against, the conclusion of the rule will always follow.

To avoid superfluous steps, the logic might attach the conclusion of the rule immediately to the intermediate result that the reasons for applying the rule outweigh the reasons against. This step seemed intuitively too big. Therefore I decided to retain one intermediate conclusion, and to emphasise the deontic nature of the reasons for and against rule application, the intermediate conclusion is that the rule ought to be applied. Clearly this decision is rather arbitrary, although not unmotivated.

A question that might be raised in this connection is whether the conclusion of a rule should not also follow if the rule is applied, even though it is not the case that it ought to be applied, and maybe even if the rule ought not to be applied. I have no univocal answer to this question.

On the one hand it seems to be the real application of the rule, not merely its owing to be applied, that leads to the conclusion of the rule. A fortiori it would follow that if a rule is applied, its conclusion follows. The question whether the rule ought to be applied is on this approach irrelevant.

On the other hand it seems irrational to apply a rule if there are no reasons to do so, or even outweighing reasons not to do so. Would an irrational op-

---

2 In earlier versions of RBL, such as in Hage and Verheij 1995, they *were* different.

eration lead to a (decisive) reason for a particular conclusion? It seems attractive to deny that.

Apparently we are stuck with a dilemma for which I have presently no solution. The best approach seems to me to allow the following rule as domain-knowledge, rather than as part of RBL:

```
applies(conds ⇒ concl) ⇒ concl
```

(If a rule applies, the conclusion of this rule follows.)

A weaker, and maybe more attractive, version would be:

```
applies(conds ⇒ concl) &
 ~ob(~applies(conds ⇒ concl)) ⇒ concl
```

Adoption of this last rule has the result that the conclusion of a rule also follows if it is not the case that the rule ought to be applied, as long as it is actually applied and it is not the case that the rule ought not to be applied.

Finally, there is also a case, not of deontic collapse, but of deontic inflation, which was not incorporated in RBL. Arguably a valid rule or principle should not be used in an argument if it ought not to be valid (cf. section II.14). This might have been incorporated in RBL by only allowing rules and principles which ought to be valid to be used in arguments. I rejected this possibility because it would lead to an infinite regress (cf. section III.5.3).

3. REASONS FOR INCOMPATIBLE CONCLUSIONS

Suppose that I receive a postcard from England which was signed by Tracy, and in which she writes me that she spends some weeks with her uncle there. This is a reason to assume that Tracy is in England. Suppose, moreover, that when I spoke Tracy a few weeks ago, she told me that she would leave for Australia and would stay there for a couple of months. This is a reason to assume that Tracy is in Australia.

Strictly, the reasons why Tracy is in England and why she is in Australia have no logical relationship with each other. Still it seems that if I have reason to assume that Tracy is in Australia, this is also a reason to assume that she is not in England, and the other way round. We have already encountered this phenomenon with incompatible legal conclusions, such as the conclusion that one rule prevails over another, and that the other prevails over the one.

This predicament can be solved by accepting the following principle:

```
incompatibility:
 Valid(incompatible(state1, state2) ⊃
  r(reason, state1) → r(reason, ~state2))
```

(If two states of affairs are incompatible, a reason why the one state of affairs obtains is ipso facto a reason why the other state of affairs does not obtain)

This cannot be turned around to the assumption that if two states of affairs are incompatible, a reason why the one state of affairs does not obtain is a reason why the other state of affairs obtains, because this would commit the fallacy of the excluded middle.

It remains to be specified when two states of affairs are incompatible. The most obvious case is when they are each others opposite:

```
(∀state1)(∀state2)N(State1 ≡ ~State2) →
 Incompatible(state1, state2)
```
[3]

(If one sentence is logically equivalent to the negation of the other, the states of affairs which they express are incompatible.)

For instance, the states of affairs that John is a thief and that he is not a thief are complementary and therefore incompatible.

The lightest form of incompatibility of two states of affairs is when they happen not to obtain both:

```
(∀state1)(∀state2)(State1 → ~State2) →
 Incompatible(state1, state2)
```
[4]

A special form of incompatibility deals with the relative weights of sets of reasons:

$$(\forall set1)(\forall set2)(\forall conclusion)\ \mathrm{Incompatible}((set1 > set2)_{conclusion},\ (set2 > set1)_{conclusion})$$

(The states of affairs that one set of reasons outweighs another one with regard to a particular conclusion, and that the other one outweighs the former one with regard to that same conclusion, are incompatible.)

3 N stands here for the traditional operator for logical necessity. Cf. Chellas 1980, p. 4.

4 Adoption of this form of incompatibility in combination with the principle `incompatibility` would add a kind of consistency maintenance to RBL. Cf. section 16.

A special legal variant would be:

```
(∀rule1)(∀rule2)(∀case)Incompatible(
  prevails_over(rule1, rule2, case)
  prevails_over(rule2, rule1, case))
```

(It is not compatible that in some case both the one rule prevails over the other, and the other over the one)

Special variants for deontic logic would be[5]:

```
(∀state)Incompatible(ob(state, ob(~state))
```

(The states of affairs that some state both ought and ought not to be the case, are incompatible)
and

```
(∀x)(∀action)Incompatible(od(x, action),
 od(x, ¬action))
```

(The states of affairs that somebody both ought and ought not to perform some kind of action, are incompatible).

This elaboration of incompatibility and its consequences might be included in RBL. In particular the principle that if two states of affairs are incompatible, a reason for the one is a reason against the other seems to hold generally. The same counts also for inconsistency as a criterion for incompatibility and for the thesis that if one group of reasons outweighs another one, it cannot also be the other way round. The other criteria seem to be (in varying degrees) less universal and are therefore less suitable for incorporation in a logic, rather than in a domain theory.

4. DECISIVE REASONS

In his work on defeasible reasoning Pollock (e.g. 1987, 1992 and 1994) assigns a central place to the notion of a reason. In this connection he distinguishes between defeasible and conclusive reasons. The background of Pollock's work is epistemology and consequently the reasons he discusses are reasons to believe, or - in my terminology - epistemic reasons. Moreover, the reasons are in his view psychological states such as perceptual states and beliefs. Nevertheless he uses the contents of these states in his definition of a defeasible reason. According to Pollock P is a defeasible (or prima facie) reason for S to believe Q, if and only if P is a reason for S to believe Q and

[5] For some definitions of the deontic predicates these incompatibilities would be inconsistencies.

there is an R such that R is logically consistent with P but (P & R) is not a reason for S to believe Q (Pollock 1987). As conclusive reasons Pollock mentions beliefs which deductively imply their conclusions.

Clearly a defeasible reason in the sense of Pollock is from a logical point of view related to reasons in the sense of RBL.[6] Moreover, there are two situations in RBL where something like a decisive reason plays a role, that is when a rule ought to be applied, which leads to a decisive reason for the rule's conclusion, and when there is an exclusionary reason, which is a decisive reason against the application of a rule or principle. Should RBL not make a distinction between decisive and defeasible reasons in a way similar to that of Pollock?

On the one hand the answer to this question ought to be affirmative, because RBL already makes use of something like decisive reasons in two cases. On the other hand, I doubt whether there are decisive reasons in other situations than the two mentioned ones. For instance, there are circumstances in which even deductively valid arguments seem not to provide decisive reasons.[7] Moreover, the mechanism of exclusionary reasons makes the use of decisive reasons superfluous from a logical point of view. A 'decisive' reason can be modelled as a non-decisive one which excludes all rules and principles which might lead to competitors.[8]

I have no outspoken opinion about whether decisive reasons should be included in RBL. Presently the role of decisive reasons is hidden in the inference rules 2, 4 and 6, and the reasons which are explicitly mentioned are all defeasible ones in the sense of Pollock.

5. DIMENSIONS OF REASONS

A reason can be seen as a kind of summary that combines the factual content of the state of affairs which makes up the reason with the significance for a particular conclusion that derives from a rule, principle, or goal. A reason for a conclusion (reasons against are similar) contributes to a conclusion, but the measure in which this is the case depends of a number of factors. These factors are what I will call the 'dimensions' of a reason, because they are all amenable to degrees.

---

6 From a philosophical point of view I reject his view that reasons are in general psychological states. Cf. section II.1.1.

7 Cf. in this connection Pollock's (1987) discussion of the lottery-paradox.

8 Cf. the discussion about the all-or-nothing character of rules in section III.10.

5.1 Relevance and weight

The most obvious dimension of a reason is the measure in which it is relevant for its conclusion. Some reasons are so relevant that their presence guarantees their conclusions. For instance, if some rule ought to be applied this may be said to be a *decisive reason* for the conclusion of this rule.

Some reasons are so little relevant that their presence hardly influences the conclusion. If, for instance, a blond hair was found on the place of the theft, this fact is a very weak reason why John, who is blond, is the thief.

Most reasons will be in between the latter kind of reason and decisive reasons. They give clear support to their conclusions, without guaranteeing the truth of the conclusions. In fact, RBL presupposes a minimum degree of relevance by stipulating that any non-empty set of reasons, and consequently also any single reason, outweighs the empty set of reasons concerning any conclusion. This excludes reasons which are so weak as the single presence of a hair of a particular colour. For sure, we would not be prepared to conclude that John is the thief for the single reason that his hair is of the same colour as a hair found at the place of the crime.

It seems to me that the dimension of relevance is the same as the dimension of weight that is involved in the weighing of reasons. A reason that is very significant will outweigh a less relevant reason.

5.2 The dimension of probability

A particular state of affairs may be very relevant for a particular conclusion, but if it does not obtain, it does not contribute to the conclusion. The state of affairs that John is a thief would be a reason for John's punishability, but this reason only obtains if John actually is a thief.

If we want to argue that John is punishable on the ground that he is a thief, we must make it plausible that John is a thief. If it is not given that John is a thief, an argument to this conclusion must be produced. Most often such an argument will not be decisive, and then we are left with a certain degree of probability that John is a thief. The reason that John is a thief for the conclusion that John is punishable is the stronger (other things equal), the larger the probability that John is in fact a thief.

It seems plausible that probability and relevance interfere, so that under circumstances a very probable, but not so significant reason can outweigh a not so probable, but more relevant reason.

5.3 The dimension of degree

Not all facts obtain to the same degree. Take for instance a pram which has been equipped with a motor. This motorised pram is to a less degree a vehicle than a car. Similarly, a dolphin (which is a mammal) is to a less degree a fish than a pike.[9] [10]

Sometimes the degree in which a state of affairs belongs to the category which lends this state of affairs its reason-giving nature can influence the measure in which the reason contributes to its conclusion. For instance, if John is a petty thief, the fact that he is a thief is a less reason for John's being punishable, than if John were a bank robber.

Presumably degrees interfere with probability and with relevance.

6. EPISTEMIC RULES AND PROBABILITY

From the three mentioned dimensions, RBL takes only the dimension of relevance into account. The probability of reason-giving facts is assumed to be a hundred percent, just as the degree in which they obtain. Probability reasoning such as Bayesian statistics takes only degrees of probability into account, while fuzzy logics take degrees into account. Ideally a logic would deal with all three dimensions.[11] In this section I show how RBL can be extended to be able to deal with probability reasoning, albeit in a very simple fashion.

Remember the distinction made in chapter II, the introduction of part D, between constitutive rules and epistemic rules. The former lead to constitutive reasons which make their conclusion true, while the latter only underlie reasons to assume a particular conclusion. In general, constitutive rules cannot be supported by probabilistic arguments. Epistemic rules can very well be supported by probabilistic arguments. If some fact makes another fact sufficiently probable, this is a reason to adopt an inference rule that allows us to infer the one fact from the other fact.

I readily admit that the following is too simplistic for legal practice, but suppose that the probability that a suspect committed the murder in case he had a motive is more than eight times so big than the probability in case he had no motive. This may be a reason to adopt the rule that if the suspect had a motive, he may be assumed to have committed the murder. In the following formalisation of this example, `p(a|b)` stands for the probability of a, given b.

---

9 Notice the parallel between on the one hand the distinction between probability and degree, and on the other hand epistemic and constitutive reasons. Cf. chapter II, the introduction to part D (KINDS OF REASONS).

10 Degrees correspond to dimensions in the HYPO-system. Cf. Ashley 1991.

11 The theory proposed by Verheij (1995) to some extent combines the three forms of reasoning by allowing the phenomenon of 'sequential weakening'. This phenomenon boils down to that the justification for the conclusion of an argument can become weaker, depending on the length of the argument which leads to it.

```
evidence_murder: motive ⊃ murderer
R( p(murderer|motive) / p(murderer|~motive)) > 8,
 ob(valid(evidence_murder)))
```

(If the chance that somebody committed a murder in case he had a motive is more than eight times so big than in case he had no motive, this is a reason why the principle ought to be valid that if somebody had a motive, this is a reason to assume that he is the murderer.)

There cannot only be probabilistic support for epistemic rules, but also for exclusionary reasons that block the application of epistemic rules. Suppose, for instance, that the probability relation between having a motive and being the murderer is much less strong in the case of policemen. It may be the case that if somebody is a policeman, the probability that he committed the murder in case he had a motive is only twice as big as in case he did not have a motive:

```
p(murderer | motive & policeman) /
 p(murderer | ~motive & policeman) = 2
```

In that case, the fact that somebody is a policeman is a reason to exclude the application of the rule `evidence_murder`:

```
R(policeman, excluded(evidence_murder))
```

This reason is based on the rule

```
exception_for_policemen:
 policeman ⇒ excluded(evidence_murder)
```

which ought to be valid because of the decreased probability that you are a murderer in case the person with a motive is a policeman:

```
R( p(murderer|motive & policeman) /
   p(murderer|~motive & policeman)= 2,
 ob(valid(exception_for_policemen)))
```

This example shows how probabilistic evidence can support a kind of Lex Specialis argument, where the application of a general rule is excluded on the basis of information that a more specific case is involved.

It is possible to generalise the examples to all epistemic rules:

```
epistemic_backing:
 p(a | b) / p(a | ~b) > threshold_value1 &
    epistemic_rule(b ⇒ a) ⊃
   ob(valid(b ⇒ a))
```

(If the odds of some conclusion, given some facts exceed a particular threshold, this is a reason why the rule of inference from these facts to this conclusion is valid.)

```
epistemic_exclusion:
 p(a | b & d) / p(a | b & ~d) < threshold_value2 &
   epistemic_rule(b ⇒ a) ⊃
 ob(valid(d ⇒ excluded(b ⇒ a)))
```

(If the presence of some particular fact sufficiently decreases the odds - from above `threshold_value1` to below `threshold_value2` - that some conclusion is true given the presence of some other facts, this fact is an exclusionary reason against application of the rule of inference that allows to draw the conclusion form those other facts.)

7. EPISTEMIC RULES

Some ways to derive rules seem so natural that it may seem strange that they are not built into RBL. For instance if A is a reason for B, and if B entails C, then surely A must be a reason for C. Still, this cannot be derived in pure RBL. From the theory

```
R(a, b)
N(b → c)
```

it cannot be derived that

```
R(a, c)
```

Analogously, from

```
Valid(a ⇒ b)
N(b → c)
```
[12]

it is not possible to derive

```
Valid(a ⇒ c)
```

nor

12 N stands here for the traditional operator for logical necessity. Cf. Chellas 1980, p. 4.

```
Ob(valid(a ⇒ c))
```

Why is this not possible? The answer is that the conclusion of this argument is a statement about the validity of a rule. It depends on the domain, under which circumstances a rule is said to be valid, or ought to be valid, and domain dependent knowledge is not part of RBL. Clearly, in a domain that contains the rule `a ⇒ b`, there will normally be a reason to adopt the rule `a ⇒ c`, but this need not be the case. That is why RBL does not allow the inference that leads to the conclusion that rule `a ⇒ c` can be derived from the given theory.

However, this is not the whole story. In the previous subsection about epistemic rules and probability, we have already seen that there are possibilities to derive epistemic rules. If the rules are epistemic ones, it is very attractive to make it possible to derive `Ob(valid(a ⇒ c))` from `Valid(a ⇒ b)` and `N(b → c)`. To this purpose the following rule might be added to RBL theories, which makes it possible to derive a more specific from a more general rule:

```
epistemic_rule(cond ⇒ concl1) &
  valid(cond ⇒ concl1)) & N(concl1 → concl2) ⇒
 ob(valid(cond ⇒ concl2))
```

(If a rule with condition `a` and conclusion `c` is an epistemic rule, and if `c` entails some other state of affairs `d`, then the rule `a ⇒ d` ought to be valid.)

One can even imagine that the following inference relations between rules are allowed:

```
epistemic_rule(cond ⇒ concl1) & valid(cond1 ⇒ concl1) &
  epistemic_rule(concl1 ⇒ concl2) &
  valid(concl1 ⇒ concl2) ⇒
 ob(valid(cond ⇒ concl2))
```

The adoption of this last rule would make the following inference possible:

```
Valid(smoke ⇒ fire) & Epistemic(smoke ⇒ fire)
Valid(fire ⇒ danger) & Epistemic(fire ⇒ danger)
∴ Ob(valid(smoke ⇒ danger))
```

(If the rule 'smoke means fire' is a valid epistemic rule, and if the same holds for the rule 'fire means danger', then the rule 'smoke means danger' ought to be valid.)

Other attractive seeming additions to RBL would be[13]:

```
Valid(
  epistemic_rule(cond ⇒ concl) & valid(cond ⇒ concl) ⊃
    valid(~concl ⇒ ~cond))
Valid(
  epistemic_rule(cond ⇒ concl) & ~concl ⊃ ~cond)
```

B. SEMANTICS FOR RULES

In the case of epistemic rules, there seem to be possibilities to derive them which are lacking in the case of purely constitutive rules. On the one hand, this suggests how RBL can be amended. On the other hand, this asks for an explanation and in the following section I will attempt such an explanation, which - I hope - also sheds additional light on the way in which rules differ from statements. The explanation centres around the distinction between directions of fit.

The difference between rules and statements based on directions of fit can be elaborated in a semantic difference between statements and rules. In the sections 9 to 15, this semantic difference is elaborated..

8. DIRECTIONS OF FIT

There is an important difference between rules and descriptive statements. Descriptions have what Searle called the *word to world direction of fit* (Searle 1979, pp. 3/4; 1983, p. 7). Rules, on the contrary, have the *world to word direction of fit.*

The distinction between directions of fit is explained by Searle by borrowing an example of Anscombe's (1957). I will use the same example. Suppose that I make a shopping list which I use in the supermarket to put items in my trolley. A detective follows me and makes a list of everything that I put in my trolley. After I am finished, the list of the detective will be identical to my shopping list. However, the lists had different functions. If I use the list correctly, I place exactly those items in my trolley that are indicated on the list. My behaviour is to be adapted to what is on my list. In the case of the detective it is just the other way round; the list should reflect my shopping behaviour. If we consider my behaviour as (part of) the world, we can say that my shopping list has the world to word direction of fit, because my behaviour must fit the words on the list. The detective's list, on the contrary, has the

---

13 The following two principles are only syntactically correct if the condition parts of the original rules are literals.

word to world direction of fit, because his list must fit the world (my behaviour).

Descriptions have the word to world direction of fit; they aim to 'correspond' to what is the case in the world. Although legal rules usually aim to take the world into account in that their contents are influenced by what is the case, they do not have the word to world direction of fit, but just the other way round: rules aim to impose their contents on the world; rules have the world to word direction of fit. For example, the rule that thieves ought to be punished makes it the case that in the world thieves ought usually to be punished.[14] It is not the case that the content of the rule depends on what is the case in the world.

Another way of stating the same kind of thing is to point out that rules are constitutive, rather than descriptive. Searle (1969, p. 33) opposed constitutive rules to regulative rules. We have seen that regulative rules, or norms, are also constitutive. In my opinion, the correct distinction is the one between constitution and description. This distinction does not coincide with the distinction between the directions of fit (unauthorised commands do not constitute obligations, but still have the word to world direction of fit), but it is nevertheless related to it.

The distinction on the basis of directions of fit between descriptions and rules is most clear in the case of purely constitutive rules. Constitutive rules derive their existence not from the facts which they constitute, but e.g. from a social practice, or from legislation. As soon as they exist, they impose their structure on the rest of the world. Thieves become punishable, vehicles with four wheels become cars, etc. Constitutive rules are ontologically prior to the facts which they constitute.

In the case of epistemic rules, this ontologically priority of the rules is still present, but less outspoken. The reason for this is that an epistemic rule is

---

[14] This characteristic of rules may be the cause of the error to consider rules as a kind of imperatives. Not everything that makes the world fit itself is an imperative. Baptising, for instance, also makes the world fit the speech act.

Peczenik 1989, p. 199/200 makes a distinction between practical and theoretical statements, which is similar to the distinction between directions of fit as illustrated by Searle's example. The distinction between constitution and description is different, however. Sentences that express deontic facts are descriptive, while deontic rules (and - for that matter - all other rules) are constitutive. The distinctions deontic/non-deontic and constitutive/non-constitutive do not coincide.

normally only justified if it corresponds to the facts.[15] For instance, the rule that thunderclouds predict rain ought only to be valid if it often rains after the appearance of thunderclouds. In other words, epistemic rules aim to fit the world, they exhibit some kind of word to world fit, just like descriptions.

Still epistemic rules are rules, and their direction of fit is primarily world to word. This becomes especially clear if one considers their constitutive function (cf. section II.20). In their inferential function, epistemic rules behave very much like universal descriptions, but it is only thanks to *ontologically prior* epistemic rules that some facts *count as* certain or probable. Moreover, epistemic rules can still fulfil their inferential and the constitutive roles if they are actually valid, even though they do not correspond to the facts and therefore ought not to be valid. If everybody considers the fact that the horizon is flat as a reason to assume that the world is flat, the flatness of the horizon is a social reason to assume that the world is flat (but cf. section III.15 on the shifting bounds of rationality).

9. POSSIBLE WORLDS

The distinction between directions of fit can be reflected in modeltheoretic semantics for logical theories which deal with rules. I will demonstrate that by giving a semantics for RBL. But first I want to say something more on modeltheoretic semantics in general.

According to the semantic notion of logical validity, an argument is logically valid if and only if it is logically impossible that the premises of the argument are true, while the conclusion of the argument is false (e.g. Copi 1978, p. 32). This notion leaves unspecified what counts in this connection as logically impossible. Modeltheoretic semantics can be regarded as a means to specify the notion of logical (im)possibility and consequently also of logical validity in the sense concerned here.

Logical validity is defined in terms of truth. Truth is a characteristic of a sentence which it has thanks to a particular relation to what is actually the case, to the way the world is. A world can be defined as the set of all the facts. A sentence is then true in a particular world if it states one of the facts that obtain in that world. For extensional logics[16], we only need to consider one world, the actual one. A sentence is then true if it states one of the facts

[15] An exception are legal rules of proof, which may be the result of legislation and which determine what counts as legal evidence. It is possible, though not very sensible, to legislate that if somebody has a good alibi, this is a reason to consider her as a suspect. Normally, however, legal rules of evidence will be precise versions of socially accepted rules of evidence, which aim to correspond to the facts.

[16] The difference between extensional and intensional logics is briefly discussed in section 13.

which obtain in the actual world, or - in other words - which actually obtain. A theory that consists of more sentences is true if all of the sentences that are part of the theory are true.

In modeltheoretic semantics, the notions of necessity and (im)possibility are explicated by making use of sets of possible worlds.[17] This seems circular because it defines possibility in terms of possibility. However, the notion of a possible world can be defined without making use of the notion of possibility itself. This feat is performed by relating possible worlds to a language.

The notion of possibility, and also that of necessity, is an elliptical one. Possibility is never just possibility, but always possibility relative to a set of constraints. Logical possibility, for example, is determined by logical constraints, and physical possibility by physical constraints. In the law we say that something is possible, if it is possible while obeying the rules of law.

A very fundamental kind of possibility is based on the constraints imposed by a language. A language determines which facts can be expressed. For example, the English language does not allow me to express that *fmfkrv i ;pw gfl*, because that string is not a well-formed sentence of English. Given a particular language, there is a set of well-formed sentences of that language. It is even possible to define a language as the (possibly infinite) set of its well-formed sentences. In many languages, in particular natural languages, sentences do not only express propositions but also (the contents of) non-declarative speech-acts such as commands. For the purposes of modeltheoretic semantics, it is assumed that all well-formed sentences are declarative, that is, express states of affairs.

Given a language which only allows declarative sentences, a possible world is defined as a set of states of affairs. This set determines the truth value, *true* or *false*, for all sentences of the language. If the state of affairs that is expressed by a sentence obtains in a possible world, this sentence has the truth value true in that world, and otherwise it has the truth value false.

So, if some toy language L has only three sentences, 'It's raining', It's clouded', and 'It's raining and it's clouded', there are eight different possible worlds, corresponding to the eight different ways in which truth values can be assigned to these three sentences. Clearly if a language allows for infinitely many well-formed sentences, there will be infinitely many possible worlds.

---

[17] I am aware that pure modeltheoretic semantics abstracts from the intuitions behind the notion of a possible world and only makes use of the characteristics that are explicitly defined for frames, models and possible worlds. Nevertheless I think that the underlying intuitions are essential to make modeltheoretic semantics a kind of *semantics*, rather than yet another uninterpreted formal system. That is why I do not hesitate to emphasise the intuitions of modeltheoretic semantics, rather than the formal definitions of models.

Notice that the notion of a possible world as defined here is related to a language. Different languages have different sets of possible worlds. Strictly it would be necessary to tag every set of possible worlds with an indicator of the language to which this set of possible worlds belongs. To facilitate my argument, I will assume for a while that the language we are talking about is fixed as the language of propositional logic, and that there is only one set of possible worlds.

10. LOGICALLY POSSIBLE WORLDS

The notion of a possible world as defined until now has nothing to do with logic whatsoever. In particular the possible worlds need not be logically possible. Actually the notion of a logically possible world needs to be defined on the basis of the more primitive notion of a possible world that is language-related. So, even if the language that defines the set of possible worlds is the language of some system of logic, not all possible worlds need to be logically possible worlds.

Assume for instance that we have a language which consists of two elementary sentences, P and Q, and one compound sentence, P & Q. Each of these sentences can be true or false, which defines eight possible worlds. From these eight possible worlds, only four are also logically possible. In the other worlds the (logical) meaning of the operator & has not been taken into account. This meaning boils down to that if two sentences are joined together by means of the connective &, the result is true, if and only if both of its constituent sentences are true. Possible worlds in which this meaning is neglected are impossible from a logical point of view.

In this example I have taken it for granted that the operator & is a logical operator and also what the meaning of this operator is. It is, however, neither a priori given that & is a logical word, nor what its meaning is. A logic specifies which (if any) of its words or expressions have a logical meaning and the nature of this meaning. Given this specification, it becomes possible to divide possible worlds into logically possible and impossible ones.

In general it holds that it is possible to specify by means of criteria which distinguish between worlds which are logically possible and which are not, what words in a language count as logical words and what their meaning is. These criteria can also be considered as constraints on *logically* possible worlds. Worlds which do not meet the constraints may be possible with regard to the language involved, but they are not logically possible. The constraints on possible worlds from the perspective of propositional logic then become:

1. a world is only logically possible if it assigns the truth value *false* to the sentence ~A if and only if it assigns the truth value *true* to the sentence A;
2. a world is only logically possible if it assigns the truth value *false* to the sentence A ∨ B if and only if it assigns the truth value *false* to both the sentences A and B.

The constraints for the other operators follow from the way in which these operators are defined in terms of the negation and the disjunction.

A consequence of these constraints is that the truth values of elementary sentences such as A and B can be assigned independently of each other, but that the truth values of compound sentences such as A & B, or A → B are fixed, given the truth value assignments of the elementary sentences.

11. LOGICALLY POSSIBLE WORLDS AND VALIDITY

It is interesting to see how the constraints on propositional logical-possible worlds determine which inferences are logically valid. For instance, the argument

P → Q
P
∴ Q

is valid because the constraints on logically possible worlds do not allow worlds in which P → Q and P are both true, while Q is false.

In general it holds that an argument is valid if the constraints on the logically possible worlds do not allow a world in which the premises of this argument are true, while the conclusion is false. Notice that this is precisely the semantic notion of logical validity.

12. RULES AND CONSTRAINTS

The distinction between descriptive sentences and rules has a counterpart in modeltheoretic semantics in the distinction between the assignment of truth values to sentences and constraints on this assignment.

Whether a descriptive sentence is true depends on the truth value it is assigned. Every elementary sentence receives its truth value in a particular world independently of all other elementary sentences, and also independently of the truth values of the sentences in all other possible worlds. The truth values of logically compound sentences is determined by on the one hand the assignments of the truth values to the elementary sentences, and on the other hand by the constraints on *logically* possible worlds.

If a rule is valid in a particular world, the descriptive sentence which expresses this fact will be assigned the truth value true. But this is not all: in this world there is also an additional constraint on the assignment of truth values to other sentences. For instance, if in a world the rule that thieves are punishable is valid, the truth value of the sentence that John is a thief influences the truth value of the sentence that John is punishable. The nature of this influence depends on the logic for reasoning with rules. If reasoning with rules were not defeasible, the constraint would be that if a sentence of the form `Thief(x)` is assigned the truth value `true`, the corresponding sentence of the form `Punishable(x)` should also be assigned the truth value `true`. Since reasoning with rules is defeasible, however, the influence of the constraints that follow from valid rules (and principles) is far more complex, as we will see in section 14.

That the validity of a rule imposes constraints on the world in which this rule is valid reflects the world to word fit of rules. It should be noticed that the direction of constraints is also world to word. However, if a possible world has some constraint on its facts, it does not mean that the corresponding rule is valid. Suppose, for instance, that in all possible worlds thieves are punishable. Does this mean that in all these worlds the rule that thieves are punishable is valid? That the answer is negative becomes clear if we consider the possibility that these worlds all have two valid rules instead: Somebody only counts as a thief if he owns a false key, and the possession of false keys is punishable. These two rules may lead[18] to (amongst others) the same constraints as the single rule that thieves are punishable, but the validity of this latter rules does not follow from the validity of the former two (cf. also section 7).

13. EXTENSIONAL AND INTENSIONAL LOGICS

If a logic is extensional, all the information that is needed to determine the truth value of a sentence is contained in one possible world. If the sentence is elementary, its truth value is directly given. If the sentence is logically compound, its truth value follows from the truth values of its constituents and the constraints on logically possible worlds.

A model of a logical theory is a set of possible worlds (including a valuation) which makes this sentence true. In case of an extensional logic, a model needs only contain one possible world, because every individual possible worlds contains all the information that is needed to determine the truth value of every sentence (in that world).

If a logic is intensional, the meanings, rather than the truth values, of the constituents of logically compound sentences are somehow relevant for the

---

[18] Whether they really lead to the same constraints depends on the nature of the constraints imposed by valid rules.

truth values of these sentences. In modeltheoretic semantics, the intensionality of a logic is reflected in the fact that a model of a theory involves more than one possible world. This can be illustrated by the semantics for conditional logic.

Suppose that > is a conditional operator. Its meaning can then be defined by saying that the sentence A > B is true in a possible world i, if B is true in all possible worlds in which A is true, and which are sufficiently close to i (Sanford 1989, p. 113). By giving an additional characterisation of the notion 'sufficiently close', it is possible to make the logical characteristics of the >-operator more precise. For my purposes, the essential point in this definition is that it has become impossible to establish the truth value of the sentence A > B in a world i, by means of the information content of i alone. The information in the worlds which are sufficiently close to i is also needed.

The connection between the conditions and the conclusion of a rule is intensional. If a thief is punishable, this is so because he is a thief. There is a connection between the characteristics expressed in the rule conditions and in the rule conclusion. Moreover, the connection which a rule creates between its conditions and its conclusion not only holds for the actual situation, but also for hypothetical situations. The rule that thieves are punishable also underlies the fact that if somebody were a thief, he would be punishable.

It seems, therefore, that the semantics for a logic for rules would need models which contain sets of possible worlds, rather than single possible worlds. Yet, this is not necessary, as is illustrated by the semantics for RBL which uses models of theories that consist of single possible worlds.

This is possible by taking an intermediate course between the semantics of extensional logics and the traditional semantics for intensional logics. In an extensional logic, the truth value of a logically compound sentence in a possible world is determined by the truth values *of its constituents* in that same possible world (that is why these sentences are said to be logically *compound*), and by the constraints on logically possible worlds.[19] According to the traditional semantics for intensional logics, the truth value of a sentence with a non-truthfunctional operator in a possible world is determined by the truth values *of its constituents* in a set of possible worlds, and by the constraints on logically possible worlds.

It is, however, also possible to let the truth value of a sentence in a possible world be determined by the truth values of *all* other sentences, and not only its constituents, *in that same possible world*. This is precisely the course

---

[19] That the information content (the meaning) of a complex expression is determined by the meanings of its constituents, is sometimes called the 'Fregian principle'. Cf. Allwood *et al.* 1977, p. 130.

that is taken in the semantics for RBL to specify the truth values of sentences like `R(a, b)`, and `Excluded(rule, case)`.

In this approach, the distinction between types of sentences should not be between logically elementary and logically compound sentences, but rather between logically primitive and logically dependent sentences. The truth values of logically primitive sentences are assigned independent of each other, while the truth values of the dependent sentences is determined by the truth values of the primitive sentences and the constraints on the relevant possible world. Logically dependent sentences will express reason-based facts (cf. section II.5). I will return to this issue in section 15, after having given a modeltheoretic semantics for RBL.

14. SEMANTICS FOR REASON-BASED LOGIC

The starting point for the semantics of RBL is the definition of an RBL-possible world. I define a possible world as a set of states of affairs. A possible world determines for every well-formed sentence of RBL whether it is true or false, depending on whether the state of affairs expressed by the sentence obtains in the concerning world.

RBL-possible worlds are a subset of the set of all logically possible worlds as defined for FOPL. In these latter possible worlds there are certain constraints that reflect the meanings of the logical operators. In a similar way RBL imposes additional constraints on RBL-possible worlds. If, for instance, in a possible world the reasons for a conclusion outweigh the reasons against this conclusion, the conclusion must be assigned the truth value `true` in this world. In general, the relations between the validity of rules, the satisfaction of rule conditions, the applicability, the exclusion and the application of a rule, the reason generated by a principle, and the conclusion that follows if some set of reasons outweighs another set are captured by means of constraints on RBL-possible worlds.

RBL-possible worlds are defined by the following constraints that come on top of the constraints for FOPL-possible worlds. In these constraints, truth always means truth in a possible world.

1. In all RBL-possible worlds, the following sentences must be true:
   a. $(\forall \mathit{reasonset})(\forall \mathit{state})$
      $(\mathit{reasonset} \neq \emptyset) \rightarrow (\mathit{reasonset} > \emptyset)_{\mathit{state}}$
   b. $(\forall \mathit{state})(\exists \mathit{case})\mathrm{Obtains}(\mathit{state}, \mathit{case}) \rightarrow \mathit{state}$
   c. Valid(applicable(*instantiated_rule*, *case*) ⊃
      ob(applies(*instantiated_rule*, *case*)))

   These sentences are, so to speak, axioms of RBL.

2. Given that the sentence `Facts` minimally entails the sentence `Cond` under some substitution σ, and that the term `iconcl` is the instance of the term `concl` under σ, it must hold that:

   If and only if:

   `Valid(`*`cond`* `⊃` *`concl`*`) ∨ Ob(valid(`*`cond`* `⊃` *`concl`*`))` is true, and
   `Obtains(`*`facts, case`*`)` is true, and
   `Excluded(`*`cond`* `⊃` *`concl, case`*`)` is false, then
   `R(`*`facts, iconcl`*`)` is true.

   (A fact is and can only be a reason if there is a valid, non-excluded principle which makes it into a reason.)

3. Given that the sentence `Facts` minimally entails the sentence `Cond` under some substitution σ, and that the term `iconcl` is the instance of the term `concl` under σ, it must hold that:

   If and only if:

   `Valid(`*`cond`* `⇒` *`concl`*`) ∨ Ob(valid(`*`cond`* `⇒` *`concl`*`))`
   is true, and `Obtains(`*`facts, case`*`)` is true, and
   `Excluded(`*`cond`* `⇒` *`concl, case`*`)` is false, then
   `Applicable(`*`facts`* `⇒` *`iconcl, case`*`)` is true.

   (A rule which is or ought to be valid, is and can only be applicable if its conditions are satisfied, and if it is not excluded.)

4a. If `Goal(`*`state`*`)` is true, then the following sentences must be true:

a. `Valid(contributes_to(`*`new_state, state`*`) ⊃ ob(`*`new_state`*`))`

b. `Valid(contributes_to(`*`new_state`*`, ~state) ⊃ ob(~`*`new_state`*`))`

c. `Valid(contributes_to(`*`action, state`*`) ⊃ od(x,` *`action`*`))`

d. `Valid(contributes_to(`*`action, ~state`*`) ⊃ od(x, ¬`*`action`*`))`

4b. If `Ob(goal(`*`state`*`))` is true, then the following sentences must be true:

a. `Ob(valid(contributes_to(`*`new_state, state`*`) ⊃ ob(`*`new_state`*`)))`

b. `Ob(valid(contributes_to(`*`new_state, ~state`*`) ⊃ ob(~`*`new_state`*`)))`

c. `Ob(valid(contributes_to(`*`action, state`*`) ⊃ od(x,` *`action`*`)))`

d. `Ob(valid(contributes_to(`*`action, ~state`*`) ⊃ od(x, ¬`*`action`*`)))`

5. If `Ob(applies(facts ⇒ iconcl, case))` is true, then `Iconcl` is true.

   (If a rule ought to be applied, its conclusion is true.)

6. Let `reasons(atom)` be {`s`: `R(s, atom)` is true}

   If `(reasons(literal) > reasons(~literal))`$_{literal}$ is true, then `Literal` is true.

   (A sentence is true if the reasons that plead for it outweigh the reasons that plead against it.)

7a. If `Excluded(rule, case)` is true, then either

```
reasons(excluded(rule, case)) >
  reasons(~excluded(rule, case))
```

or

```
Ob(applies(instantiated_conditions ⇒
  excluded(rule, case), case2))
```

is true.

(If a rule is excluded, it is so on the balance of reasons, or on the basis of a rule.)

7b. If `Ob(state)` is true, then either

```
reasons(ob(state)) > reasons(~ob(state))
```

or

```
Ob(applies(
  instantiated_conditions ⇒ ob(state)))
```

is true.

(If a state of affairs ought to be the case, it is so on the balance of reasons, or on the basis of a rule.)

7c. If `Od(x, action)` is true, then either

```
reasons(od(x, action)) > reasons(~od(x, action))
```

or

```
Ob(applies(
  instantiated_conditions ⇒ od(x, action)))
```

is true.

(If somebody ought to perform some action, it is so on the balance of reasons, or on the basis of a rule.)

The constraints 7a-7c express the reason-based nature of rule-exclusions and deontic facts.

15. SEMANTICS FOR RULES

Which conclusions can we draw from the discussion in the previous sections for the semantics for rules? I think that there are three conclusions, one negative and two positive.

The negative conclusion is that it is not necessary to use models of more than one possible world to deal with rules. Indeed, rules do not only deal with what is actually the case, but also with hypothetical situations. But this does not mean that they describe hypothetical situations and that it is necessary to consider hypothetical situations to determine whether a rule is valid.

The crucial distinction in this connection is that between a constraint on logically possible worlds, and sentences which are true in more than one possible worlds. Constraints lead to sentences which are true or false in all possible worlds, but not every sentence which is true or false in all possible worlds is directly based on a constraint. (Cf. the example about thieves with false keys in section 12.) Rules are to be represented by constraints, and not by sentences which are true in a set of possible worlds.

A more practical argument, which leads to the same conclusion, is that there need not be a set of sentences which can represent the constraints imposed by rules. For instance, the constraint formulated under number 6 makes use of a meta-language construction which cannot be expressed in the object-language of RBL. It can therefore not be replaced by a set of one or more sentences which are to be true in all RBL-possible worlds.

Moreover, even if there are sentences which can represent the constraint, it is highly doubtful whether they can represent the meaning of the sentence from which they follow. For instance, if the rule

made_by_legislator(*rule*) ⇒ valid(*rule*)

is valid in a possible world, this imposes constraints on the other facts in that world, amongst which the constraint that the following sentence is true:

(∀*r*)made_by_legislator(*r*) →
 Valid(*r*) ∨ (∃*reason*)R(*reason*, ~valid(*r*)) ∨
 Excluded(made_by_legislator(*rule*) ⇒ valid(*rule*))

(If a rule is made by the legislator, this rule must be valid, or there is a reason against its validity, or the rule that rules made by the legislator are valid was excluded.)

It seems far-fetched, however, to say that this complex sentence expresses the meaning of the sentence

Valid(made_by_legislator(*rule*) ⇒ valid(*rule*))

The only meaning of this sentence is in my opinion that the rule

made_by_legislator(*rule*) ⇒ valid(*rule*)

is valid. The rest is 'merely' the logical consequence of the validity of this rule.
Since semantics deals with the meanings of sentences, it would be incorrect to represent the meaning of the statement that a rule is valid by means of its consequences (not its meaning) in a set of possible worlds.

The two positive conclusions deal with the question how rules are to be represented semantically. The first of them is that rules are to be treated as logical individuals, and that every statement about rules which does not contain logical operators (and the rule formulation by itself does *not* contain logical operators) is logically elementary. In principle it should be possible to assign a truth value to the sentence that a particular rule is valid, independently of all other primitive sentences. Exceptions to this principle can only be based on the validity of other rules or principles (e.g. rules of recognition) which impose constraints on the possible world in which the rule is valid. The example discussed above illustrates such an exception.

The second positive conclusion is that if a rule is valid in a particular possible world, it imposes constraints on the combinations of (other) facts *in this same world*. Notice that the constraints imposed by valid rules are confined to the worlds in which these rules are valid. In this respect they appear to differ from the logical constraints which hold for *all* logically possible worlds.
This appearance is deceptive. Logical constraints only hold for logically possible worlds, and logically possible worlds are precisely those worlds in which logical rules are valid. It is also possible to define the set of legally possible worlds, in which a set of legal rules is valid. In these worlds thieves will usually be punishable, owners can usually revendicate their goods, etc. ...

The essential semantics for rules therefore seems to be that if a rule (or principle) is valid in a particular possible world, this imposes constraints on the other facts which obtain in that world. The precise nature of these constraints can be subject of discussion.

C. REASON-BASED LOGIC IN COMPARISON

RBL in its present version is not the only way to deal with the peculiarities of reasoning with rules. I have mentioned a number of possible extensions and modifications of the RBL. But there are other logics for defeasible reasoning. In the following sections I will offer a relatively abstract discussion of these nonmonotonic logics. It is not my purpose to discuss the advantages and disadvantages of particular systems of logic, but rather to have a look at the fundamental ideas which underlie them and to evaluate these ideas.

I discuss four different approaches to defeasible reasoning, that is consistency maintenance approaches, default logic, conditional logics, and logics based on the comparison of arguments. I will evaluate these approaches with regard to three issues that have turned out to be important where reasoning with rules is concerned. These issues are how well the concerning logic can deal with:

- exceptions to rules,
- conflicts of reasons,
- arguments about rules.

Exceptions to rules will generally be easy for nonmonotonic logics, because they were designed to deal with the defeasibility of arguments. However, if we leave conflicting reasons out of consideration, we encounter two kinds of exceptions. There may be an exclusionary reason against the application of a rule, and there may be non-decisive reasons against the application of a rule which have to be weighed against reasons for application. It will turn out that not all nonmonotonic logics can deal with this distinction, because it presupposes the possibility to argue *about* rules.

Conflicts of reasons will also not produce many problems, because arguments which lead to incompatible conclusions were one of the main inspirations for the development of nonmonotonic logics. It will turn out, however, that the accrual of reasons, which is an important characteristic of conflicts of reasons, cannot be dealt with by most alternatives for RBL.

Arguments about rules will be problematic for all logics which treat rules as ordinary sentences of the logical language, but also for default logic, which treats rules as inference rules.

16. CONSISTENCY MAINTENANCE APPROACHES

One main source of inspiration for nonmonotonic logics is the phenomenon that human knowledge is not always consistent (to say the least) and that humans are nevertheless capable to use this inconsistent knowledge without experiencing serious problems. A possible explanation for this capability is that humans normally do not take all their knowledge in consideration when they deal with a particular issue, but only a subset. As long as this subset is consistent, there are no problems.

This 'solution' for the problem of inconsistent knowledge can be given a logical rendering by developing logics which deal with maximal consistent subsets of theories which, as a whole, may be inconsistent. The consistent subsets can then be dealt with by a traditional logic, such as predicate logic.

Logics which take this approach may be called *consistency maintenance approaches*. I will first give a relatively abstract discussion of consistency maintenance approaches, and then say something more about one particular system.

16.1 Maximal consistent subsets

The basic idea behind consistency maintenance approaches is that from an inconsistent theory two or more consistent subsets are taken. These subsets are to be maximal in the sense that it is not possible to add more sentences from the original theory without creating an inconsistency.

This approach can be refined by considering a theory T as consisting of two parts, each of which can theoretically be empty. One part is a set of all the sentences that contains the 'hard' knowledge of T and the other part is a set of defaults. Let us call the hard knowledge K and the defaults D. It then holds that T = <K, D>.

If all the defaults from D can be used in combination with the facts from K without leading to inconsistency, reasoning with T is dealt with by a monotonic logic. If the defaults of D cannot all be applied in combination with the facts of K, a new theory 'T is generated by adding a subset D' of D to K, such that all defaults of D' should be consistent with K. T' = <K, D'>. Reasoning with T' is again dealt with by a monotonic logic. If K is inconsistent, there will be no sets T'.

Often it will be possible to combine many different subsets of D with K. For each of these combinations there is a corresponding set of sentences that can be derived from them. These different sets of derivable sentences are called the *extensions* of T. Cf. figure 1, where D1, D2 and D3 are subsets of the set of defaults D. These subsets lead, in combination with the knowledge K, to respectively the extensions E1, E2, and E3. Cf. figure 1.
Take for instance the theory

```
Thief(x) → Ob(punished(x))
Minor(x) → Ob(~punished(x))
Thief(john) & Minor(john)
```

The hard knowledge of this theory consists of

```
K: {Thief(john) & Minor(john)}
```

The defaults consist of

```
D:  {Thief(x) → Ob(punished(x)),
     Minor(x) → Ob(~punished(x))}
```

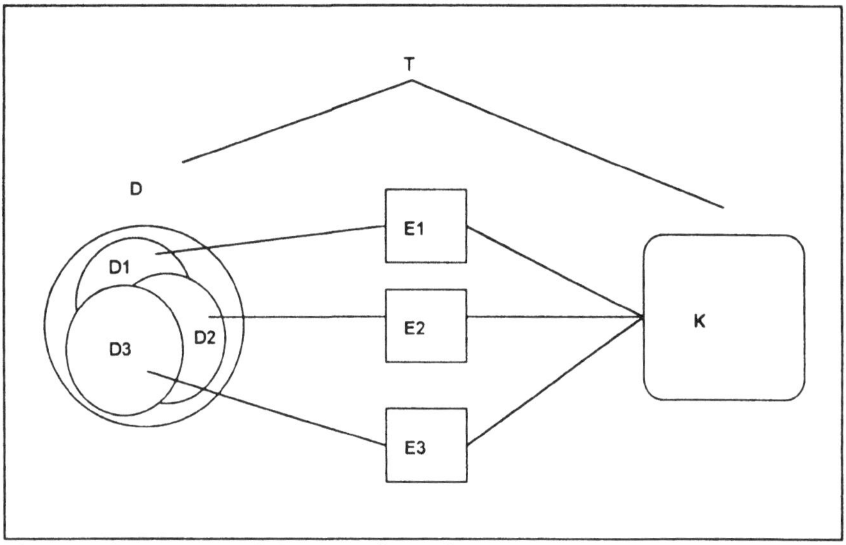

Figure 1: The parts and the extensions of a theory T.

To maintain consistency, D is divided into

D1: {Thief(x) → Ob(punished(x))}

and

D2: {Minor(x) → Ob(~punished(x))}

Both the extension E1, based on S1 = {K, D1}, and the extension E2, based on S2 = {K, D2}, is consistent and the result of applying *all of the applicable defaults* from D1, respectively D2 to the facts of K. This leads to

E1 = Th(K ∪ {Thief(x) → Ob(punished(x)), Ob(punished(john))})[20]

and

E2 = Th(K ∪ { Minor(x) → Ob(~punished(x)), Ob(~punished(john))})

Clearly, the results in the two extensions are not compatible. According to E1, John ought to be punished, while according to E2, he ought not.

16.2 The multiple extension 'problem'

In a consistency maintenance approach, an inconsistent theory can have more than one extension and it depends on which extension is chosen whether a

[20] The operator Th stands for the deductive closure of a set of sentences.

particular sentence is derivable. In our example, it is not clear whether John ought to be punished because he is a thief, or that he ought not to be punished because he is a minor. Still, this is precisely what we would like to know. We have the phenomenon that a theory often has more than one extension and that it depends on the extension which sentences follow from the theory. This phenomenon is sometimes called the *multiple extension problem*.

It must be noted, however, that the problem is not so problematic. If nothing else is given than a theory with rules that lead to incompatible outcomes and facts that satisfy the conditions of these rules, it only seems natural that more than one outcome (or no outcome at all) is arguable. The theory contains a conflict, and it is not a *logical* problem if this conflict is made explicit in the form of multiple extensions.

The question what can be derived from a theory which has more than one extension can be given two extreme answers. The one extreme answer is that a sentence follows from a theory if it is contained in at least *one* of the extensions of the theory. Another defensible approach would be to say that a sentence only follows from a default theory if it is part of *all* the extensions of this theory. These two approaches have respectively been called the 'brave' and the 'cautious' approach (e.g. Ginsberg 1987, p. 14), because they allow relatively many, respectively few sentences to be derived from a theory. In many nonmonotonic logics these two extreme answers are avoided by distinguishing between the different extensions, and preferring one or more of them above others. Such preferences will be discussed in the next section.

The problem of multiple extensions becomes a logical one, if the theory also contains information as to how the conflicting rules relate to each other. For instance, if the theory somehow contains the information that the rule about minors prevails over the rule about the punishing of thieves, and not the other way round, there should be logical means to take this into account and to derive, in our example, that John ought not to be punished.

In RBL-terminology this comes down to the demand that the logic must have means to deal with the weighing of reasons. In the terminology of extensions, the demand becomes that the logic should have means to prefer one extension above the others. The preferred extension then determines which sentences can be derived from the original theory.

16.3 Brewka's theory of preferred subsets

In the general framework for consistency maintenance as sketched in the previous section, there is a distinction between the sentences that contain hard knowledge on the one hand, and the defaults on the other hand. If the elements of a theory are ordered so that some sentences are 'higher' than others, it becomes possible to refine the fundamental distinction between hard knowledge and defaults. The sentences that represent knowledge are assigned the highest place in the ordering, and the rules are given a lower place; in that way the distinction between knowledge and rules is realised in a relative, rather than in an absolute way.

Brewka's (1989) theory of preferred subsets generalises this approach. Informally, this theory boils down to that one starts with a (possibly inconsistent) set T of sentences of e.g. first order predicate logic, and an ordering over these sentences. The set is divided into a number of layers L_1 ... L_n, with the understanding that all sentences in a layer have the same place in the ordering, where the sentences in L_1 have the highest place, and the sentences in L_n have the lowest place. Each of the subsets may be inconsistent.

Preferred subsets are constructed in the following way. First a maximal consistent subset of L_1 is constructed. This subset is complemented with as many sentences from L_2 as is possible without the result becoming inconsistent. Sometimes, it will not be possible to add any sentences from L_2, because every addition would lead to an inconsistency. In that case, no sentence from L_2 is added to the subset of L_1.

This procedure of complementing the set is repeated with sentences from L_3 etc., until L_n has been dealt with. The result of this procedure is a preferred subset of T.

The distinction between hard and soft knowledge can on this approach be realised by putting all the hard knowledge of T in L_1 and placing all rules in L_2. However, the rules can be ordered among themselves by dividing them over more than one category, with the relatively preferred rules in the higher categories.

16.4 Evaluation of consistency maintenance approaches

As their name already indicates, consistency maintenance approaches aim at maintaining consistency. That makes them very suitable to deal with the situation where one reason outweighs another reason, because these situations will be modelled by different extensions, where the one extension is preferred above the other one.

But what happens in case there are three reasons, two of which are by themselves outweighed by the third one, but in combination outweigh the third one? Consider the example that thieves ought to be punished, just as mistreators, but that minors ought not to be punished. If a thief is a minor, he should not be punished, assuming that being a minor outweighs being a thief where the issue of punishing is concerned. The same counts if the minor is a mistreator. However, if a minor is both a thief and a mistreator, he should be punished, because being a thief and a mistreator are two reasons for punishing that together outweigh being a minor. If we try to deal with this situation by means of prioritisation, we obtain:

```
1:  Thief(john)
    Mistreator(john)
    Minor(john)
2:  (∀x)Minor(x) → Ob(~punished(x))
3:  (∀x)Thief(x) → Ob(punished(x))
    (∀x)Mistreator(x) → Ob(punished(x))
```

This theory has only one preferred subset, that is

```
{Thief(john), Mistreator(john), Minor(john),
  (∀x)Minor(x) → Ob(~punished(x))}
```

This subset leads to the conclusion that John should not be punished. The reason why this unattractive conclusion is drawn is that the rules are compared one by one, with the effect that the strongest rule wins. Because rules underlie reasons, it is possible to translate the prioritisation on rules into the decision which of two reasons outweighs the other one. If we make this translation, the comparison of *two* rules comes down to weighing *two* reasons. The present procedure then leads to the result that the strongest reason decides what will be the conclusion.

However, reasons should not be compared one by one, but set by set. That is why prioritisation on rules leads to the wrong results in the case that more than two reasons must be weighed and the strongest reason is contained in the weakest set.

There is a possibility to 'solve' the problem. Consider the following formalisation of the same case:

```
1:  Thief(john)
    Mistreator(john)
    Minor(john)
2:  (∀x)Minor(x) & ~(Thief(x) & Mistreator(x)) →
     Ob(~punished(x))
    (∀x)Thief(x) & (~Minor(x) ∨ Mistreator(x)) →
     Ob(punished(x))
    (∀x)Mistreator(x) & (~Minor(x) ∨ Thief(x)) →
     Ob(punished(x))
```

This formalisation neatly leads to the desired results and seems to show that prioritisation can also deal with the conflict of more than two reasons. The preferred subset contains all the sentences of both levels and leads to the conclusion that John should be punished.

However, as the superfluousness of the prioritisation (all sentences are included in the preferred set) might already have warned us, this solution is unattractive because it hides the weighing of the reasons in the reformulated premises of the theory. Here we have a case of adapting the premises to obtain the wanted results, while the logic is kept fixed.[21] Summarising we can say that a consistency maintenance approach as described in this and the previous section can handle the weighing of two reasons, but cannot handle the weighing of sets of reasons.

Consistency maintenance approaches *as such* are also unable to deal with exceptions to rules and with reasoning about rules. Exceptions to rules which are not based on the conflict of reasons must explicitly refer to the rules to which they are an exception. If rules are treated as sentences of the object language, it is not possible to refer to them in the object language. Moreover, consistency maintenance approaches have no logical means to deal with exceptions which do not involve that the conclusion of the rule is false, that is with pure undercutters.

Because it is not possible to refer to rules, it is also not possible to reason about rules. This does not mean that consistency maintenance approaches cannot be adapted to make it possible to reason about rules. But it does mean that mere consistency maintenance is not sufficient to deal with all important aspects of reasoning with rules.

17. DEFAULT LOGIC

Consistency maintenance approaches attempt to deal with the defeasibility of reasoning with rules by making a different use of a traditional logic. Reiter's default logic takes another approach by treating defaults as a kind of inference rules that are not part of the logical language itself. A theory of default logic consists of a set of sentences that can be used in a 'normal' way to make inferences, and a set of defaults which can only be used in a restricted way.

A default contains three elements, namely a prerequisite, a justification, and a consequent. For instance, a legal default could have the following elements:

prerequisite: *x* is a thief
justification: The crime is not prescribed
consequent: *x* ought to be punished.

In the notation of Reiter it would look as follows:

$$\frac{\texttt{Thief}(x)\ :\ \texttt{M}\ \sim\texttt{Prescribed crime}}{\texttt{Ob}(\texttt{punished}(x))}$$

---

[21] It is interesting to compare the formalisation of the rules in the present example with the way in which the outcome of colliding forces is described in sentences that describe all possible cases. Cf. section III.1.

Defaults can be considered as instructions how to extend an incomplete theory. The incomplete theory is given in the form of a number of sentences, and the defaults indicate how this set of sentences can be extended. If the prerequisite of the default is a consequence of the theory, the consequent of the default can be added to the theory in case that the justification of the default is consistent with the theory.

In our example this would mean that if it can be derived that John is a thief, and it is consistent with the theory that the crime is not prescribed, then the sentence that John ought to be punished can be added to the theory. If, however, it follows from the theory that the crime is prescribed, it is not possible to add that John ought to be punished.

It is important to see the difference in role of the prerequisite on the one hand, and the justification on the other hand. To extend a theory with the consequent of a default, the theory must already contain the prerequisite. It is not necessary that the theory contains the justification; instead it suffices that the final extension of the theory does *not* contain the *denial* of the justification. Informally, it can be said that to 'derive' the consequent of a default, one needs to know that the prerequisite is true, but as far as the justification is concerned it suffices that it is not *known* to be false. Just a lack of information suffices, although it is of course also all right if the justification is known to be true.

An important category of defaults consists of thc so-called *normal defaults*. A normal default is characterised by that its justification is identical to its consequent. The following would for instance be a normal default:

$$\frac{\texttt{Thief(x) : M Ob(punished(x))}}{\texttt{Ob(punished(x))}}$$

In the natural language formulation of a normal default, it is natural to leave the justification away. The example normal default would therefore be formulated as 'Thieves ought to be punished'.

17.1 Extensions of a theory

A default theory consists of a number of sentences and a number of defaults. An extension of a default theory is a second set of sentences, that includes the sentences of the default theory and is closed under deduction. A final characteristic of an extension is that it is not possible anymore to apply one of the defaults of the theory to obtain new sentences. All defaults that could be applied have already been applied to make the extension as big as possible. An extension is a *maximal* set of sentences that results from applying defaults to the original set of sentences.[22]

The following example illustrates the phenomenon of extensions. A default theory T consists of the sentences:

```
Thief(john)
Minor(john)
```

and the following defaults:

```
d1: (∀x)(Thief(x) > Ob(punished(x)))
d2: (∀x)(Minor(x) > Ob(~punished(x)))
```
[23]

By applying default 1, the extension of T becomes

```
E1 = Th({Thief(john), Minor(john), Ob(punished(john))})
```

This extension cannot be extended anymore by applying defaults, because the application of default 2 is blocked by the sentence `Ob(punished(john))`.

By applying default 2, the extension of T becomes

```
E2 = Th({Thief(john), Minor(john), Ob(~punished(john))})
```

This extension cannot be extended anymore by applying defaults, because the application of default 1 is blocked by the sentence

`Ob(~punished(john))`.

We find that theory T has two extensions, namely E1 and E2. According to Reiter, each extension can be considered to contain a number of beliefs that can rationally be held.

17.2 Semi-normal defaults and undercutters

If the justification of a default contains not only the default's consequent, but also one or more other conditions, the default is called *semi-normal*. An example of such a semi-normal default would be:

$$\frac{\texttt{Thief}(x)\ :\ \texttt{M (Ob(punished(}x\texttt{)) \& \textasciitilde Prescribed crime)}}{\texttt{Ob(punished(}x\texttt{))}}$$

The distinction between normal defaults and semi-normal ones is important because normal defaults are little more than means of consistency mainte-

---

[22] Precise definitions of extensions can be found in Reiter 1980.

[23] I use the operator > to designate normal defaults, that is defaults, the justification of which is identical to their consequent. For instance, the formula A > B stands for the default:

$$\frac{A: M(B)}{B}$$

nance. These defaults can be applied if and only if application does not lead to an inconsistency.

Pure consistency maintenance, as it is obtained through the use of normal defaults, can deal with rebutters, but not with undercutters. Undercutters make it possible to block the application of a rule without taking recourse to the denial of the rule conclusion.

To obtain the effect of undercutters, semi-normal defaults are necessary (or defaults which even lack the negation of the consequent in their justification). If the crime is prescribed, the default mentioned in the last example does not lead to the conclusion that the thief ought to be punished, even though the prerequisite of the default is satisfied and the extension does not include that the thief ought not to be punished.

17.3 Evaluation of default logic

An important advantage of default logic, which it shares with other consistency maintenance approaches, is that it provides us with means to deal with inconsistencies which in traditional logics would follow from the application of rules with incompatible conclusions. In this way, default logic can deal with conflicting reasons. By using semi-normal defaults, default logic can also deal with undercutters.

Another advantage of default logic as a means to represent rules is that defaults are strictly not part of the logical language, but are a kind of inference rules. As a consequence, they only allow for Modus Ponens-like inferences. In particular it is not possible to use defaults for inferences of the forms Modus Tollens, Hypothetical Syllogism, and Contraposition. Moreover, defaults cannot be derived from the denial of their antecedents of the truth of their consequents. In fact, because defaults are not part of the logical language proper, there is no way at all to derive defaults.

The advantage that defaults are not part of the logical language proper is at the same time a disadvantage, however. Because defaults are not part of the logical language, it is impossible to reason about them. As a consequence, it is, for instance not possible to weigh reasons for and against the application of a default.

A final disadvantage of default logic is that it can only deal with arguments which are defeasible because the application of a rule is blocked. In particular it cannot deal with the weighing reasons which is not pairwise. The reasons for this are essentially the same ones as those which were mentioned in section 16.4 in connection with consistency maintenance approaches.

18. CONDITIONAL LOGICS

Conditional logics are characterised by having a non-truth-functional conditional operator. The logical behaviour of this operator must be defined by the concerning conditional logic. Intuitively, this behaviour must involve that the consequent of the conditional will normally be true if its antecedent is true.

Before evaluating conditional logics with regard to how well they can deal with rules, I will illustrate them by a brief discussion of a particular system of conditional logic, that is the system proposed in Morreau 1994.[24]

18.1 Morreau's system

Morreau defines a weak conditional > by means of which it is possible to represent rules. The rule that thieves ought to be punished can be represented by means of the sentence `(∀x)Tx > Ob(p(x))`. A prima facie fact can now be represented by the conjunction of an instantiated rule and the facts that satisfy the conditions of the rule instantiation: `Ta & (Ta > Ob(p(a)))`.

Literally this sentence means that `a` is a thief, and that if `a` is a thief, `a` ought to be punished. The conditional > is so weak that it does not allow arguments of the form Modus Ponens. So it is not possible to derive `Ob(p(a))` from `Ta & (Ta > Ob(p(a)))`.

Intuitively the conditional sentence `a > b` may be read as meaning that `b` is the case in all situations (possible worlds) in which `a` is the case and in which everything holds that tends to go with `a`. The use of this operator makes it possible to distinguish between theories which provide *prima facie* support for a conclusion, and theories which provide *all-things-considered* support.

To make this possible in his logic, Morreau defines an ordering on possible worlds based on the number of exceptional actions. An individual `a` of type `T` is exceptional if it holds that `(∀x)Tx > Cx`, but nevertheless `Ta & ~Ca`. In other words, exceptionality is defined by the fact that a prima facie consequence does actually not hold.

A world W_1 stands in the relation =< to a world W_2 (W_1 =< W_2) if the exceptional individuals in W_1 are a subset of the exceptional circumstances in W_2. Let us call this relation *less exceptional*. If W_1 is less exceptional than W_2 and also the other way round, these two worlds are said to be *equally exceptional*.[25]

---

[24] Morreau's system is confined to a deontic logic for ought to do. In this discussion I generalise his system to a logic for rules in general.

[25] The names *less exceptional* and *equally exceptional* stem from the present author, not from Morreau.

This last relationship can in turn be used to define the relationship of *minimal satisfaction*. A possible world W_1 minimally satisfies a set of sentences T if:

1: all sentences in T are true in W_1, and
2: there is a possible world W_2 such that all sentences in T are true in W_2, then W_1 and W_2 are equally exceptional.

In other words, a possible world minimally satisfies a theory if there is no possible world that also satisfies this theory and which is strictly less exceptional. This means that all exceptional circumstances in such a world are the consequence of what is entailed by this theory.

The notion of minimal satisfaction can be used to define some-things-considered support and all-things-considered support for a sentence:

A theory T provides *some-things-considered support* for a sentence S if there is at least one model N, containing a world W, such that W minimally satisfies T, and such that S is true in all possible worlds in all models which are equally exceptional as W.

A theory T provides *all-things-considered support* for a sentence S, if S is true in all possible worlds in all models that minimally satisfy T.

Suppose that we have the rules

```
(∀x)Tx > Ob(p(x))
```

(Thieves ought to be punished),

and

```
(∀x)Mx > Ob(~p(x))
```

(Minors ought not to be punished).

Suppose, moreover, that John is both a thief and a minor. Since nothing is given about the relative weight of being a thief and a minor, there will be some worlds in some models which minimally satisfy this theory in which John ought to be punished, but there will also be such worlds in some models in which John ought not to be punished. Therefore, the present theory provides some-things-considered support for both the facts that John ought and that he ought not to be punished. It does not provide all-things-considered support for either fact, however. To obtain all-things-considered support, it is necessary to somehow indicate the relative weight of the two factors. The language of Morreau's logic does not provide means to do that.

18.2 An evaluation of conditional logics

Since rules are in a conditional logic normally represented by means of a conditional sentence, that is a sentence of the object-language, it is in general not possible to reason about rules. In this respect conditional logics are rather similar to consistency maintenance approaches. As a consequence, conditional logics will, just as consistency maintenance approaches, in principle be able to deal with conflicting reasons, but not with undercutters. And neither will they provide facilities for arguments about rules, including arguments about whether a rule ought to be applied

Moreover, conditional logics have an additional drawback. If rules are represented by means of conditional sentences, rules will be 'true' (probably to be interpreted as 'valid') if its constituents have the appropriate truth values in normal possible worlds. However, the validity of a rule is normally (epistemic rules are an exception; cf. section 7) independent of the truth values of its constituents. If the validity of a rule goes together with particular truth values of its constituents in normal worlds, this does not imply that the rule is valid *because of* these truth values. It may be just the other way round: the valid rule imposes constraints on normal worlds which lead to certain combinations of truth values.

Nevertheless, the semantics for conditional logics work precisely the other way round. The truth values of sentences with a conditional operator depend on the truth values of the constituent sentences in normal worlds. The semantics seems to treat conditional sentences, which ex hypothesi represent rules, as a kind of descriptive statements (cf. section 15).

In fact, these logics make it impossible to distinguish rule formulations from universal hypothetical statements. For instance, the rule that thieves ought to be punished becomes indistinguishable from the statement that if somebody is a thief, he ought to be punished. Although the truth of this statement (if it is true) will probably be based on the validity of the rule (but cf. section 12), there is still a difference between the rule that makes the statement true and the statement that is made true by it.

It is possible to enhance a conditional logic by providing possibilities to refer to rules. That would make it possible to represent undercutters and to reason about rules. This approach is taken in e.g. the work of Gordon (1994). The disadvantage that rules and conditional statements cannot be distinguished is essential for conditional logics however, and cannot be overcome. From the perspective of the present work, which stresses the fundamental difference between rules and statements, this disadvantage is serious.

19. ARGUMENT-BASED LOGICS

Argument-based logics are built around the idea that given a set of premises and some system of logic, there can be a number of arguments which possibly lead to conflicting conclusions. It is also possible that one argument has as its conclusion that a subargument of another argument does not hold. In such cases, these arguments are not compatible and they need to be compared in order to determine which argument 'survives'. In the end a number of arguments survive, and the conclusions of these arguments are justified on the basis of the original set of premises. Other arguments are defeated, and their conclusions are not justified. Finally some conflicts of arguments may end undecided, and the conclusions of these arguments so to speak 'hang in the air'.[26]

19.1 PS-logic

A recent version of an argument-based logic is the logic proposed in Prakken and Sartor 1995 (PS-logic for short). RBL and PS-logic can to a large extent be translated into each other. That is why I will pay relatively much attention to a comparison between RBL and PS-logic. An essential difference between the two is that RBL takes the notion of a reason as central, which almost automatically leads to the result that the comparison takes place between *sets* of reasons in the form of weighing reasons. Almost all argument-comparison logics compare arguments one by one[27], and as a consequence have difficulties if larger sets of reasons (arguments) have to be weighed.

In the following subsections I will compare RBL to PS-logic to show both how similar they are in some respects, and to argue why the reason-based approach is still to be preferred.[28]

---

[26] Examples of such logics are the work of Pollock (e.g. 1987), Simari and Loui 1992, Prakken 1993, Vreeswijk 1993, and Dung 1995. Not all argument-based logics have the category of undecided conflicts of arguments.

[27] By reconstructing an argument, so as to include two or more reasons into one argument, this characteristic of argument-based logics can be circumvented. This has all the disadvantages of adapting the premises, however. Cf. section I.3.5 and also section 16.4 of this chapter.

[28] I will omit some technical details which are not essential for the comparison between PS-logic and RBL. This means that the description of PS-logic is not sufficiently precise to evaluate PS-logic on its own. I expect, however, that it is sufficiently precise for the comparison with RBL. Moreover, the terminology used in the comparison is not that of Prakken and Sartor 1995, but my own.

19.2 Arguments

The central notion in PS-logic is that of an argument. An argument is a tree of rules, where the conclusion of the one rule is one of the conditions of the following rule. Premises are rules without conditions.

Reasons in RBL are comparable to the joint conditions of the last rule in a chain. This means that an argument in PS-logic corresponds to one reason in RBL, with the difference that an argument contains its conclusion, while a reason in RBL does not contain its conclusion yet, although it is known for which conclusion a reason pleads. Take for instance the argument a → b → c. In RBL-terminology, b would be a reason for c.

In PS-logic there are two kinds of rule conditions, strong and weak ones. Strong conditions are the ones which must be shown to be satisfied to apply the rule. Weak ones are assumed to be satisfied unless their contrary is shown; they are satisfied by default. The weak conditions which are part of an argument, are called the assumptions of this argument.

In the terminology of PS-logic, one might say that each RBL rule has two weak conditions, namely that the rule is not excluded, and that if there are reasons against the application of the rule, they do not outweigh the reason for application based on the rule's applicability.

19.3 Conflicts of arguments

In PS-logic arguments can conflict. There are two kinds of conflict. One argument is said to *rebut* another argument if the conclusions of the two arguments are complementary. This is the case of conflicting reasons in RBL.

One argument *undercuts* another argument if the conclusion of the former argument is the complement of one of the assumptions of the latter argument. An argument which undercuts or rebuts another argument is said to *attack* that other argument. In RBL this is the case of exclusionary reasons against the application of a rule or principle. The situation in RBL where there are both reasons for and against the application of a rule is an intermediate case.

If an argument undercuts another argument, the former is said to *defeat* the latter. In case of two arguments which rebut each other, the *stronger* argument of the two defeats the other one. (If both arguments are equally strong, they both defeat the other argument.) Which argument is the stronger is determined by another argument, which has as its conclusion that some argument is stronger than another argument. This argument with a conclusion concerning the relative strength of other arguments is comparable to weighing information in RBL.

19.4 Three categories of arguments

A conflict between two arguments cannot be solved by looking only at the arguments involved in that conflict. It is possible that some argument A1 is invalidated by an argument A2, and therefore cannot invalidate the argument A3 anymore. A3 'survives' because it is saved from defeat through the help of A2.

This is comparable with the situation in RBL where the reason R1 which pleads for a conclusion C does not have competition from a reason R2 which pleads against C, because the rule which would lead to R2 is excluded.

Because it can only be determined which arguments survive by considering all arguments at once, the definition of justified arguments, the ones which win and justify their conclusions, can only be defined in terms of sets of arguments.

Given a set of rules (including rules without conditions) it is possible to construct a number of arguments. These arguments are divided into three categories, the *justified* ones, the *overruled* ones, and the *defensible* ones. Cf. figure 2.

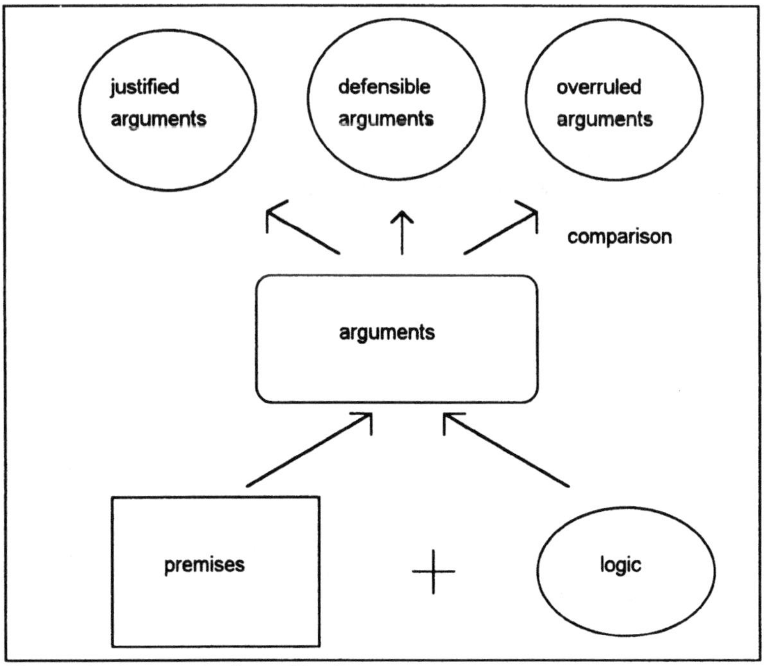

Figure 2: Argument-based logics

The justified arguments are those arguments which are not attacked at all, or are only attacked by arguments which are defeated by a(nother) justified argument. The overruled arguments are the ones which are defeated by a justified argument. The defensible arguments are the arguments which are neither justified, nor overruled.

In RBL, overruled arguments would not lead to reasons at all. Defensible arguments would in RBL fall in one of two subcategories. If the unsolved conflict, which makes that the arguments are not justified, belongs to a subargument which leads to a reason, the argument does not generate a reason. If the unsolved conflict concerns the reasons that plead directly for or against the conclusion, the arguments lead to reasons, but the necessary weighing information to decide the collision of reasons is lacking. In both cases PS-logic and RBL lead to the same conclusion, namely that the final conclusions of the arguments cannot be derived. The constructions used are somewhat different, however.

In the case of justified arguments, PS-logic and RBL are rather similar. A justified argument in PS-logic is one where the chain of reasons that leads to a conclusion is uninterrupted and where the final reason is stronger than any reason against the same conclusion. The main difference with RBL is that in PS-logic a justified argument justifies its conclusion on the basis of one single reason. This reason is stronger than any other reason which pleads in a different direction, but the conclusion is still based on one reason. In RBL, however, every conclusion is based on the weighing of the *sets of reasons* for and against that conclusion. Very often one set will consist of only one reason, and the other set of at most one reason, but this does not subtract from the principle that in RBL it is sets of reasons which determine the conclusions, and not single reasons. As a consequence, the weighing information in RBL deals with sets of reasons, rather than with pairs of reasons.

It would be relatively easy to modify PS-logic so that the relation of strength which now holds between individual arguments, would hold for sets of arguments. With that modification, PS-logic would lead to the same results, and along essentially the same line as RBL.[29]

There remains an important difference, however. In RBL the notion of a reason takes the central place, and there is a two step-procedure that consists of collecting and weighing reasons. Both of these steps are on one and the same level of argumentation. In PS-logic the notion of an argument plays the central role, and the two step-procedure consists of collecting and comparing all arguments. The comparison of arguments is necessarily on another level of

---

[29] This may not be fully correct for some deviant arguments in which rules are used that refer to themselves and to each other. Cf. section IV.8. For those cases, PS-logic might offer a slightly different solution than RBL.

argumentation, although it is possible to model the second level in the same way as the first level.

19.5 An evaluation of logics based on the comparison of arguments.

Argument-based logics as such do not specify the nature of the arguments which are to be compared, nor the criteria by means of which they are to be compared. By adopting a good underlying logic to represent the arguments, and standards which compare the arguments in an attractive way, these logics can be made into powerful tools for dealing with rules. We have seen how a slight modification can turn PS-logic into a logic which can achieve practically the same results as RBL.

An essential difference remains that argument-based logics divide arguments which originally seemed to be one, into basic arguments and arguments about arguments. This seems not so intuitive to me.

D. TWO METAPHORS OF REASONING

At the beginning of this book I wrote that reasoning with rules is different from reasoning with hypothetical statements. I hope that I have provided sufficient reasons and illustrations to make this thesis feasible. In the chapters II and III I developed an informal model of reasoning with rules, goals, and principles. In the chapters IV and V this model was developed formally, and in part C of this chapter the result of that development was briefly compared with other logics for defeasible reasoning. In this final part of the book I want to tie some strings together by juxtaposing principles and statements again, and by showing how the difference between these two is reflected in two different ways of looking at arguments.

20. TWO METAPHORS

Metaphors are very important for our view of the world (Lakoff and Johnson 1980). They strongly influence how we look at phenomena, and as a consequence how we try to solve problems in certain areas. Metaphors can, for that reason, be seen as central elements in scientific paradigms. Just as the quality of a paradigm strongly influences the success of a research program based on this paradigm, the quality of a metaphor is to a large degree determinative for the success of a direction of research. In fact, the metaphor underlying a paradigm may be seen as part of the hard core of a research program, where the various theories built on the metaphor are the protective belt of the program. (cf. Lakatos 1970, pp. 132f.)

A common view of valid reasoning is that valid arguments make in their conclusions information explicit that was implicitly available in the premises. The theory that consists of the premises of an argument is considered as a *container filled with information*. Valid arguments show us parts of the contained information. The *container metaphor*, especially its elaboration in terms of possible worlds, plays a central role in much of our thinking about valid reasoning and logic. Fruitful as this metaphor may have been for much logical theorising, it hinders, I think, an adequate analysis of reasoning with rules.

Based on a brief characterisation of the role of argumentation in everyday life, I will propose another metaphor for arguments, the *metaphor of colliding forces*. In this metaphor, the notion of a reason for a conclusion plays a central role. I will show how the proposed metaphor makes sense of various forms of defeasibility.

21. THE CONTAINER METAPHOR AND POSSIBLE WORLDS

The container metaphor is often elaborated in terms of possible worlds. A possible world is a complete collection of states of affairs, that is a collection of states of affairs for which it holds that every state of affairs obtains in it or not. A sentence divides the set of all possible worlds into the set of worlds in which this sentence is true, and the set of worlds in which this sentence is false. Analogously, every set of sentences (theory) divides the set of possible worlds into two sets, the models and the non-models of the theory.[30]

Given this relation between a theory and the set of its models, it is possible to give an attractive definition of a valid argument. Each possible world can be considered as a container of information. Those possible worlds that are models of a particular theory, have a certain amount of information in common. In fact, the common information of all these possible worlds is precisely the information contained in the theory whose models they are. As a consequence, any sentence that contains information that is also contained in the theory will be true in all models of this theory. That the conclusion of a valid argument can only contain information that was also contained in its premises becomes in possible world terminology: *An argument is valid if and only if its conclusion is true in all possible worlds in which all of its premises are true.*

The notion of logical validity as expressed by means of possible worlds is essentially *semantic*. It makes use of the truth values of sentences in possible worlds to determine whether an argument is valid or not. In a calculus that is interpreted as a logic, the rules of inference define the *syntactic* notion of

[30] Notice that a model is here just one possible world.

validity. An argument is valid if its conclusion can be produced from the premises by means of the rules of inference that belong to the calculus. Logical calculi are influenced by the possible worlds metaphor insofar as they make their rules of inference reflect the semantic notion of validity.

It should be noticed that the container metaphor itself is much less precise than its elaboration in terms of possible worlds. The intuition behind the metaphor is that a valid argument consists of two parts. On the one hand there are premises which together give us a certain amount of information about the world. This is the information which goes, so to speak, into the container. On the other hand we have the conclusion which also contains some information. The idea behind the container metaphor is that an argument is valid if the information contained in the conclusion is part of the information contained in the premises. In other words, the information of the conclusion should be in the container.[31]

22. THE INFORMATION CONTENT OF RULES

If rules are represented as a kind of information conveying sentences (statements), this is completely in accordance with the container metaphor, which considers all elements of a theory as pieces of information that are joined together as the basis for derivations. However, in section 8, that deals with directions of fit, I have argued that in opposition to statements, rules have no information content. They are constitutive and have the world to word direction of fit.

But is not it the case that rules, even if they do not have it as their primary function to convey information about the world, nevertheless *indirectly* contain information? For example, if the rule that thieves ought to be punished is valid, thieves ought usually to be punished. The validity of the rule makes it the case that certain facts obtain, or rather, because of the defeasibility of reasoning with rules, tend to obtain. In the semantics of RBL, this indirect information content is expressed by means of constraints on all possible worlds which connect particular consequences to the fact that a rule is valid in a world. So there is a clear connection between rules and the facts that obtain in the world.

The mistake in this objection that rules at least indirectly have an information content is that it suggests a wrong picture of the relation between the

---

[31] Possible world semantics, or modeltheoretic semantics, is a way to make the notion of information content that is connected with a set of sentences, precise. As a technical device, this type of semantics can however be stretched to cover completely different views of logical validity. An example of this can be found in section 14, which provides a possible worlds semantics for RBL, a logic which is absolutely not based on the container metaphor.

validity of the rule and the corresponding facts in the world. The facts in the world are there because of the logically prior validity of the rule. The rule is not valid because of the corresponding facts in the world. As I argued in section 12, it is even possible that the facts in the world, or even a set of possible words, which correspond to a rule may hold even thought the concerning rule is not valid.[32]

23. THE PRAGMATIC NOTION OF VALIDITY

We may conclude that it is unattractive to treat rules in arguments as if they were statements. This conclusion returns us to the issue of semantic validity. Does it make sense to work with the semantic notion of validity in case of arguments based on rule application? My answer to this question would be negative, because the whole issue of the information content, around which the semantic notion of validity is built, is meaningless in connection with rules. It is possible to have formal theories of reasoning with rules, but they cannot be based on the container metaphor and its corresponding notion of semantic validity. As an alternative for the semantic notion, I will therefore introduce the pragmatic notion of validity.

23.1 Validity and effectiveness

The pragmatic notion of validity is defined in terms of *effectiveness* of argumentation. Argumentation is the speech act in which a line of reasoning is brought to the fore. Only argumentation as an actual event can be effective; a line of reasoning can metaphorically be said to be effective if its use in argumentation tends to be effective. In a similar fashion, argumentation can be said to be valid if it employs a line of reasoning that is valid.

There is a connection between logical validity (as an unanalysed notion) and the effectiveness of means to convince an audience. Means of conviction that are never effective, under whatever circumstances, are not valid means. On the contrary, valid means of conviction will be normally effective. A deductively valid argument, for instance, would never have counted as valid if it would most of the times be ineffective.

We found that valid arguments will normally be effective. Is it possible to turn the connection between validity and effectiveness around, and say that argument types that are usually effective, are also valid? I think that the answer to this question should *in general* be affirmative, but that there are three conditions that must be fulfilled. The first condition is that the *connection* between effectiveness and validity is confined to argument *types*. The second

---

[32] Cf. also section 15.

condition is that what is adduced in arguments of an effective type should also be considered as *reasons* for the conclusion. The third condition, finally, is that an effective argument type should usually not loose its effectiveness if the rule of inference that defines this argument type is *criticised* on the basis of other standards.

23.2 Effectiveness and validity in connection with argument types

Not every argument that turns out to be effective, is ipso facto valid. People tend to make mistakes, also in their judgement of arguments, and this may lead to the effectiveness of bad argumentation. However, people do not always make mistakes. If a type of argument is most of the times effective, this very fact means that this type of argument is considered to be a suitable type of argument for the conclusion at stake, or - in other words - that it is (informally) valid.[33] Of course, I assume here that the other two conditions for validity are also satisfied.

If validity is a characteristic of argument types, it is important to know how arguments can be divided into the relevant types. Here the notion of a *rule of inference* comes in. Rules of inference must abstract from some of the details of the arguments they govern. If only for practical reasons, there cannot be a rule of inference for every individual argument; a rule must state the validity of classes of inferences, which are identified by a number of characteristics identified in the rule. A rule of inference specifies which characteristics of an argument determine whether the argument is valid. An argument type is valid if arguments of this type are licensed by a rule of inference.

If an audience uses a rule of inference, it will both recognise arguments based on this rule as valid, and normally be convinced by these arguments. It is not possible to use a rule of inference, and still be normally unconvinced by arguments based on these rules. A rule with such dubious effects can hardly be called a rule of *inference* anymore. That is why valid arguments will usually be effective arguments too.

23.3 Causes and reasons

Suppose that it would be an effective strategy for an attorney who wants a suspect to be convicted, to point out that the suspect is black. Does this make the argument that somebody is black a valid one for the thesis that this person should be convicted?[34]

---

[33] Cf. section II.10 on the dispositional nature of reasons.

[34] Here I use the word 'argument' in the sense of something that is adduced *within* a line of reasoning.

Pointing out that the suspect is black may trigger unconscious mechanisms that would not be sanctioned by the persons subject to them, if they would be aware of them. Effectiveness of arguments only implies validity if the causal connection between the arguments and their effects is approved by the persons for whom this connection exists.[35] Such approval can take place in the form of adducing the arguments as the *reason* (not only the cause) why the conclusion was adopted. In other words, the facts adduced in the argument should not only *explain*, but also *justify* the conviction in the eyes of the audience.

Of course, explicit approval is only possible in those cases in which the convinced person acknowledges the arguments as the cause of his conviction. This need not be the case in all cases of conviction. However, for an argument type to be valid it is necessary that the persons for whom the type is effective approve of this effectiveness *if they are aware of it*.[36]

23.4 Rules of inference should withstand criticism

Until now, I discussed rules of inference as if they were rules adopted by individual persons. In the end, this seems to be correct. Rule following behaviour ultimately comes down to behaviour of individuals. Still, the validity of arguments is usually evaluated by means of standards that are in practice in a social group. Rules of inference are normally social rules.

What counts as valid in one society or period of time, is based on the rules of inference used in that society at that time; it may be completely invalid in another society or period. The standards of validity are relative to a particular audience. Still, this does not mean that it is impossible to argue about standards. Even in a racist society it is possible to argue against discrimination on the basis of race. Such arguments will only be effective (and valid) if this society adopts additional standards that make it possible to evaluate the first-mentioned standards. The result of this evaluation may be that the racist standards are wrong and consequently that it is invalid to argue for a person's conviction by pointing out that he is black.[37]

23.5 The fact-value distinction

It may seem that the pragmatic notion of logical validity is based on a confusion between the evaluative notion of validity and the factual notion of effectiveness. This appearance is deceptive. The pragmatic notion of validity is based on rules of inference (standards for the validity of arguments) and is as

---

[35] Cf. section II.11.2 on unwanted associations.

[36] Cf. section II.11.1 on the consciousness of reasons.

[37] Cf. section III.5.3 on the validity of social rules.

such evaluative. An argument is valid if it is in accordance with a valid rule of inference.

Effectiveness of arguments plays a role in the analysis of the existence (validity) of rules of inference. Whether a rule of inference exists (whether it is valid) is a purely factual matter, and whether an argument is in accordance with such a rule is also a purely factual matter. Therefore, the validity of an argument is a purely factual matter, and the crucial facts have, in the pragmatic view, to do with the effectiveness of types of argumentation.

Still, it may be objected that I confuse the internal and the external point of view here (cf. Hart 1961, pp. 55/56 and 86-88). The pragmatic definition of validity only gives the conditions under which an argument is considered as valid within a particular community. As such, it is an analysis of validity from the (moderately) external point of view. The evaluation of arguments by means of logical criteria presupposes a commitment to those criteria, and is therefore from the internal point of view.

The reply to this objection is that this distinction is correct, but irrelevant for logical purposes. I may use a standard in making an evaluative statement. In that case I take the internal point of view, and do not relativise the evaluation to the validity of the standard. I seem to accept the standard. However, the truth value of the evaluative statement still depends on the validity of the standard. It does not matter whether the internal or the external point of view is taken, a standard must be valid in order to support evaluative judgements.

Since a logical theory is involved with the truth (or the acceptability) of conclusions, the internal/external distinction does not play a role in it. An external theory that specifies the truth conditions for evaluative judgements, for instance about the validity of arguments, also specifies under which circumstances the evaluations are justified.

23.6 Rules of inference are social rules

Many readers will already have noticed that the account of logical validity that is presented here comes down to the following theory:

An argument is valid if it is in accordance with the social rules or principles of inference which are valid in the group to which the reasoner belongs.

The tendency to effectiveness of valid arguments is logically connected to the account of the validity of social rules and principles. The demand that the relevant characteristics of arguments are not only the cause, but also the justification of the acceptance of the conclusion corresponds to the demand that the connection between reasons and their conclusions should be conscious. And, finally, the demand that rules of inference should withstand criticism corresponds to the general demand that a person who employs a principle should approve, or at least not disapprove, of it.

This view of valid reasoning is a consequence of the more basic assumption that reasoning is a kind of rule or principle following behaviour, which is similar to other kinds of rule or principle following behaviour. The general theory of reasoning with rules etc. which I proposed in this book also holds for reasoning with inference rules. This basic assumption is also reflected in the definition of logically possible worlds as those worlds in which some logical rules are valid (cf. section 15). Logically possible worlds are different from, e.g. legally possible worlds, but the difference is a difference in the rules which are assumed to be valid, and not something more fundamental.

A consequence of this view, which was not elaborated in this book, is that it is not necessary to make RBL-possible worlds a subset of the possible worlds according to predicate logic. Instead the rules of predicate logic could be treated as rules which might be valid in some RBL-possible world.

24. THE FORCES METAPHOR OF REASONING

The pragmatic notion of validity that was defined above is completely different from the semantic notion. It is much more connected to social practices and human behaviour, and less to the meaning and the truth conditions of sentences. Although there seems to be room for both the semantic and the pragmatic notion of logical validity, I think that the pragmatic notion is more useful if we deal with principles and rules. To make this more clear, I will develop an alternative metaphor of valid reasoning, the metaphor of *colliding forces*.

A rational audience that is subjected to arguments that try to convince it of a particular conclusion, or of its denial, can be compared to a physical body that is subject to a number of colliding forces (cf. section III.1 for another exploration of the physics-parallel). Just as the combination of the forces determines in which direction the body will actually be moved (accelerated), the combination of the adduced reasons determines whether a rational audience will accept the conclusion or its negation, or refrain from judgement.

The forces that act upon a physical body are determined by the facts of the situation at hand, and by the applicable laws of nature. In fact, the forces can be considered as instantiations of the physical laws. None of the forces by itself determines the behaviour of the physical body; only in their interaction they cause the body to move. Clearly, if there is only one force, that force by itself determines what will happen. In this case, the one force should be considered as the combination of all the forces.

The relation between a physical law and a force is not straightforward. Indeed, in simple cases, the magnitude of the force can simply be computed by filling in the parameters in the formula that represents the law. The gravitation on Earth can, for instance, be computed by filling in the mass m of the accelerated body in the formula G = 9.8m. The scope of this law is restricted, however. The law only applies near the surface of planet Earth. In a similar fashion, the Newtonian laws of gravitation only apply if the concerned velocities are not extremely high. In short, a law does not apply to a particular case if this case falls outside the scope of the law.

The relation between a physical law and its instantiations, the forces that occur in a particular case, is similar to the relation between a principle and the reasons that are based on it. If a principle applies to a particular case, the facts that make the principle applicable (that match with the conditions of the principle) become a reason for the conclusion. A reason is comparable to a force; it pulls a rational audience towards acceptation of the conclusion for which it is a reason.

The purpose of the comparison between a body that is subjected to forces, and an audience that is subjected to arguments, is to suggest that the conclusion from a set of premises is the outcome of the interactions of the reasons that can be based on these premises, and that the role of principles, which make facts into reasons, is comparable to that of forces, which make facts into causes. The comparison may be deceptive, because not all 'forces' that act on an audience represent reasons for accepting a particular conclusion. It is not my intention to suggest that a conclusion can validly be drawn from a set of premises, if the effect of adducing these premises is that the audience comes to accept the conclusion. That is why I wrote about the influences of reasons on a *rational* audience.

To those who want to point out that the notion of a rational audience will probably be defined in terms of the arguments which they accept, I answer that they are correct. There is no Archimedean point that defines the notion of rationality and which serves as an independent standard both for the rationality of arguments and of audiences. Rationality is defined in a social practice on the basis of a critical attitude which humans can take towards their own behaviour, including the behaviour of taking critical attitudes. Cf. my remarks on the shifting bounds of rationality in section III.15.

The metaphor of colliding forces is more suited to reasoning with principles than to reasoning with rules. The reason for this is that rules are somewhat in between principles and statements (cf. section III.2). Rules are like statements in that if they are (ought to be) applied to a case, their conclusions always follows. But they are like principles in that there can be reasons for and against their application. The forces metaphor of reasoning still holds for the weighing of these reasons.

25. SUMMARY

With the discussion of the two metaphors of reasoning, the argument of this book has returned to its beginning. There I argued that rule applying arguments should not be modelled as arguments of the form Modus Ponens. In the chapters II and III I attempted to show how principles and rules are different from statements and why reasoning with them should be modelled differently. In the chapters IV and V, I have made an elaborated proposal for such a different way of modelling. In this final chapter, the different themes of this book were connected.

The central distinction of this book is the distinction between descriptive sentences and constitutive principles. Descriptive sentences have the word to world fit, and their truth depends on an independently existing world. Principles have the world to word direction of fit. They are not true or false, but they constrain the possible combinations of facts in the world. Rules take a position in between principles and descriptive sentences.

Descriptive sentences have an information content. A suitable metaphor for reasoning with them is the container metaphor. The corresponding notion of logical validity is the semantic one: a conclusion follows from a theory if and only if it is true in all models of this theory.

Principles have no information content, but they function as constraints on combinations of facts. A suitable metaphor for reasoning with principles is the colliding forces metaphor. The corresponding notion of logical validity is the pragmatic one: a conclusion follows from a set of premises if the reasons based on this set of premises for the conclusion outweigh the reasons that plead against it. Reason-Based Logic is an example of how the pragmatic notion of validity can be cast into a logic.

Aarnio, A. (1987). *The Rational as Reasonable. A Treatise on Legal Justification*. D. Reidel Publishing Company, Dordrecht.

Albert, H. (1968). *Traktat über kritische Vernunft*, Siebeck, Tübingen.

Alchourrón, C.E. (1993). Philosophical Foundations of Deontic Logic and the Logic of Defeasible Conditionals. J.-J. Ch. Meijer and R.J. Wieringa (eds.), *Deontic Logic in Computer Science*. John Wiley & Sons, Chicester, pp. 43-84.

Alchourrón, C.E. and Bulygin, E. (1991). The Expressive Conception of Norms. R. Hilpinen (ed.), *New Studies in Deontic Logic*, D. Reidel Publishing Company, Dordrecht e.a., pp. 95-124.

Alexy, R. (1978). *Theorie der juristischen Argumentation*. Suhrkamp Verlag, Frankfurt am Main.

Alexy, R. (1979). Zum Begriff des Rechtprinzips, *Rechtstheorie*, Beiheft 1, pp. 59-87.

Alexy, R. (1985). *Theorie der Grundrechten*, Nomos Verlagsgesellschaft, Baden-Baden.

Allwood, J. L., G. Andersson and Ö. Dahl (1977), *Logic in Linguistics*, Cambridge University Press, Cambridge e.a.

Anscombe, G.E.M. (1957). *Intentions*, Blackwell, Oxford.

Anscombe, G.E.M. (1958). On Brute Facts, *Analysis*, vol. 18, pp. 69-72.

Ashley, K.D. (1991). Reasoning with cases and hypotheticals in HYPO. *International Journal of Man-Machine Studies*, vol. 34, pp. 753-796.

Baker, G.P. (1977). Defeasibility and Meaning. P.M.S. Hacker and J. Raz (eds.) *Law, Morality and Society*. Clarendon Press, Oxford, pp. 26-57.

Branting, L.K. (1991). Reasoning with Portions of Precedents, *Proceedings of the Third International Conference on Artificial Intelligence and Law*, ACM, New York, pp. 145-154.

Brewka, G. (1989). Preferred subtheories: an extended logical framework for default reasoning. *Proceedings of the 11th International Joint Conference on Artificial Intelligence, 1989*, pp. 1043-1048.

Carnap, R. (1956). *Meaning and Necessity*, 2nd ed., University of Chicago Press, Chicago and London.

Castañeda, H.N. (1970). On the semantics of ought-to-do. *Synthese* 21, pp. 449-468.

Chellas, B.F. (1980). *Modal logic; an introduction*. Cambridge University Press, Cambridge e.a.

Copi, I.M. (1978). *Introduction to Logic*. 5th ed. MacMillan Publishing Co., New York.

Dalen, D. van (1983), *Logic and Structure*, Springer Verlag, Berlin e.a.

Dung, P.M. (1995). On the acceptability of arguments and its fundamental role in nonmonotonic reasoning, logic programming and n-person games. *Artificial Intelligence* 77, number 2, pp. 321-357.

Dworkin, R. (1978). *Taking Rights Seriously*, 2nd ed., Duckworth, London.

Fuller, L.L. (1958). Positivism and Fidelity to Law: A Reply to Professor Hart, *Harvard Law Review* 71, pp. 630-672.

Geffner, H. and J. Pearl (1992). Conditional entailment: bridging two approaches to default reasoning, *Artificial Intelligence* 53, pp. 209-244.

Ginsberg, M. (ed.) (1987). *Readings in Nonmonotonic Reasoning*, Morgan Kaufmann Publishers, Palo Alto.

Goodman, N. (1978). *Ways of worldmaking*, Hackett Publishing Company, Indianapolis and Cambridge.

Gordon, Th. F. (1994): The Pleadings Game: An Exercise in Computational Dialectics, *Artificial Intelligence and Law* 2, pp. 239-292.

Hage, J.C. (1986). The Objectivity of Value Judgments. *Rechtstheorie*, vol 17, pp. 501-507.

Hage, J.C. (1987). *Feiten en betekenis; een verhandeling over ontologie en praktische rede*, PhD-thesis, Leiden.

Hage, J.C. (1991). An Alternative for Deontic Logic. C. van Noortwijk, A.H.J. Schmidt and R.G.F. Winkels (eds.), *Legal Knowledge Based Systems. Aims for Research and Development*, Koninklijke Vermande BV, Lelystad, pp. 59-69.

Hage, J.C. (1993). Monological Reason Based Logic. *Proceedings of the Fourth International Conference on Law and Artificial Intelligence*, ACM-press, New York, pp. 30-39.

Hage, J.C. (1994). Reason Based Logic: General Considerations and some Applications. I. Carr and A. Narayanan (eds.) *Proceedings of the Fourth National Conference on Law, Computers and Artificial Intelligence*. University of Exeter, pp. 70-79.

Hage, J.C. (1995). Teleological reasoning in reason-based logic. *Proceedings of the Fifth International Conference on Artificial Intelligence and Law*, ACM Press, New York, pp. 11-20.

Hage, J.C. (Model). A Model of Legal Reasoning and a Logic to Match. To appear in a special issue on legal reasoning of *Artificial Intelligence and Law* (1996).

Hage, J.C. and H.B. Verheij (1994). Towards a logic for reasoning with norms. J. Breuker (ed.) *Proceedings of the ECAI-94 Workshop on Artificial Normative Reasoning*, pp. 160-177.

Hage, J.C. and H.B. Verheij (1995). Reason-Based Logic: a logic for reasoning with rules and reasons. *Law, Computers and Artificial Intelligence*, vol. 3, nrs. 2/3, pp. 171-209.

Hare, R.M. (1952). *The Language of Morals*. Oxford University Press, Oxford e.a.

Hare, R.M. (1963). *Freedom and Reason*, Oxford University Press, Oxford e.a.

Hart, H.L.A. (1949). The Ascription of Responsibility and Rights. *Proc. of the Aristotelian Society*, 49, pp. 171-194.

Hart, H.L.A. (1961). *The Concept of Law*, Clarendon Press, Oxford.

Hilpinen, R. (ed.) (1971), *Deontic Logic: Introductory and Systematic Readings*, D. Reidel Publishing Company, Dordrecht e.a.

Hintikka, J. (1971). Some Main Problems of Deontic Logic. R. Hilpinen (ed._, *Deontic Logic: Introductory and Systematic Readings.*, D. Reidel Publishing Company, Dordrecht e.a, pp. 59-104.

Hofstadter, D.R. (1980), *Gödel, Escher, Bach: an Eternal Golden Braid*, Vintage Books, New York.

Hohfeld, W.N. (1913). Fundamental Legal Conceptions as Applied in Judicial Reasoning, 23 *Yale Law Journal*, 16.

Hull, D.L. (1974), *Philosophy of Biological Science*, Prentice-Hall, Englewood Cliffs.

Kelsen, H. (1945). *General Theory of Law and State*, Russell and Russell, New York.

Kelsen, H. (1960). *Reine Rechtslehre*, 2nd ed., Franz Deuticke, Wien.

Kelsen, H. (1979). *Allgemeine Theorie der Normen*. (K. Ringhofer und R. Walter hrsg.) Manz-Verlag, Wien.

Lakatos, I. (1970). Falsification and the Methodology of Scientific Research Programs. I. Lakatos and A. Musgrave (eds.), *Criticism and the Growth of Knowledge*, Cambridge University Press pp. 91-196.

Lakoff, G. (1987a). *Women, Fire, and Dangerous Things. What Categories Reveal about the Mind.* University of Chicago Press. Chicago and London.

Lakoff, G. (1987b). Cognitive models and prototype theory. U Neisser (ed.), *Concepts and Conceptual Development. Ecological and intellectual factors in categorization*, Cambridge University Press, pp. 63-100.

Lakoff, G. and M. Johnson (1980). *Metaphors we live by*, The University of Chicago Press, Chicago and London.

Larenz, K. (1983). *Methodenlehre der Rechtswissenschaft*, 5th ed., Springer Verlag, Berlin e.a.

Loui, R.P. (1995). Hart's Critics on Defeasible Concepts and Ascriptivism. Proceedings of the Fifth International Conference on Artificial Intelligence and Law, ACM, New York, pp. 21-30.

Lukaszewicz, W. (1990). *Non-Monotonic Reasoning; formalization of commonsense reasoning*. Ellis Horwood, London e.a.

MacCormick, D.N. (1974). Law as institutional fact, *The Law Quarterly Review* 90, pp. 102-129. Also in D.N. MacCormick and O. Weinberger, *An Institutional Theory of Law*, Reidel, Dordrecht 1986, pp. 49-76.

MacCormick, D.N. (1978). *Legal Reasoning and Legal Theory*, Clarendon Press, Oxford.

MacCormick, D.N. (1993). Argumentation and Interpretation in Law. *Ratio Juris*, vol. 6, pp. 16-29.

MacCormick, D.N. and O. Weinberger (1986), *An Institutional Theory of Law*, Reidcl, Dordrecht e.a.

MacCormick, D.N. and Summers, R.S. (1991). *Interpreting statutes: a comparitive study*, Darthmouth Publishing Company Limited, Hants and Brookfield.

Marx, M. (1977). Interessenjurisprudenz und Freirechtslehre. A. Kaufmann und W. Hassemer (hrsg.), *Einführung in Rechtsphilosophie und Rechtstheorie der Gegenwart*, Müller Juristischer Verlag, Heidelberg e.a., pp. 97-102.

Mendelson, E. (1987). *Introduction to Mathematical Logic*, 3rd ed., Wadsworth & Brooks/ Cole Advanced Books and Software, Belmont.

Morreau, M. (1994). Prima Facie and Seeming Duties, A.J.I. Jones and M. Sergot (eds.), *Deon '94*, Proceedings of the second international workshop on deontic logic in computer science, pp. 221-251.

Naess, A. (1978). *Elementaire argumentatieleer*. Ambo, Baarn.

Peczenik, A. (1983). *The Basis of Legal Justification*, Lund.

Peczenik, A. (1989). *On Law and Reason*, Kluwer Academic Publishers, Dordrecht e.a.

Pollock, J.L. (1987). Defeasible Reasoning. *Cognitive Science* 11, pp. 481-518.

Pollock, J.L. (1992). How to reason defeasibly, *Artificial Intelligence* 57, pp. 1-42.

Pollock, J.L. (1994). Justification and defeat, *Artificial Intelligence* 67, pp. 377-407.

Prakken, H. (1993). *Logical tools for modelling legal argument*, PhD-thesis, Amsterdam.

Prakken, H. and G. Sartor (1995). On the relation between legal language and legal argument: assumptions, applicability and dynamic priorities, *Proceedings of the Fifth International Conference on Artificial Intelligence and Law*, ACM, New York, pp. 1-10.

Putnam, H. (1975). *Mind, Language and Reality; Philosophical Papers, vol. 2*, Cambridge University Press.

Putnam, H. (1981). *Reason, Truth and History*. Cambridge University Press, Cambridge e.a.

Raz, J. (1972). Legal Principles and the Limits of Law, *Yale Law Journal* 81, pp. 851f.

Raz, J. (1975). *Practical Reason and Norms*, Hutchinson, London.

Raz, J. (1978a). Introduction. J. Raz (ed.) *Practical Reasoning*. Oxford University Press, Oxford, pp. 1-17.

Raz, J. (1978b). Reasons for actions, decisions, and norms. J. Raz (ed.), *Practical Reasoning*. Oxford University Press, Oxford, pp. 128-143.

Raz, J. (1979). Legitimate Authority. J. Raz, *The Authority of Law*, Clarendon Press, Oxford, pp. 3-27.

Raz, J. (1986). *The Morality of Freedom*. Clarendon Press, Oxford.

Raz. J. (1993). On the autonomy of legal reasoning. *Ratio Juris*, vol 6, nr. 1, pp. 1-15.

Reiter, R. (1980). A logic for default reasoning. *Artificial Intelligence* 13, pp. 81-132.

Rosch, E. (1978). Principles of categorization. E. Rosch and B.B. Lloyd (eds.) *Cognition and Categorization*, Erlbaum, Hillsdale.

Ross, W.D. (1930). *The Right and the Good*, Clarendon Press, Oxford.

Ruiter, D.W.P. (1993) *Institutional Legal Facts. Legal Powers and their Effects*. Kluwer Academic Publishers, Dordrecht e.a.

Sanford, D.H. (1989). *If P, then Q. Conditionals and the Foundations of Reasoning*. Routledge, London and New York.

Sartor G. (1991). The Structure of Norm Conditions and Nonmonotonic Reasoning in Law, *Proc. of the Third International Conference on Artificial Intelligence and Law*, ACM Press, pp. 155-164.

Searle, J.R. (1964). How to Derive 'Ought' from 'Is', *Philosophical Review* 73, pp. 43-58.

Searle, J.R. (1969). *Speech acts. An essay in the philosophy of language*. Cambridge University Press.

Searle, J.R. (1978). Prima Facie Obligations. J. Raz (ed.), *Practical Reasoning*, Oxford University Press, Oxford.

Searle, J.R. (1979). A Taxonomy of Illocutionary Acts, *Expression and Meaning*, Cambridge University Press, Cambridge e.a., pp. 1-29.

Searle, J.R. (1983). *Intentionality. An essay in the philosophy of mind*, Cambridge University Press.

Searle, J.R. (1995). *The construction of social reality*. The Free Press, New York.

Simari, G.R. and R.P. Loui (1992). A mathematical treatment of defeasible reasoning and its implementation. *Artificial Intelligence* 53, pp.125-157.

Smith, E.E. (1989). Concepts and Induction. M.I. Posner (ed.), *Foundations of Cognitive Science*, MIT Press, Cambridge, pp. 501-526.

Smith, E.E. (1990). Categorization. D.N. Osherson and E.E. Smith (eds.), *Thinking. An Invitation to Cognitive Science, vol. 3*. MIT Press, Cambridge Mass. and London, pp. 33-54.

Soeteman, A. (1989). *Logic in Law. Remarks on Logic and Rationality in Normative Reasoning, Especially in Law*. Kluwer Academic Publishers, Dordrecht e.a.

Strawson, P. F. (1971). *Logico Linguistic Papers*, Methuen, London.

Summers, R.S. (1978). Two types of substantive reasons: The core of a theory of common-law justification. *Cornell Law Review* 63 nr. 5, pp. 707-735.

Tammelo, I. und H. Schreiner (1977). *Grundzüge und Grundverfahren der Rechtslogik*, Verlag Dokumentation Saur KG, München.

Taylor, P.W. (1961). *Normative discourse*. Greenwood Press, Westport.

Toulmin, S.E. (1953). *The Philosophy of Science; An Introduction*, Hutchinson & Co., London.

Toulmin, S.E. (1958). *The Uses of Argument*, Cambridge University Press, London and New York.

Valente, A. (1995). *Legal Knowledge Engineering. A Modelling Approach*. PhD-thesis. IOS Press, Amsterdam.

Verheij, H.B. (1995). The influence of defeated arguments in defeasible argumentation. M. de Glas and Z. Pawlak (eds.) *WOCFAI 95. Proceedings of the Second World Conference on the Fundamentals of Artificial Intelligence*, pp. 429-440. Angkor, Paris.

Verheij, H.B. and J.C. Hage (1994). Reasoning by analogy; a formal reconstruction. H. Prakken, A.J. Muntjewerff and A. Soeteman (eds.), *Legal knowledge based systems; the relation with legal theory*, Koninklijke Vermande, Lelystad, pp. 65-78.

Vreeswijk, G.A.W. (1993). *Studies in Defeasible Argumentation*. PhD-thesis, Amsterdam.

Weinberger, O. (1986). Facts and Fact-descriptions, D.N. MacCormick and O. Weinberger, *An Institutional Theory of Law*, Reidel, Dordrecht 1986, pp. 77-92.

White, A.R. (1975). *Modal Thinking*. Basil Blackwell, Oxford.

White, A.R. (1984). *Rights*. Clarendon Press, Oxford.

Wittgenstein, L. (1953). *Philosophical Investigations*, Basil Blackwell, Oxford.

Wright, G.H. von (1963). *Norm and Action*, Routledge and Kegan Paul, London.

Law and Philosophy Library

1. E. Bulygin, J.-L. Gardies and I. Niiniluoto (eds.): *Man, Law and Modern Forms of Life.* With an Introduction by M.D. Bayles. 1985 ISBN 90-277-1869-5
2. W. Sadurski: *Giving Desert Its Due.* Social Justice and Legal Theory. 1985 ISBN 90-277-1941-1
3. N. MacCormick and O. Weinberger: *An Institutional Theory of Law.* New Approaches to Legal Positivism. 1986 ISBN 90-277-2079-7
4. A. Aarnio: *The Rational as Reasonable.* A Treatise on Legal Justification. 1987 ISBN 90-277-2276-5
5. M.D. Bayles: *Principles of Law.* A Normative Analysis. 1987 ISBN 90-277-2412-1; Pb: 90-277-2413-X
6. A. Soeteman: *Logic in Law.* Remarks on Logic and Rationality in Normative Reasoning, Especially in Law. 1989 ISBN 0-7923-0042-4
7. C.T. Sistare: *Responsibility and Criminal Liability.* 1989 ISBN 0-7923-0396-2
8. A. Peczenik: *On Law and Reason.* 1989 ISBN 0-7923-0444-6
9. W. Sadurski: *Moral Pluralism and Legal Neutrality.* 1990 ISBN 0-7923-0565-5
10. M.D. Bayles: *Procedural Justice.* Allocating to Individuals. 1990 ISBN 0-7923-0567-1
11. P. Nerhot (ed.): *Law, Interpretation and Reality.* Essays in Epistemology, Hermeneutics and Jurisprudence. 1990 ISBN 0-7923-0593-0
12. A.W. Norrie: *Law, Ideology and Punishment.* Retrieval and Critique of the Liberal Ideal of Criminal Justice. 1991 ISBN 0-7923-1013-6
13. P. Nerhot (ed.): *Legal Knowledge and Analogy.* Fragments of Legal Epistemology, Hermeneutics and Linguistics. 1991 ISBN 0-7923-1065-9
14. O. Weinberger: *Law, Institution and Legal Politics.* Fundamental Problems of Legal Theory and Social Philosophy. 1991 ISBN 0-7923-1143-4
15. J. Wróblewski: *The Judicial Application of Law.* Edited by Z. Bańkowski and N. MacCormick. 1992 ISBN 0-7923-1569-3
16. T. Wilhelmsson: *Critical Studies in Private Law.* A Treatise on Need-Rational Principles in Modern Law. 1992 ISBN 0-7923-1659-2
17. M.D. Bayles: *Hart's Legal Philosophy.* An Examination. 1992 ISBN 0-7923-1981-8
18. D.W.P. Ruiter: *Institutional Legal Facts.* Legal Powers and their Effects. 1993 ISBN 0-7923-2441-2
19. J. Schonsheck: *On Criminalization.* An Essay in the Philosophy of the Criminal Law. 1994 ISBN 0-7923-2663-6
20. R.P. Malloy and J. Evensky (eds.): *Adam Smith and the Philosophy of Law and Economics.* 1994 ISBN 0-7923-2796-9
21. Z. Bankowski, I. White and U. Hahn (eds.): *Informatics and the Foundations of Legal Reasoning.* 1995 ISBN 0-7923-3455-8
22. E. Lagerspetz: *The Opposite Mirrors.* An Essay on the Conventionalist Theory of Institutions. 1995 ISBN 0-7923-3325-X
23. M. van Hees: *Rights and Decisions.* Formal Models of Law and Liberalism. 1995 ISBN 0-7923-3754-9
24. B. Anderson: *"Discovery" in Legal Decision-Making.* 1996 ISBN 0-7923-3981-9

25. S. Urbina: *Reason, Democracy, Society.* A Study on the Basis of Legal Thinking. 1996
ISBN 0-7923-4262-3
26. E. Attwooll: *The Tapestry of the Law.* Scotland, Legal Culture and Legal Theory. 1997
ISBN 0-7923-4310-7
27. J.C. Hage: *Reasoning with Rules.* An Essay on Legal Reasoning and Its Underlying Logic. 1997
ISBN 0-7923-4325-5

KLUWER ACADEMIC PUBLISHERS – DORDRECHT / BOSTON / LONDON

GPSR Compliance

The European Union's (EU) General Product Safety Regulation (GPSR) is a set of rules that requires consumer products to be safe and our obligations to ensure this.

If you have any concerns about our products, you can contact us on ProductSafety@springernature.com

In case Publisher is established outside the EU, the EU authorized representative is:

Springer Nature Customer Service Center GmbH
Europaplatz 3
69115 Heidelberg, Germany

Batch number: 10607214

Printed by Printforce, the Netherlands